Jesus Christ
The Word Incarnate.

CONSIDERATIONS

GATHERED FROM THE WORKS OF THE

ANGELIC DOCTOR

St. Thomas Aquinas.

BY

ROGER FREDDI, S J.

TRANSLATED FROM THE ITALIAN

By F. J. SULLIVAN, S. J.

ST. LOUIS, MO. 1904.

Published by B. HERDER,

17 South Broadway.

NIHIL OBSTAT.

S. Ludovici, die 30. Dec. 1903.

F. G. HOLWECK,
Censor theologicus.

IMPRIMATUR.

✠ JOHN J. GLENNON,
Archbishop, St. Louis.

St. Louis, Mo., Dec. 30, 1903.

— BECKTOLD —
PRINTING AND BOOK MFG. CO.
ST. LOUIS, MO.

The undersigned, Superior of the California Mission of the Society of Jesus, in virtue of faculties granted to him by the Very Reverend Louis Martin, General of the same Society, hereby permits the publication of a book entitled "Jesus Christ, the Word Incarnate", translated into English by the Rev. Florence J. Sullivan, S. J., from the Italian of the Very Rev. Roger Freddi, S. J., the same having been approved by the censors appointed to revise it.

JOHN P. FRIEDEN, S. J.

St. Ignatius College,
  San Francisco, Cal.
    November, 21, 1903.

TO THE READER.

The title itself of this book, intelligent and devout reader, gives you to understand the matter treated of, the source from which it is taken, in what manner and to what end it is proposed.

The matter is Jesus Christ, not viewed however in every respect, but simply as the Word Incarnate. If it shall please God to grant us life, time and sufficient strength, we shall endeavor to offer you some time other considerations, drawn from the same pure sources of the angelic doctor, which regard Jesus Christ in his sacraments, especially in the Eucharist and in his Sacred Heart. But for this time we confine ourselves to consider him only as the Word of God, and the Word Incarnate, that is, we limit ourselves to that matter which is dealt with by St. Thomas in his *summa theologica*, both in the first part where he treats of the Person of the Word, and in the third part where he treats of the Incarnation.

With this we have now indicated from what source the whole matter of the present volume is taken. It is taken from the works of the angelic doctor St. Thomas, chiefly from the *summa theologica*, but sometimes also from his other works, according as suited the various subjects which we had to explain. This will give you the reason why we omitted several points, by treating which we

(iii)

would have been able to render our labor more complete. We have omitted them, because they were not found in St. Thomas. For it was our intention in writing these pages, to confine ourselves, in explaining them, to the doctrine of St. Thomas and no other. Nor is it even said in the title that these considerations are composed by us, but only gathered, for such they are in truth; and, therefore, whatever is found praiseworthy in them, is all to be ascribed to the merit of the holy doctor, not to our credit. Imagine a gardener who goes about through the beds of his garden, rich with every kind of flowers, selecting and putting those together which suit his purpose. Is it he that gives to these flowers the loveliness of their tints, or the elegance and variety of their forms, or the fragrance of their odors? Not at all; he does nothing more than to cull them, and join them together in a bunch. The same we have done ourselves. From the works of the angelic doctor, which are truly a most flowery garden, we have gone about selecting and gathering that which served our argument, and we have put it together, arranging it in the form of considerations.

But why have we preferred a form like this? Because best adapted to the aim we had in view. By considerations, at least in common use, is understood not indeed any study of truth, but a study which tends directly, it is true, to enlighten the understanding with the knowledge of truth, but is also indirectly calculated to inflame the will with the love of good. This is precisely what we proposed to ourselves in compiling this little work; that is, to invite and assist you to study Jesus Christ in order to know him, and to know him in order to love him. Hence it is that we have chosen the form and manner of considerations.

Still this has not been our only intention. Besides feeding the reader in mind and in heart, we also intended by this means to feed at the same time those who may have to break the bread of the divine word. To speak from the pulpit of Jesus Christ, oh! how necessary it is, especially in our age; but to speak properly of him, at the same time, oh! how difficult it is, for with Jesus Christ there are connected the most sublime and profound mysteries of our religion, such as are those of the Trinity and Incarnation. Therefore, to diminish somewhat this difficulty for the sacred orators, we have endeavored to furnish them compendiously in the present book with abundant and safe materials on this point. And for this reason we wished to extract them from no other mines than from the pure and most precious mines of Aquinas, who discoursed on everything so well and so divinely, but above everything on Jesus Christ. We shall end by wishing to our readers the same good augury with which St. Peter concluded his second letter: "But increase in grace and in the knowledge of our Lord and Saviour Jesus Christ. To him be glory both now and unto the day of eternity. Amen." (2 Pet. III, 18.)

INVOCATION TO OUR LORD JESUS CHRIST.

Most amiable Jesus, thou art a good, a most delightful good, the greatest good, a pure and infinite good as to thy divinity, a good incomparably superior to any other created good as to thy humanity, a good most deserving, that all hearts should love thee with all their strength. Wherefore the saints and angels of heaven all burn with the most ardent love for thee; they feed on thy love, they are happy in thy love, and with thy love they shall be, to their inexplicable delight, always satiated and always thirsting, throughout eternity. But why mention the angels and saints? The infinite love of thy divine Father, O Jesus, in thee, and in thee alone, is fully gratified from all eternity.

Yet, O Jesus, among men, few are they who love thee earnestly. The greater number, forgetful or regardless of thee, run madly after paltry, fleeting and deceitful goods, unfit to satisfy the cravings of their hearts. Whence, O Jesus, ever comes a monstrosity so deplorable? Why do those, who are so sensitive towards thy creatures, show themselves so strangely insensible to thee? It is because they do not know thee, O Jesus. If they knew thee, if they understood something of thy perfections, of thy goodness, of thy ineffable charity, oh! what a fire of love would be enkindled in their breasts! But thou art for them a good unknown, and therefore not appreciated, and therefore not loved.

But we, O Jesus, we do not wish to be in the number of those most unfortunate blind ones. We desire to love thee, yea, and at any cost; and to love thee, we wish to know thee; and to know thee, we wish to study thee. This most delightful and noble study we now intend to undertake at once, confiding not, indeed, in our own poor abilities, but in the assistance which we confidently expect from thee, O Jesus, who art the uncreated wisdom, and fountain of all wisdom. And we expect this aid with so much the more confidence, as our master and patron in this study will be thy most beloved saint, whom thou wast pleased to illustrate with thy divine light to such a high degree, that he shone in thy Church like a sun, and even in this life knew thee and loved thee, not as a man of earth, but as an angel of paradise.

INDEX.

CHAPTER I.

Jesus Christ the Word Incarnate.

The Study of Christ.

Consider that it is the property of wisdom to contemplate the highest cause, and to judge and arrange every thing according to it. The highest cause, however, may be understood in two ways, either in some determinate kind or absolutely. That wisdom which contemplates the highest cause in some determinate kind will be wisdom in that particular kind, for example, in medicine, architecture, or the like. That wisdom which contemplates the highest cause absolutely, will be absolute wisdom. Now the absolutely highest cause is God: therefore the true absolute wisdom is that which considers God and divine things.

This being granted, it will be evident that among all the studies, to which men can apply themselves, the study of wisdom is the most perfect, the most sublime, the most useful, and the most pleasing.

It is the most perfect, not only because the object is most perfect, but also because the more a man devotes himself to the study of wisdom, the more does he partake even now of the perfection of the true happiness, which consists solely in the contemplation of God: hence the Wise Man calls

him already blessed, who is engaged in this study.
"Blessed the man who shall abide in wisdom."
(Eccli. XIV, 22.)

It is the most sublime, because by it man is
raised to a most special likeness of God, since this
is the same study, so to say, in which God is oc-
cupied from all eternity with infinite delight: and
all things, which he does and ordains, he does and
ordains according to wisdom: "Thou hast made
all things in wisdom." (Ps. CIII, 24.) And as
likeness is a cause of love, so the study of wisdom
helps wonderfully to beget a mutual friendship
between God and man; for this reason it is written
of wisdom, that it is an infinite treasure for men,
and that those who use it, have part in the friendship of God: "For it is an infinite treasure to men,
whilst they that use it, become the friends of
God." (Wisd. VII, 14.)

It is the most useful, because wisdom brings
with it every good: "Now all good things came to
me together with her." (Wisd. VII, 11.) And
the love of wisdom leads to the everlasting kingdom: "Therefore the desire of wisdom bringeth to
the everlasting kingdom." (Wisd. VI, 21.)

It is the most pleasing, because conversing
with wisdom has nothing of bitterness, and to live
together with it, causes no irksomeness, but joy
and gladness: "For her conversation hath no
bitterness, nor her company any tediousness, but
joy and gladness." (Wisd. VIII, 16.)

The study of Christ is the very study of wisdom.

Consider that the study of Christ is the very study of wisdom: since Jesus Christ is like a most precious living book and life, "in whom are hidden all the treasures of wisdom and knowledge." (Coloss. II, 3.) And therefore, if we wish to study wisdom, we have only to try to read and understand according to our abilities, this divine book, which is Christ.

Let us see then how all the treasures of wisdom and knowledge are contained in Christ. God has diffused the riches of his wisdom over all his works: "And he poured her out upon all his works." (Eccl. I, 10.) But these riches, thus spread around, cannot be called treasures, because we do not give that name to riches scattered around, but only to riches collected together. Therefore the treasures of the wisdom and knowledge of God are the riches of his wisdom and knowledge collected together in that most pure and infinite act, by which God comprehends himself, and in himself every other thing. In as much as he comprehends himself, the divine act unites all the riches of wisdom, which is the cognition of divine things; in as much as he comprehends creatures, he unites all the riches of knowledge, which is the cognition of created things. Now the Word of God is the most perfect image, the adequate expression, and so to say, the subsistent and consubstantial definition of this same act; and for this reason also all the same treasures of divine wisdom and knowledge are contained in the Word.   See then how in Christ the Word of God all the treasures of wisdom and of knowledge are united.

It is added, however, that these treasures are hidden.   But they are not in themselves hidden, nor for the blessed in heaven, who contemplate the Word face to face; but they are hidden for us wayfarers.   The Word of God is, as we have said, similar to a book in which all the divine wisdom is most clearly described; but as for us there are two things, that keep this book occult to us, the imperfection of our intellect, which is dimmed with a thick mist, and the veil of human flesh, with which the Word is invested.   Still we too with the divine aid, may read some portion of that book, provided we apply ourselves earnestly to study it.   The darkness with which our mind is naturally obscured, is in a great measure, dissipated by the light of faith, which is just like a lamp that is lit in the midst of darkness; and the veil of humanity which covers the book is not so thick as not to let something come out from it: the more so as the characters of this divine book send forth rays of the most vivid light.   Nay more whilst that veil on the one hand is an impediment to us, on the other it is of assistance to us in the study of this book; because we would not be able to bear the splendors of the rays of the divinity, if they were not tempered and accommodated to the weakness of our vision by the veil of the humanity.

The study of Christ the best of all studies.

After what has been said in the two preceding points, there can be no doubt, that the study of Jesus Christ is the most perfect, the most sublime, the most useful, and the most pleasing of all studies. It is not wonderful then, if the great Apostle St. Paul loudly protests, that he was satisfied with the knowledge of Christ, and of Christ crucified: "For I judged not myself to know anything among you, but Jesus Christ, and him crucified." (1. Cor. II, 2.) And again referring to the most noble knowledge of Jesus Christ, he says, that it is among all things the most eminent, and that he holds every other thing not only of no account, but even considers it a detriment: "But indeed I esteem all things to be but loss for the excellent knowledge of Jesus Christ, my Lord." (Philip. III, 8.)

Should we not then apply ourselves with great courage and ardor to the delightful study of this science? And the fruit of our study should be, not only to enlighten the understanding, but also to inflame our will, so that our knowledge may become the principle of charity. Then indeed will our knowledge be true wisdom, and like to Christ the uncreated Wisdom, who is not Wisdom only, but Wisdom whence eternally proceeds uncreated Love.

Chapter II.

Christ the Word of God.

Consider first what is understood by a word. A word is that which is uttered to signify something by him that speaks. We distinguish a threefold manner of a word, according to the three manners of speech: the oral, the written, and the mental word. The oral word is that by which a man speaks to others present; the written word is that by which a man speaks to others distant either in place or time; the mental word is that by which a man, or rather his intellect speaks to himself. The oral and the written word are called external words; the mental word is called internal. Of these two, it is clear, that the external word is naturally posterior to the internal one, because it is the sign and effect of the latter. Yet the name of word was first applied to the external, and thence transferred to the internal, because the external word being more sensible, is better known to us than the internal one.

But what is this internal word properly? It is not the intellective power, for this is the cause which produces it. Nor is it that virtual likeness of the object, which is called the species impressed, for this is, as it were, a seed which fecundates the intellect and determines it to

(6)

generate the intellective act; and thus is presupposed by the act, as the seed is by the plant, whereas the word is the term produced by the intelligent act. Neither is it the action itself of understanding, for the word is not the action of understanding, but that which the mind forms by understanding, just as the statue is not the action itself of the sculpturing, but that what the sculptor forms by his action.

The word is therefore the ideal expression of the object, which the mind produces in itself by understanding. Imagine that there were a canvas which of itself would have the virtue to paint itself, and thus of representing of itself, in itself and to itself its original; this representation would be its word, by which it would express to itself the same object represented. Now that which no canvas can do, the mind does by understanding. It paints of itself, in itself and to itself, an image of the object, which it understands; and this image thus painted by the mind is what is called its word. Wherefore the mental word has a twofold relation: one to the mind as the principle from which it proceeds, the other to the object, as the intellectual image of it.

Observe finally that the object understood by the intellect may be either the intellect itself, or some other thing, as for instance, the sun, a plant or some thing else. When the object is some other thing, the word will be only an ideal image of that thing, say for example, that of the sun. But when the intellect understands itself, then the word will be the ideal image of the intellect itself, from which it proceeds.

The mental word is in every intellective nature.

Consider that the mental word is found not only in man, but also in every intellective nature; because it is necessary that every intellect while understanding, should express the object which it understands, and this expression is the word. Now the intellective nature may be human, angelic or divine. Correspondingly there will be the human word, the angelic word and the divine word. And the divine word is that of which it is written that it was from the beginning: "In the beginning was the Word." (John I, 1.) For the reason that the human and the angelic word have been made, whilst the divine word was not made, but all things were made by it. This can be said of the divine Word alone.

The better however to understand properly what the Divine Word is, let us examine in what it agrees with, and in what it differs from our word. It agrees with our word in three things. First, our word is in the subject itself, which understands the thing of which the word is the ideal expression; in like manner the word of God is in God himself, who understands himself, and in himself all things: and therefore it is said, "The Word was with God." (John I, 1.)

Secondly, our word proceeds really from the one that understands, as from its principle; and in like manner the word of God proceeds really from

God understanding, as from its principle, and consequently it refers really to the principle, from which it proceeds, and is really distinct from it; and for this reason also it is said, that the 'Word was with God,' thus denoting a like distinction between the word of God and God who speaks it.

Thirdly, our word is a likeness of the object understood by us; and in a similar way, the word of God is a likeness of the object understood by God. These three things belong to the essence of the mental word, and consequently take place not only in the human word, but likewise in the divine word. However, the divine word differs from ours in three other respects. The first difference is, that our word is first in potency, and afterwards in act, whilst the divine word is always in act, and is therefore co-eternal with God. And therefore it is said: "In the beginning was the Word." The second difference is that our word is imperfect, and does not express all the objects to which the intellective force of our mind extends, but only some of them, and therefore we have need of many words. But the divine word is infinitely perfect, and expresses all that is contained in the knowledge of God, who says it; consequently it is not multiple, but single. The third difference is, that our word is not the essence itself of the soul, but is an accident superadded to it, whereas the divine word is not an accident but God himself: "And the Word was God." (John, I, 1.) Because in God, the intellect, the intellective act, the principle from which the word flows, and the word are not distinct from the essence, but are the one sole and same divine essence.

Yet the word is distinct from its principle, in as much as it proceeds from it. Hence the word is a divine person; because it subsists in the divine nature, distinct on account of the relation of origin from the principle that begets it, which also subsists in the same divine nature. Now he is called a person in regard to any intellective nature, who subsists in that nature, distinct from all the others, who subsist in that same nature, both when the nature is the one selfsame in all merely according to species, as is the case in creatures, and also when it is one and the same as to number, as is verified in God.

What it means to say that Christ is the Word of God.

Let us consider the meaning of the expression Christ is the Word of God. It means that Christ is not an other person from the Word of God, but the same person of the Word, in as much as He subsists not only in the divine nature, but also in the human nature assumed by him. Therefore between Christ and the Word there is no difference in the person, but there is an inadequate difference in the natures, because the word implies simply the divine nature; and Christ, besides the divine nature, implies also the human nature, and thus Christ means the word of God incarnate. From this it follows that Christ can be called the Word of God also in an other sense, namely, by analogy to our oral word. We employ the oral word to make our mental word perceptible and manifest to others; and in a similar way the divine Father made in Christ his invisible Word perceptible and manifest to us. This is the reason why God after having spoken to men in different ways by the mouth of his prophets, spoke at last to us by the incarnation of his Word, that same only and divine Word, which he speaks to himself from all eternity: "God having spoken on divers occasions, and many ways, in time past, to the fathers by the prophets, last of all in these days hath spoken to us by his Son." (Heb. I, 1. 2.) And again: "The only begotten Son, who is in the bosom of the Father, he hath declared him." (John, I, 18.)

CHAPTER III.

Christ the Son of God.

Consider that the Word proceeds from its principle by true generation, and therefore proceeds as Son. Now what is understood by generation? It means the production of a living being from a living being; for only in living beings can generation properly take place. It is not sufficient, however, that a living being derive its origin in whatsoever manner from an other living being, to be said to be generated. In addition it is required, that the generator produce the originated from his own substance, and communicate to it his own very nature; for example, if the generator is a man, he must communicate the human nature to the originated. Besides this, it is required that he communicate it in virtue of his intrinsic activity: and so Eve cannot be said truly to have been generated by Adam, even though she proceeded from his substance and partook of his very nature, for the reason that she did not proceed through the intrinsic activity and fecundity of Adam, but through the extrinsic operation of God.

Finally, for generation it is necessary that the generated proceed from the generator in such a manner, that in consequence of the mode itself of its procession, it be an image of the generator.

Now all this is realized most perfectly in the production of the divine Word. The Word proceeds from its principle, as God living from God living, and has received from it not a nature of the same kind, but its identical divine nature; and therefore it proceeds not only from the substance, but according to the whole substance of the producer. It proceeds in virtue of the intrinsic activity and fecundity of its principle, because the divine intellect has in itself, and of itself most fully and always in act, the productive virtue of its Word. It proceeds as the image of the principle from which it derives, precisely because it proceeds as the Word; for the word is essentially the image of the object understood by the intellect, and is therefore the image of the intellect itself whenever the intellect understands itself. Now the divine intellect produces its own Word by understanding and comprehending itself adequately. Hence the Word of God is essentially the image of the same divine intellect from which it derives. It cannot then be denied, that the Word of God proceeds by true generation, not otherwise than does every child proceed from its parents, by true generation. Nay, the generation of the divine Word is so much the more true and more perfect than that which may be found in creatures by how much the life of the generator and of the generated is more perfect in God; by how much the production from the substance of the producer is more perfect; by how much the communication and the unity of the nature in both, is more perfect and more intimate;

by how much the intrinsic principle of fecundity
is more essential, and more completely in act; and
by how much the Word generated is the more
conformable and the more adequate expression of
the generator.

Consider particularly a twofold difference that
there is between the most perfect generation of the
Word, and the true, but imperfect generation that
is proper to beings having living bodies, and
especially to animals. In this the conception of
the offspring is different from its birth. By conception the offspring begins to exist in the parent,
as a fruit which still adheres to its tree; by birth
it becomes detached and separated from the parent:
and the reason of this is, because by mere conception
the offspring has not yet attained its ultimate perfection, so as to be self-supporting and live of
itself. It is needful therefore that it be carried
and supported for some time by the parent. But
in the generation of the Word there is no difference
between the conception and the birth, because the
Word is generated from eternity in all the plenitude of its infinite perfection. Hence of the divine
wisdom, which is the Word, it is sometimes said
that it was conceived: "The depths were not as
yet, and I was already conceived." Prov. VIII, 24;
sometimes it is said to have been brought forth:
"Before the hills I was brought forth"; to denote
always its perfect and eternal generation. It is
said, however, to be conceived, to show especially
its permanence in the generator; it is said to be
brought forth, to indicate especially its distinction
from the generator.

And this is the first difference between the generation of the Word and the carnal generation of animals. The other difference is, that in the generation of animals a twofold generative principle concurs; one as the active principle which is called the father; the other as the passive principle, which is called the mother. Hence of the things that appertain to the generation of the offspring, some regard the father, others the mother. But in the generation of the Word of God, there is but one sole generative principle, and that is the divine Father, to whom on that account, is attributed all that regards the generation of the Word. To understand how this can be, consider what takes place, even in our mind. When our mind thinks on an object, it conceives also its word, which is an ideal image of the object thought on. Now such a word is as an offspring both of the mind and of the object thought on. Of the mind, because it conceives it; of the object thought on, because that fecundates and determines the mind to produce a word like itself. Whenever therefore the mind thinks on an object different from itself, the object thought on, is, as it were, the father of the word conceived by the mind, since it performs the part of the active and fecundating principle; and the mind is, as it were, the mother of the word, because it acts the part of the passive principle, by conceiving and carrying in itself the word. But when the mind thinks on itself, then it acts at the same time as father and mother of the word, and therefore every thing that regards

the generation of the same is to be attributed to it.
A similar reasoning applies to our case. The
divine mind produces its Word by comprehending
itself, and hence it is the sole generative principle
of the Word.

Christ the only-begotten and first-born Son of God.

Consider that Christ is the only-begotten and
first-born Son of God.   He is the only-begotten
Son: "And we saw his glory, the glory as of the
only-begotten of the Father, full of grace and
truth." (John 1, 14.)   "The only-begotten Son,
who is in the bosom of the Father, he hath declared
him." (John 1, 18.)   And indeed the Word of
God can be only one, whether on the part of the
act which generates it, or on the part of the Word
itself.   On the part of the act which generates it,
for the reason that it is a sole act, most simple,
most pure, and infinitely intelligent, and moreover
necessarily expresses by its Word all that it comprehends.   On the part of the Word itself, because
it is a perfect Word, and thus is an adequate expression, and therefore an infinite expression of the
divine intellect whence it proceeds.   But if in God
the expressive act is one only, and expresses all
with one word, it is clear that in God there can be
but one word.   This however does not prevent,
but rather it follows from this, that outside of God
there may be countless expressions more or less
inadequate of this his infinite Word, which however multiplied they may be, yet will never be able
to express what the sole Word of God expresses.

But Christ is called not only the only-begotten, but he is called likewise the first-begotten. He is called thus first of all in relation to all creatures: "Who is the image of the invisible God, the first-born of every creature." (Colos. 1, 15.)

And for what reason? Not only because he was begotten before all creatures, but also because he is the principle of every creature: "For in him were all things created." (Colos. 1, 16.) He is the principle for three reasons; by the creation of all things: "By him and in him were all things created"; (Colos. 1, 15.) by the distinction and order established among them: "For in him were all things created in heaven and on earth, whether visible and invisible, whether thrones or dominations or principalities or powers"; (Colos. 1, 16.) and by their preservation in being: "And by him all things consist." (Colos. 1, 17.)

In the second place however and chiefly, Christ is called the first-born in regard to those creatures to which he wished to communicate a likeness and participation of his divine filiation, by raising them to the adoptive filiation of God: "For whom he foreknew he also predestinated to be made conformable to the image of his Son, that he might be the first-born amongst many brethren." (Rom. VIII, 29.) Of such likeness and participation of the divine filiation of Christ, one is proper of men on earth, and is imperfect; the other is proper of the blessed in heaven, and is perfect. The imperfect is that which is had through grace, and is called imperfect, because it imports only a renova-

2

tion of spirit: "Be ye renewed in the spirit of your mind." (Eph. IV, 23.) And moreover in the spirit itself it is partly deficient: "For we know in part, and prophecy in part." (1. Cor. XIII, 9.) The perfect is that which shall be had by glory, which shall extend also to the body: "Who will reform the body of our lowliness made like to the body of his glory." (Philip. III, 21.) And in the soul it shall be without defect. And this is that perfect adoption which we are yet expecting, and for which we sigh and groan in the depths of our hearts: "Even we ourselves groan within ourselves, waiting for the adoption of the sons of God, the redemption of our body." (Rom. VIII, 23.)

The adoptive filiation of God.

Let us consider a little more minutely what concerns this adoptive filiation of God, and the quality both of the adopter and of the adopted. A man is said to adopt another as son, when he admits him to the participation of his inheritance, to which naturally he would have no right. And in like manner it is said, that God adopts men as children, in as much as through his infinite bounty, he admits them to the participation of his inheritance, to which naturally they would have no right. But in what does the inheritance of God consist? By an inheritance of some one is meant those goods which form his riches. Now that which forms the riches of God, is the fruition of God himself; for God needs not other goods outside of himself, but is rich in himself and of himself, and is completely happy by the enjoyment of himself. Therefore the inheritance of God is the fruition of God, that is to say, the happiness proper of God. And when he adopts men as children, he admits them to share in this happiness, which is natural to himself, but supernatural to them. And since man of himself is unable to attain such beatitude which transcends the power of his nature, God himself renders him capable through the gift of grace. Hence we see how much superior the divine adoption is to the human one. Man does not make the adopted fit but supposes him such, and therefore adopts him; whilst God, on the contrary, supposes man to be not fit, and, by adopting him, renders him fit for the attainment of the heavenly inheritance.

As to what regards the adopter, it might be asked whether the adoption is proper of the Father only, or is common to all the three divine persons. I answer that it is common to all the three divine persons. Notice in fact the difference there is between the natural Son of God and the adopted sons of God. The natural Son of God is begotten, not made; but the adopted sons of God are made: "To them he gave power to be made the sons of God." (John 1, 12.) Now to generate in God is proper solely of the first person; and therefore to the first person only it appertains to be the Father of Christ. But to produce any effect whatever in creatures, is common to the whole Trinity, by the oneness of the nature; for where the nature is one, the operative virtue and the operation must also be one; and, consequently, to be our Father belongs not only to the first person, but to the whole Trinity. It is true that, although our adoption belongs in reality to all three of the divine persons, yet sometimes by appropriation it is ascribed singularly to one or the other under different respects. It is ascribed to the Father, as to the first author of it; it is ascribed to the Son, as to the exemplar; it is ascribed to the Holy Ghost, as to him who imprints in us the likeness of that exemplar, viz., the brightness of that grace which makes us conformable to the divine splendor of the Son.

Next we shall consider what creatures are capable of being adopted in this manner by God. Evidently those only that are rational. Adoptive filiation is a likeness of natural filiation. Now this likeness of the natural filiation of God can be found only in rational creatures. And in truth, the Son of God proceeds naturally from the Father, as the mental word, and is one sole thing with the Father. Now creatures can be like to such word in three ways. In the first place, only as to the exemplary cause, in such a manner as the material edifice is like to the idea which is in the mind of the architect: and in this way all creatures are similar to the eternal Word, for the reason that they have all been made through the Word. Secondly, the creature is similar to the Word, not only in kind as to the exemplary cause, but also by being conformed to it also in its intellectual being, just as the knowledge which is generated in the mind of the scholar, is conformed to the word which is in the mind of the teacher: and in this manner, only the rational creature resembles the Word. Thirdly the creature is like to the Word of God, even according to the unity which it has with the Father in nature: and this similarity is effected through the grace and charity, by which creatures are made partakers of the same divine nature, and united with God and with one another by the closest and most intimate bond. This was the likeness which Christ besought of his divine Father for the faithful: "That they all may be one, as thou Father in me, and I in thee, that they also may be one in us . . . . that they may be one, as we also are one." (John XVII, 21. 22.) And this likeness supposes the others, and is properly that which constitutes the adoptive filiation of God: because to those who are in this manner made like to the Son of God, is due the eternal inheritance. It is plain, then, that the divine adoption belongs only to rational creatures; not however to all, but merely to those who have supernatural charity, which is poured out into our hearts by means of the Holy Ghost: "The charity of God is poured out into our hearts by the Holy Ghost who is given to us." (Rom. V, 5.) Hence it is, that the Holy Ghost is called the Spirit of adoption of sons: "But you have received the Spirit of adoption of sons." (Rom. VIII, 15.)

Christ the natural and not adopted Son of God.

Consider that Christ, even as man, is the natural, and not the adopted Son of God. The reason is, because filiation properly appertains to the per-

son, not to the nature.   Now Christ, even as man,
is not a different person from the divine person,
but is always the same person of the Word, begotten from eternity by the Father, and therefore the
natural Son of God, and in no wise adopted.   Nor
can it be said that at least the human nature of
Christ, if regarded by itself, may be called the
adoptive Son of God.   It cannot, for the reason
already advanced.   Because the human nature of
Christ does not subsist in itself, but in the Word:
and hence it cannot be affirmed of it, that it is
either the adopted or the natural Son, but it must
be said, that it belongs to that person who is the
natural Son of God; just as the hand of John cannot be said to be the natural son of Zebedee, nor
the hand of Esther the adoptive daughter of Mar-
docheus: but of both it is necessary to say that
these are part of that person, to which the natural
or adoptive affiliation belongs.

Chapter IV.

Christ the Image of God.

Consider that in every image two properties are necessary: likeness and derivation from its exemplar. First of all, likeness is necessary. Not however any kind of likeness, for example not one according to the generic nature, nor one according to an accidental quality which may be common to several different species. Thus it cannot be said, that a plant is the image of the soil from which it springs; or that the nest is the image of the bird that builds it, although they agree in the generic nature of corporal substance. In like manner it cannot be said, that the lily is the image of snow, although it resembles it in whiteness. It is necessary, moreover, that this likeness be either in the specific nature, as it is between father and son, or at least in some accidental quality, which would be, as it were, a sign proper of the species, as is particularly the figure: as is, for example, between the king and his image stamped on the coin. The other property required in an image is, that it be derived from its prototype according to the likeness of it. Hence one egg is not an image of another, however very similar they may be to each other, both in the specific nature and the figure, because the one has not its origin from the other. These two properties, then, are sufficient of themselves for what is essential in an image. The image, however, will be the more perfect, the nearer it approaches equality with its prototype: and it will be totally perfect when it is entirely equal to it, in such a way that there be nothing in the prototype, which is not expressed in the image.

Christ the most perfect Image of God.

Consider that Christ, being the Word and natural Son of God, is on this very account the most perfect image of God: "Who is the image of the invisible God." (Colos. 1, 15.) Because for this reason he has likeness to the Father, has origin from the Father, has entire equality with the Father, nay, the same nature of the Father; for there cannot be total equality with God, except in the identity of nature; and hence he is also called the 'figure of his substance' (Heb. 1, 3), the figure of the substance or of the essence of God, since he represents the very essence of God, and represents it as the adequate and subsistent image in that same essence. From this we see how different is the mode in which the Son of God is the image of the Father, and that by which man is the image of God. The Son of God is the image of the Father as a son is the image of the king his father, and even much more so, for the king and the king's son, though they have the nature of the same species, yet it is distinct, whereas the Son of God and the Father have one and the very same nature. Man is the image of God, as the effigy of the king, impressed on the coin, is the image of the king which represents the king in some mode, but subsists in a nature of another species. Therefore man is not the perfect, but the imperfect image of God, and is by so much the more inferior to his exemplar by how much the nature of man is distant from that of God, that is to say, infinitely. And as an indication of such imperfection, man is not said solely to be made the image, but to the image of God: "And God created man to his own image" (Gen. 1, 27), since the particle 'to' expresses a movement of that which tends to a distant term. But the Son of God is called simply the image of God, and not to the image of God.

The manner in which Man may be the Image of God.

Consider again more particularly in what manner man may be the image of God. He is the image of God both as regards the divine nature, and as regards the Trinity of the persons. First, as regards the nature. The image, as we have seen, should represent its exemplar in some way, according to its specific nature, and, consequently, according to the ultimate difference which is constitutive of the specific nature. Now man, like every other creature endowed with intelligence, represents God, not only in being and in living, but also in understanding, which is, as it were, the ultimate difference in respect to the divine nature. Indeed, from the shadow of the divine nature we are able to judge of the nature itself. The shadow

of the divine nature is that finite participation of
the perfections of God, which is found in creatures.
See then among these participated perfections,
which is the ultimate, viz., that which presupposes
all the others, and completes, so to say, the divine
nature participated and shadowed in its effects.
Evidently it is the perfection of understanding.
Man, therefore, and every intellectual creature is
truly an image of God, as regards the nature.   He
is also an image, as regards the Trinity of the
Persons.   The three divine persons are distinct
from each other in this, that the Son proceeds from
the Father, as the word of the intellect, and the
Holy Ghost proceeds from the Father and from the
Son, as love of the will.   Now in man and in all
rational creatures in the same manner there is the
word which proceeds from the intellect, and the
love which proceeds from the will.   And therefore
in such creatures there shines a likeness of the
Trinity, and a likeness which, in a certain sense,
may be called a representation of the species, since
it represents separately the processions, the dis-
tinctions, the properties of the three divine persons, and on this account can justly be called an
image of the Trinity.

   Observe, moreover, that the image of God, both
as to nature and as to the Trinity, can exist in man
in three different modes.   The first mode is according to the natural aptitude he has to know and to
love God; and this first mode is seated in the very
nature of the intellectual soul.   The second mode
is, in as much as man knows and loves God, in act

or in habit, supernaturally, yet imperfectly; and
this second mode is attained by grace.   The third
mode is, in as much as man knows and loves God
supernaturally, in act and perfectly; and this third
mode is proper of the state of glory.   The first
kind of image is common to all men; the second is
common only to the just; the third to the glorified.
The first is never lost; the second and the third are
lost, or hindered by sin.

Even irrational creatures represent the divine nature.

Consider that even irrational creatures represent
in some form both the divine nature, and the
Trinity of the Persons, yet this representation is
more imperfect, and therefore does not deserve the
name of image, but rather of vestige.   A vestige
implies three things: resemblance, the imperfection of the resemblance, and that it be the effect
of the thing whose vestige it is, and that from it
we may attain a knowledge of its cause.   Now in
all creatures, even the irrational, there is found
some similitude of God, either more or less imperfect; all are the effect of the Creator, and from
them all we can rise to a knowledge of him.   So
then even in creatures without intelligence a vestige of God is found, not only in respect to the
divine essence, but also in respect to the Trinity;
but in respect to the Trinity the representation is
more faint and remote, and on that account also
further from the perfection of the image, and nearer
to the imperfection of the vestige.

But in what does such a representation consist? In irrational creatures there is not the principle of the word, the word and the love, as in the rational ones, yet there is in them a trace which indicates that they are found in their Maker. They all have a participated being, they have a determinate species, they have an ordination to some good as their end. The participated being reveals the principle whence it springs; and thus points out the person of the Father, who is the first principle, because a principle without a principle. The species reveals the word of which it is the imitation, as the form of the house reveals the word which is in the mind of the architect; and thus points out the person of the Son, who is the Word of God. The ordination to good reveals the love of him, who has produced them, since it is the property of love to wish good, and to ordain to good; and in this way it points out the person of the Holy Ghost, who is the Love proceeding from the Father and from the Son.

Chapter V.

Christ the Wisdom, the Art, the eternal Law, the Light, the Power of God, and splendor of his glory.

Consider that although wisdom be the attribute of the divine essence, and therefore common to all the divine persons, nevertheless it is usually attributed to Christ by appropriation: "But we preach Christ the power of God, and the wisdom of God." (1 Cor. I, 23, 24.) Let us understand well the meaning of such appropriation. To appropriate means nothing more than to make one's own that which is common, so that to appropriate an attribute to a divine person, simply means to make proper of that person an attribute which of itself would be common to the whole Trinity. And for what reason is it made proper of that person? Certainly not because it belongs in reality more to that one than to the others, for that would be opposed to the perfect equality, which exists among them, but because it has a greater affinity with that which is proper to one person, than it has with that which is proper to the others, and for that reason, is more fit to show us the property of that person, rather than of the others. For such reason goodness is appropriated to the Holy Ghost, since goodness has a special affinity to

(29)

what is proper of the Holy Ghost, who proceeds as love; and goodness is the object of love. In a like manner power is appropriated to the Father; because power has the nature of a principle and therefore has more resemblance with the property of the Father which is that of being the origin of the whole Trinity. And for the same reason wisdom is appropriated to the Son, because it has more conformity with the property of the Son, wisdom being the gift of the intellect, and the Son proceeding from the Father as a word from the intellect. It is true, however, that if we do not say wisdom simply, but wisdom begotten or proceeding from the Father, then we do no longer express a common attribute, but the property itself of the Son, which is to be wisdom, as the Father, and the same wisdom as the Father is; but wisdom begotten by the unbegotten wisdom of the Father.

Different titles of Christ by appropriation.

Consider that as Christ is called the Wisdom of God, he is also styled the Art of God, the eternal Law, the Light, the Power of God, and the like. All these titles are likewise ascribed to Christ by way of appropriation. He is styled the Art, because the Word of God expresses all that is contained in the knowledge of God, and therefore expresses not only the divine essence, but also creatures; with this difference, however, that in respect to God, it is expressive only, whilst in respect to creatures it is at the same time both operative and expressive. In regard to God, it is the image; in regard to creatures it is the exemplar. In regard to God it has not the nature or character of art, but of the most perfect wisdom, in as much as it is the concept, and adequate and subsistent expression of God, for wisdom consists precisely in conceiving and expressing with the mind the highest cause, which is God; but in relation to creatures it has the nature of most perfect art; for art is the right rule of things that are feasible by the artificer, as it exists in his mind. Thus the art of the architect is the right rule of the edifice; the art of the sculptor of the statue; the art of the captain of the conduct of the army; now the Word of God is the right rule of all things, that are feasible by God. Hence it is written, that all creatures were made by God through his Word: "All things were made by him." (John I, 3); for the Word, as we have said, is the perfect norma of all things, by which God the Supreme Artificer does all that he does. And this is what the Psalmist meant, when he sang: "For he spoke, and they were made" (Ps. XXXII, 9); he spoke, that is he produced the Word, and they were made, and by this his Word all things were made. And since the cause of the creation and of the preservation of things is one and the same, it follows that all things having been made by the Word, are also preserved in their being by the Word. Hence we read in the psalms that from the word of the Lord the heavens have their stability; "By the Word of the Lord, the heavens are established." (Ps. XXXII, 6.)

And the apostle affirms of Christ, that he it is who by his powerful word sustains whatever things there are: "And upholding all things by the word of his power." (Heb. I, 3.) Observe, however, a very notable difference between the Word of God and the idea, which is in the mind of the created artificer. The latter is not subsistent of itself, but is an accidental form; therefore it cannot be said of it, that it acts, for to act is the proper of the suppositum, but it can be said only that the suppositum acts through it. The idea of the house which is in the mind of the architect, does not itself make the house, but it is the architect who in virtue of it, acts and makes the house.

On the contrary the Word of God is God itself subsistent, and therefore not only the Father operates by it, but the Word operates also together with the Father: "I was with him forming all things." (Prov. VIII, 30.) Thus did the divine Wisdom affirm of itself: "My Father worketh until now, and I work." (John V, 17.) Thus also affirms the same incarnate wisdom. From this we can see how and for what reason the eternal law also is appropriated to the Word of God. For the reason that as art appertains to the divine wisdom, in as much as it is productive of creatures, so also the eternal law appertains to the divine wisdom in as much as it is the ruler of the same. And in truth, just as art is the norma of the divine wisdom in as far as it is the rule and exemplar of the things feasible to God, so also the eternal law is the rule of the divine wisdom in so far as it is directive of all the acts and movements, which regard each single creature. And as all the other laws spring from the eternal law, and from it draw their vigor, hence it is that the eternal Wisdom which is the Word of God must be said to be the first source of them all. By it kings reign, lawgivers ordain what is just; in virtue of it princes command, and judges administer justice. "By me kings reign, and lawgivers decree just things: by me princes rule, and the mighty decree justice." (Prov. VIII, 15.)

The Word of God is also called Light: "That was the true light which enlighteneth every man that cometh into this world" (John I, 9); for as the material light manifests to the eyes corporeal objects, so the Word manifests truth to the mind; since, as well as all other things, and even more especially all intellectual cognition, it is produced from God by the Word, and according to the image of the Word. Much more, however, is the Word the light and fountain of light in respect to the supernatural light of grace and of glory, which the more divine it is, the more it must be said to proceed from the Word of God, as from the supreme efficient and exemplary cause. If notwithstanding the light of the Word, darkness still remains both in the natural and supernatural order, this is not a defect of the Word, since its light is infinite, but it is a defect of those who either can not, or wish not to receive its light, and for this reason, although the Word shines like the sun in their midst, these remain in darkness:

3

"And the light shineth in darkness, and the darkness did not comprehend it." (John, I, 5.)

Lastly the Word is styled the Power of God, and in like manner the Arm of God, or Right Hand of God, because by him all things were made. The Father does all things by the Son. But that does not mean, that the Father has not in himself the power of working, or that the Son works in the manner of an instrument or minister of the Father; but it means that the Father in communicating his essence to the Son, communicates also to Him the power of working, and not a different, but his own identical power, the only difference being that the Father has it of himself whilst the Son has it of the Father. Hence it is that the Father operates by the power of the Son, and by his own power, since the power of the Son is the same as that of the Father, and the Son operates by the power of the Father and by his own power, since the power of the Father is the same as that of the Son. For this reason the Apostle says of the Son, that 'he is upholding all things by the word of his power;' thus indicating that the power with which he sustains all things in their being, is not alien, but his own power. Note too that the Apostle does not say, upholding by his power, but by the word of his power, in order to denote that as the Father does all things by the Word, so the Son also does all things not by an other word but by the very same Word as the Father does, that is by itself, which is the Word replete with all the power of the Father.

Christ the splendor of God's glory.

Consider why Christ is called the splendor of the glory of God: "Who being the splendor of his glory, and the figure of his substance." (Heb. I, 3.) Ponder in the first place in what the glory of God consists, and in what the splendor of his glory consists. Glory is commonly defined 'a clear knowledge with praise.' Glory then is a manifest and certain knowledge of another's goodness or excellence which deserves praise. Hence we can easily perceive, that glory will be greater or less according as the goodness possessed by some one is greater or less. Hence it is that the glory of creatures will always be imperfect, because their worth is necessarily finite and participated. Only the glory of God is absolutely perfect, and therefore it alone by antonomasia deserves the title of glory; because God is goodness itself subsistent, and consequently his goodness is essential and infinite. But even in regard to God, one is the glory that comes to him from creatures, and the other the glory that comes to him from himself. The glory that comes to him from creatures is always infinitely below his dignity, because the knowledge however great that creatures can have of his goodness, will always be limited, and therefore, will always be infinitely inferior to the merit of the object. Only the glory then which comes to God from himself can simply and completely be called the glory of God, because he alone has a knowledge of his perfection which is in all and entirely adequate to it, since it is an infinite knowledge of an infinite perfection. Hence it is clear in what the glory of God is placed: it is placed in the knowledge which God has of himself. And because the knowledge of divine things is called wisdom, this knowledge of God, which is the glory of God, is at the same time the most true, the most perfect and infinite wisdom.

But what does the splendor of this glory signify? Wisdom is light, so much the more vivid as the act of cognition is more pure and more perfect. Therefore the wisdom of God, which is his glory, is as a sun of infinite light. The splendor is the manifestation which the light makes of itself, and is also itself light, but light of light; light radiated from radiant light, and is, as it were, coetaneous with the source from which it springs, for there is no sensible difference of time between the rising of the sun and the diffusion of its splendors. Now the Word of God is the manifestation of the Father and of his wisdom, as by his Word the Father declares himself and his wisdom. Wherefore the Son ascribes to himself the manifestation of the Father and of his name: "Father, I have manifested thy name to the men thou hast given me." (John XVII, 6.) Moreover the Word itself also is wisdom, but wisdom of wisdom, light of light, because wisdom radiated from the wisdom of the Father.

Nor is there an order of time between the radiating wisdom of the Father and the radiated wisdom of the Son, for the one is coeternal with the other, and they are distinct only by the order of origin, in as much as the Son is the wisdom begotten eternally from the unbegotten wisdom which is the Father. Here then we have the how and the why of Christ the Word of God, being styled the splendor of the glory of God. Neither is he splendor only, but the source of splendor, for the reason that he is the principle of every splendor in every kind. He is the principle of every splendor in the supernatural order, because from the Word of God spring those splendors which are called the splendors of the saints: "With thee is the principality in the day of thy strength in the splendors of the saints." (Ps. CIX, 3); and they are the splendors of wisdom, of grace and of beatitude, by which the saints themselves are illuminated and rendered splendid to the image of the Son of God. He is the principle of all spiritual splendor in the order of nature, because every word that gleams in the human mind, is but a faint reflection of the Word of God. He is also the principle of every corporeal splendor, which is a remote and analogical imitation and participation of the uncreated and infinite splendor of the Word.

Chapter VI.

Christ is Life and the Book of Life.

Consider first of all what is understood by life. Certainly no one can doubt that life belongs to animals. But when is it that the animal may be said to live? When it can move itself; and as long as it has the power of moving itself, it is said that it lives. And when it can no longer move itself, but is moved only by another, it is then said to be no longer living, but dead. It is plain, then, that life consists in that activity which a thing has of moving itself. But bear in mind that by motion here we mean to indicate not merely local movement, but also any operation by which the thing actuates and perfects itself, as would be, for example, to feel and to understand.

Three different grades of life.

Consider that we must distinguish three different grades of life, one more perfect than the other: the vegetative, the sensitive, and the intellective life. In what does the difference between these three lives consist? In the greater or less perfection, according as the living being has in itself the principle of its motion or of its operation.

In every operation we must distinguish three things: the end to which the operation is directed,

(38)

the form in virtue of which the agent is made able and ready to act, and the execution itself of the work.   Take for example the action of painting; the end will be the profit which the painter expects to realize; the form will be the idea, which he has in his mind, of the object which he intends to paint; and the execution will be the disposition of the colors on the canvas according to the idea which is formed in his mind.   This being so, plants have within themselves the principle of their operation as to the execution, since they have within themselves the principle of their growth and sustenance, but do not have it as to the form and the end.   In respect to these two things they do not move themselves, but are moved, because they have them determined by nature; hence we see that plants live, but they have a less perfect life.   Again brute animals have in themselves the principle of their operations, not only as to the execution, but even as to the form.   The wolf which, seeing the sheep, runs to attack it, moves itself both as regards the execution of running towards the sheep, and as regards the form which is the principle of its running, since it has not such form inborn from nature, but it procures it for itself by its senses: as in this case, the form is that sensible likeness of the sheep received into the visual potency of the wolf.   Yet even the brute animals do not propose to themselves the end of their operations, but have it predetermined by nature, through whose instinct they act.   Hence the life of brute animals is less imperfect than that of plants, yet it is still imperfect itself. Lastly, living creatures gifted with intelligence have in themselves the principle of their operations, not only as to the execution and form, but also as to the end; for the reason that it is proper of the intellect to know the proportion between the end and the means, and to adapt the one to the other. And consequently their life is the most perfect of all. However even in the intellective life there are found various degrees of perfection, according as it is more or less independent of the extrinsic, and more or less inward. The lowest degree of perfection regards the intellective life of men, seeing that our intellect to understand depends on the external sensible object, and on phantasm. The intellective life of the angels is more perfect, since their intellect, in order to understand, has no need of phantasms, nor of borrowing intelligible species from objects, for it understands itself by itself, and the other things ouside of itself, by the species connatural to itself. Nevertheless, even in the angels the intellective life does not reach ultimate perfection, because even in them the understanding is not entirely independent of extrinsic causes, at least of the first cause; and besides, although their intellective act and the word are intrinsic to them, still it is not their very essence, because in them being and understanding are not the same thing. There remains then the greatest degree of perfection, which belongs to the intellective life of God, because in the intellective life of God supreme is the inwardness, and supreme is the independence from the extrinsic.   Supreme is the inwardness, for in God the intellective act and the word are not distinct from his very essence.   Supreme the independence from the extrinsic, for as in God, being is entirely, exclusively, solely, and essentially from itself, so also understanding, which in him is the same thing as being, is entirely, exclusively, and essentially from itself.

All things created are life in a certain sense.

Consider how all things created, in as much as they are in the Word, are life, and this in two ways; both as they are viewed in relation to the Word, and as they are viewed in relation to the things themselves existing in their own proper nature.   First in relation to the Word, since the Word is life, and likewise the idea of the creature, which is in it, and is identified with the essence itself of the Word, is life too, and life of the Word. Next in relation to the creature existing in its own proper nature, in as much as the creature which is in the Word ideally moves in a certain way, and brings itself out towards real existence in its own proper nature.   Now life, as we have seen, consists in this, that a thing have the activity of moving itself; and hence the idea of the creature which glows in the Word, can in some way be said to be the life of the creature itself.

The book of life.

Consider that the book of life in God is called so metaphorically, by a similitude taken from human things. Men are accustomed to write in a book the names of those who are chosen for some special office or dignity. Now all the predestined are chosen by God for eternal life. Hence the knowledge that God has of those who are predestined to glory, is called the book of life; and it is said that their names are written in this book, because as writing is permanent, and is a sign of what is to be done, so the knowledge in the divine mind is stable, and is in God, as a sign of those who are to arrive at eternal happiness. This is that knowledge which is the seal of the solid foundation of the house of God, which are his elect: "But the sure foundation of God standeth firm, having this seal: 'The Lord knoweth who are his'." (2. Tim. II, 19.) This is the knowledge which Christ said he has of his sheep: "I am the good shepherd, and I know my sheep" (John X, 14.); and which on the last day he will declare he never had of the reprobate: "And then I will profess unto them: I never knew you." (Mat. VII, 23.)

Hence we infer that the book of life is properly so called in regard to the life of glory, not to the life of grace; and that those inscribed in such a book, strictly speaking, are only the elect, or those ordained by God to eternal glory. And of these it is most true, that no one is ever blotted out from the book of life, for the reason that the ordination of the divine predestination can never fail. Still in a wider sense it can be said that all those are written in the book of life, who are ordained to

eternal life in virtue of grace, by which they are
sanctified, seeing that whoever has grace, is thereby worthy of eternal life.   And these can be blotted
out, since the ordination of grace may fail, as grace
itself can be lost by mortal sin.   Nor must we
think this implies change in the knowledge of God,
as though he first sees, and then does not any longer see the ordination of some one to eternal life;
but it only implies a change in the term which
God from eternity sees first to be ordained to life,
and afterwards not to be, owing to the loss of grace.

But why is the book of life in a special manner
attributed to Christ?   The knowledge of the predestined, it is true, is common to the whole Trinity, so also is the book of life, yet it is attributed
to the Son, for although common to all the three
Divine Persons, still it has more likeness to that
which is proper of the Son, than to that which is
proper of the Father and of the Holy Ghost, since
the Son proceeds as the word from the intellect,
and the book of life appertains to the knowledge
of the intellect.   Still the Father is said to be the
head of the book, and that he himself is also
written, for interpreters understand concerning the
Divine Father those words: "At the head of the
book it is written of me." (Ps. 39, 8.)   He is said
to be the head of the book, to signify that he is
the principle from which the Son, to whom the
book of life is attributed, has his origin.   He is
said also to be written, to signify that to be written
in the sense above explained, although it be attributed to the Son, is not however proper only of
the Son, but common also to the other Persons.

Christ the book of life also in another sense.

Christ may be called the book of life also in another sense, namely, as man and as a model; for in him we see how we must live so as to reach eternal life, and above all, this title of the book of our life applies to our Lord Crucified. This is that book which the Apostle invites us to peruse, in order to fortify us in our course of life: "By patience let us run to the fight proposed unto us, looking on Jesus, the author and finisher of faith, who having joy proposed unto him, underwent the cross." (Heb. XII, 1, 2.) Nor is he satisfied, that we peruse it only, but he wishes us to think on it repeatedly and attentively: "For think diligently upon him, who endureth such opposition from sinners against himself." (Heb. XII, 3.) Why so? Because on the cross the virtues of Christ shine with a most vivid light. There is shown the most perfect humility and obedience: "He humbled himself, becoming obedient unto death, even the death of the cross." (Philipp. II, 8.) There is shown filial piety: "He saith to the disciple: Behold thy mother." (John XIX, 27.) There patience and meekness: "He shall be led as a sheep to the slaughter, and shall be dumb as a lamb before his shearer, and he shall not open his mouth." (Is. LIII, 7.) There especially is shown the most ardent charity and most tender mercy towards men in general, and to the very executioners in particular: "And walk in love, as Christ also hath loved us, and hath delivered himself for us, an oblation and a sacrifice to God, for an odor of sweetness." (Eph. V, 2.) "Jesus said: Father, forgive them, for they know not what they do." (Luke XXIII, 34.) We might continue recounting in like manner all the other virtues, as Christ on the cross wished to afford us the most sublime and evident examples of them all. Finally, he there gave us an example of final perseverance in the same, by continuing the practice of them up to his last breath.

CHAPTER VII.

Christ the Beauty of God.

There are three elements that constitute beauty: integrity and proportion, together with a lustre which greatly enhances and gives prominence to both. Of this there is no doubt in sensible beauty. When is a painting said to be beautiful? When it is complete; when it has the due proportion both of its parts among one another, and of its whole with the original; and in fine, when it has that vivacity of light and that brightness of tint which become it. These three elements united make the sensible object pleasing to behold, and for that reason beautiful, for according to the well-known definition: those things are beautiful which please the sight. What is said of sensible beauty in regard to the sense of sight, must be understood also proportionally with regard to the sense of hearing; for this sense also in its own way perceives and relishes the beautiful, as we not only call a flower beautiful, a painting beautiful, but also call melody beautiful. Therefore even here these same three elements are required, but in a form suitable to this sense. Due integrity is required which here will not be simultaneous in space, but successive in time; due consonance of the various notes with each other is required; due clearness is required, which here will not be the clearness of light, but the clearness of sounds.

But there is not only a sensible and material beauty; there is also an intellectual and spiritual beauty, which equally, nay even much more than the sensible, when seen pleases, not seen however by the senses, but by the intellect. Such is the beauty which belongs also to abstract truths, and the greater the evidence with which they are set forth, and the greater the order, the variety and multiplicity of the consequences with which they are enriched, the greater also it will be. Such is the beauty of the moral virtues; such the beauty of spiritual substances, as human souls and angels are. Such, above all, is the beauty of the supernatural gifts of grace and of glory, which are a more intimate and more eminent communication of the beauty proper of God. And also in this intelligible and spiritual beauty, the elements from which it results are those that we have mentioned: the integrity of the perfection which belongs to the thing in its kind; the proportion and unity in the variety and multiplicity real or virtual of the parts, or quasi parts which relate to it; the clearness which renders it conspicuous, not to the senses, but to the intellect.

From this we can easily understand that spiritual beauty will be the more excellent according as the perfection is more excellent, that is, the more sublime and the more multifold virtually; according also as the proportion and unity in this multiplicity will be more excellent, and according as the spiritual clearness of the object will be more excellent. Now this being so, who can doubt that in God there is a supreme and infinite beauty? For in the divine essence the sublimity and virtual multiplicity of perfection is supreme and infinite; and in this virtual multiplicity supreme and most orderly is the proportion; supreme and most simple is the unity, and supreme and infinite is the splendor, to such a degree, that only the infinite strength of the divine eye can bear the dazzling lustre.

Hence it is, that the divine essence pleases by being seen, and with its vision delights and beatifies the saints, and beatifies them the more, the better it is seen, and the more intense is the divine light which enlightens and comforts their minds. Nay, even God's infinite happiness itself consists in nought else but in his contemplating with infinite delight the infinite beauty of his essence.

The divine beauty is appropriated to the Son.

Consider that the divine beauty, although it be common to the whole Trinity, still it is appropriated to the Son, on account of the special likeness which it has to what is proper of him according to the three elements, which constitute beauty. As to the integrity of perfection, because the Son, just by being the Son, has in him truly and fully all and the same nature of the Father. As to the due proportion, not only because the Son has in himself the same most simple unity in the infinite virtual multiplicity which the Father has, having the same essence, but, moreover, because he is the image of the Father, perfectly equal to the exemplar of which he is the expression. As to the splendor, for the reason that the Son, in as much as he is the Word, is the light and splendor of the divine intellect. Therefore Christ, by being the Son, the Image, and Word of God, is the Beauty of God. Nor is he only the divine beauty itself, but is also the source of all beauty. Every other beauty is but a rivulet which flows from this fountain, seeing that every thing is beautiful, in as much as it is in some way an image, or at least a vestige of the Word, the consubstantial image of God. All the beauty, then, which is spread out among visible creatures, which sometimes charm us so much, is but the faintest shadow of the beauty of the Word, which of itself infinitely enamors the heart of God. All the sweetness of the most harmonious concerts, which afford us so much delight, is but a most distant echo of that melody of infinite sweetness, which "came out of the Most High, the first-born before all creatures." (Eccl. XXIV, 5.) Much more, then, is every intelligible and spiritual beauty but an imitation, a copy, and ray of this Sun of beauty, which is the Word. And in fine, if the supernatural beauty of grace and of glory incomparably surpasses every other created beauty, it is, because in virtue of it we are made, in a most singular manner, 'conformable to the image of the Son of God.'

4

The beauty of Christ's humanity.

Consider from what has thus far been said, how great also must be the beauty of the glorious humanity of Christ. It is true, that as long as we are detained in the darkness of this present state, we can never describe it with words, nor picture it with the imagination, nor even form to ourselves with the mind a clear idea of it. Still we can understand at least, that such a beauty ought to be the greatest and beyond dispute, superior to whatever other beauty is outside of God, whether in the natural or supernatural order. And indeed in the blessed the beauty of the soul is the more sublime, the higher the degree of glory to which they are raised. Why so? Because the higher their glory is, the nearer they are to the source itself of beauty, which is the Word, and therefore the more they partake of its influence. As to the body its beauty is but a reflexion of the beauty of the soul, which communicates to it the brightness of its glory, and on this account Christ said of the just, that in the resurrection they will be bright as the sun: "Then the just shall shine as the sun in the kingdom of their Father." (Matth. XIII, 43.) Consequently this splendor of corporal beauty will be the greater, according as the splendor of the spiritual beauty, from which it has its origin, will be greater. From this then we may argue what must be the beauty of the soul and of the body of Christ. The soul of Christ is not only the nearest to the Word, the beauty of God and the fountain of all that is beautiful, but is wholly immersed in this fountain of beauty. But why say immersed? Because it is united to it in a manner the most ineffable, most intimate, and substantial, and therefore who can describe the torrents of beauty by which it is inundated? As for the body of Christ, it too, in its own way, is teeming with the beauty of the Word. Not only because the beauty of the soul is transfused into it, but moreover, because it is also conjoined substantially to the same Word. What then shall we say? We shall say that as it is written of the Word, that it is the brightness of the eternal light, the unspotted mirror of God's majesty and the image of his goodness: ''The brightness of eternal light, the unspotted mirror of God's majesty, and the image of his goodness.'' (Wisd. VII, 26): so it may be affirmed in a certain way, that the most sacred humanity of Christ is, as it were, an unspotted and most clear mirror, in which the divine beauty of the Word is reflected and shines most vividly. It shines in the soul spiritually, and in the body corporally, that is conformably to the nature and capacity of the one and the other. It shines in both, not infinitely, it is true, yet in a degree most sublime, most singular, and without comparison more eminent than in any other creature whatever.

CHAPTER VIII.

Mission of Christ.

Consider that in the idea of a mission a two-fold relation is included; one is of the person sent towards the one that sends; the other is of the person sent, towards the term to which he is sent, for every one that is sent, is sent by some one to some term. As to the one who sends, it is required that the person sent, proceed in some manner from him, and consequently, that the one who sends, have in some way the nature of a principle in relation to the one sent. This can be in three ways; either by command, as the master sends his servant, or by counsel, as the counsellor of the king sends him to war; or by origin, as the fountain sends forth its waters, the sun its rays, the tree its blossoms. As to the term, it is required that the one, who is sent, begin to exist there in some mode, either because he was not there at all before, or because he was not there in that mode in which he begins to be there now. This holds good in general of every mission, whether in creatures or in God, for it pertains to the very essential notion of a mission. Therefore even in God a mission implies this double relation, but without the imperfections. By consequence, even in God the one that is sent should proceed from the one that sends; not however by command or counsel, since that implies inferiority, as he who commands is superior in authority, and he who counsels is superior in wisdom; but solely according to the procession of origin. And as regards the term, it is necessary that the divine person, who is said to be sent, should not now begin to exist where he was not before, for this is repugnant to his immensity; but that where he was before in one mode, he should begin to exist in a new mode.

Hence we infer, that properly speaking, to send can pertain only to those divine persons, who have the nature of principle, namely to the Father in respect to the Son, and to both the Father and the Son in respect to the Holy Ghost. On the contrary, to be sent can pertain only to those who proceed, that is to the Son and to the Holy Ghost. Accordingly neither the Holy Ghost can properly be said to be the one that sends, nor the Father the one that is sent. Observe then the difference between sending and coming or dwelling. By sanctifying grace all the three divine persons come and abide in the soul: "We will come to him, and make an abode with him." (John XIV, 23.) Yet not all three are sent, but only the Son and the Holy Ghost. Hence we understand also how the mission of the divine person is not eternal, but temporal. The reason is because, as we have seen, the mission essentially includes two things, one of which is eternal, and the other temporal. The procession of the person from his principle is eternal, whilst the new mode of the person's existence in the term is temporal. Hence it is that a mission is accomplished in time. Nor does this imply the least change in the divine person, but in the creature alone.

The mission is both visible and invisible.

Consider that the mission of the divine person may be visible or invisible; not as regards the eternal procession of the person that is sent from his principle, since that is always invisible and ineffable, but as to the temporal effect, according to which the person sent, begins in some new way to be in the term to which he is sent. The mission therefore will be said to be visible, if the temporal effect is sensibly manifested in some form. It will be said to be invisible if the temporal effect does not appear to the senses, but is merely spiritual. The mission of the Holy Ghost on the apostles in the cenacle was visible, because there the effect of the inward sanctification of their souls was shown visibly in the tongues of fire which appeared over them. The mission of the same divine Spirit is invisible, at least ordinarily, in those who receive baptism, for the reason that the effect of spiritual regeneration, which is effected by this sacrament, is not sensibly manifested.

Christ's mission both active and passive.

The mission of Christ may be taken either actively or passively, or even in this sense, that Christ be the term to which the mission is made;

and with truth, in all these three meanings it can be taken, provided it is rightly understood. And in the first place, if taken actively, it means that Christ is the person who sends, and it is said in relation to the Holy Ghost. Now it is most true, that Christ has sent, and does send the Holy Ghost, sometimes visibly, sometimes invisibly. And he himself has declared it several times: "But when the Paraclete shall come, whom I will send you from the Father, the Spirit of truth who proceedeth from the Father." (John XV, 26.) "If I go not, the Paraclete will not come to you; but if I go, I will send him to you." (John XVI, 7.) "When he had said this, he breathed upon them, and said to them: receive ye the Holy Ghost." (John XX, 22.) Notice here that Christ said, he would send the Holy Ghost ' from the Father and who proceeds from the Father ', so that we may know that it is not he alone, that sends him, but he together with the Father, seeing that the Father and the Son are one and the same principle, as well of the procession of the Holy Ghost, as of the mission.

Christ's passive mission.

Consider the passive mission of Christ, that is, in as far as he is the person sent. But bear in mind, that we treat here of Christ as God, but not as man. Consider first of all the invisible mission. Generally the invisible mission of the Divine Persons is effected by the gift of sanctifying grace, since by this gift the Divine Persons invisibly, it

is true, but really begin to exist in the creature in
a new mode. God exists in all creatures by his
essence, power, and presence as the first cause in
its effects. But besides this mode, which is common through the gift of sanctifying grace, God
begins to be in the rational creature in a quite
special manner, namely, as one known in one
that knows him, as the beloved in the lover, and
as one known and loved with supernatural and
deiform acts, and as a most affectionate friend most
intimately present; and according to this special
mode, God is said not only to be in the creature,
but also to dwell in it as in his temple. This being
understood, it is evident that by this new manner
of existing in the creature, we have the passive
mission, as of the Holy Ghost from the Father and
from the Son, so also of the Son from the Father,
since there is added to the eternal procession the
other constituent element of the mission, which is
precisely to begin in a new mode in the term.

It may be asked whether, and how the invisible
mission of the Son is distinct from the invisible
mission of the Holy Ghost. As to the origin of
the one that sends, they differ no doubt, in the
same form as the generation, by which the Son
proceeds from the Father, and the passive spira-
tion, by which the Holy Ghost proceeds from the
Father and from the Son, differ. As to the supernatural gifts by which the Divine Persons dwell in
the creature, these are in reality the effect of all the
three Divine Persons, not otherwise than the other
works of God which are termed 'ad extra.' Never-

theless, they are attributed by appropriation to one Person rather than to the other, according as they resemble and manifest that which is proper of that Person, rather than that which is proper of the other. We must, therefore, distinguish in these supernatural effects that which has the notion of root, and that which has the notion of fruit, which grows from such a root. The root is the habit itself of sanctifying grace; and the fruits are reduced to two, to the enlightenment of the intellect by the gift of wisdom, and to the inflaming of the will by the gift of charity. As far, therefore, as concerns the root of grace, the two invisible missions of the Son and of the Holy Ghost do not differ. But they differ in the fruits, for the invisible mission of the Son, who proceeds as the mental word, is considered in relation to the enlightenment of the intellect by the gift of wisdom; and the invisible mission of the Holy Ghost, who proceeds as love, is considered in relation to the inflaming of the will by the gift of charity. It does not follow, however, from this, that these two invisible missions can be separated, but rather the contrary; for the reason that love presupposes the enlightenment of the intellect; and the enlightenment of the intellect, that it may be to the image of the Word, must be productive of love, since the Word is Wisdom breathing eternal Love.

Christ's visible mission.

Consider the visible mission of the Son of God. That mission was accomplished in the incarnation, when the Divine Person of the Word made himself visible in the visible nature assumed by him. In order the better to understand this mission, compare it briefly with the visible mission of the Holy Ghost, and examine in what it differs from it. It differs in three things. First in the visible mission of the Holy Ghost, the visible creature is only an indication of the invisible mission; but not the term to which the mission is directed. Thus the fire, which appeared over the Apostles, was a sensible indication of the charity diffused into their hearts, — but the term of the mission was the Apostles themselves, not the fire. On the contrary, in the visible mission of the Son, the visible creature, which was the human nature, was not only that by which, and in which the invisible mission manifested itself, but was at the same time the term to which the mission was made; because the Divine Person of the Word was sent to the human nature, and in it began to exist in a new mode. In the second place in the visible mission of the Holy Ghost, the visible creature is not conjoined substantially to the Holy Ghost, but only refers to it as one of its external signs, whereas in the visible mission of the Son, the human nature was assumed by the Word in unity of person. In the third place, the Holy Ghost, even in the visible mission, is always sent by the Father and by the Son; but the Son is sent only by the Father. And if it is sometimes said of Christ, that he was sent by the Holy Ghost, according to the words of Isaias: "The Spirit of the Lord is upon me, because the Lord hath anointed me; he hath sent me to preach to the meek." (Isaias LXI, 1.), this is to be understood of a mission, not properly, but improperly so called. The mission properly so called regards the Divine Person, and it is clear that the Divine Person of the Word cannot be sent by the Holy Ghost, since it does not proceed from the Holy Ghost. The mission, improperly so called, regards Christ according to the human nature, in which he is less than the Holy Ghost, as he is less than the Father, and less than himself, in as much as he is God; and consequently Christ, so far as he is man, can be said to be sent by the Holy Ghost, as also by the Father, and by himself.

Christ the term of the invisible and visible mission.

Consider that Christ was, moreover, the term both of the invisible and visible mission; not indeed as God, as is evident, but as man. Therefore, in relation to Christ the invisible mission of the Son and of the Holy Ghost was effected in the beginning of his conception, but not afterwards. For what reason? it may be asked. Because from that first instant he received all the fulness of grace, of wisdom, and of charity. The visible mission of the Holy Ghost was realized in the baptism and in the transfiguration : in the baptism under the form of a dove; in the transfiguration under the form of a luminous cloud. Observe, however, a difference between the visible mission made to Christ and the visible mission made to others, for

instance, to the Apostles. The visible mission
made to others indicates the invisible mission
which is accomplished in them at that same time;
but the visible mission made to Christ was not an
indication of a new invisible mission which was
operated in that instant, but of the invisible mission
which, as we have just said, was already perfectly
accomplished in him from the first moment of his
conception.

CHAPTER IX.

The Incarnation.

The work of the incarnation consists in this, that the second person of the most Holy Trinity, who subsists in the divine nature from all eternity, began in time to subsist also in the human nature assumed by him: whence as by the subsistence in the divine nature he is true God from all eternity, so also by the subsistence in the human nature he became in time true man. And this was accomplished without any alteration in the Divine Person, which by such a union with the human nature neither gained nor lost any perfection, in the same manner as when God drew the world from nothing, he was not changed, nor was any point of perfection diminished, or increased in him; but all the change was on the side of the creatures, which passed from not being into being.

The Divine Word, therefore, united himself to the humanity, not laying aside his grandeur, but assuming our littleness, not lowering his divinity, but exalting our nature, and uniting it to his own with the closest union, nay, the greatest of all, if the supreme union of the Divine Person be considered, in which the two natures are united, and with a union consequently not accidental, but most truly substantial. Because although the two natures remain distinct from each other, and do not constitute a third nature composed of both, yet they are united in the one sole and same person, to which the one and the other really belong. Just as in us the soul and the body are substantially joined together, not only on account of the unity of nature which they form, but also on account of the unity of the Person, which subsists together in the one and in the other.

Union of the human nature and the Divine Person.

Consider two consequences of this most wonderful union between the human nature and the Divine Person, which will help us to understand this mystery a little better, so far at least, as a mystery may be understood by us.

The first consequence is, that although only one Person of the Blessed Trinity became incarnate, namely the Son, yet by reason of the incarnation of this Person, the Father also and the Holy Ghost, who are not united substantially, it is true, to the humanity of Christ, dwell in it by a new and most special title, in such a manner, that if they were not in it by essence, by power and presence, as they are in all created things, nor by grace, as they are in all the just, they would nevertheless be there by this other most singular title solely proper of Christ. And what is this title? It is the identity of nature and the necessary mutual indwelling of the Divine Persons in each other; from which it results that where one Person is, it cannot be but that the others also will be found with it; and, therefore, since the Person of the Word is in the humanity of Christ, it can not be that the Father himself and the Holy Ghost are not there.

Nevertheless, the Word alone is in the humanity as subsisting in it; the Father and the Holy Ghost are there simply as abiding therein; and, consequently, the Word alone was made man, and not the Father nor the Holy Ghost.

The other consequence is, that between the divine and the human nature in Christ there occurs a species of circuminsession similar to that which exists among the Divine Persons in the Trinity. By the term circuminsession theologians mean the reciprocal inexistence of the three Divine Persons in each other, of the Father in the Son, of the Son in the Father, of the Holy Ghost in the Father and in the Son, and of the Father and Son in the Holy Ghost, by reason of the unity of the nature, which is the same and common to the three Divine Persons. Consequently, unity of nature is the foundation, and the bond, as it were, of such reciprocal indwelling among the three Divine Persons. Now as in the Trinity the three Persons are united in one nature, so in Christ the two natures are united in one Person; and hence, as in the Trinity, by the unity of nature, the three Persons mutually indwell in each other, so also in Christ, by the unity of Person, the two natures mutually indwell in one another. This is the reason why we said, that between the two natures in Christ, there is a certain circuminsession similar to that which takes place in the Trinity. But to avoid mistake, we must observe a two-fold difference that is found between the two. In the Trinity the real distinction is between the Persons, and the unity is in the nature; in Christ the real distinction is between the natures, and the unity is in the Person. In the second place, in the Trinity all the three terms, which reciprocally indwell in each other, that is, all the three Divine Persons are identified with the divine nature, which is the bond of their reciprocal inexistence in each other; in Christ, only one of the terms, viz. the divine nature, is identified with the Divine Person, which is here the bond of the mutual indwelling of the two natures; the other term, that is to say, the human nature, although it is made proper of the Divine Person and substantially united to it, remains however always really distinct from it, and infinitely diverse.

The end of the incarnation.

The end of the incarnation was to repair human nature fallen from primitive justice, by removing the stain of the guilt and the debt of punishment, both as to original sin, and to all the other sins superadded to it. It is said however with truth, that Christ came into the world principally to blot out original sin, for he desired most to take from us that sin which was our greatest evil. Now original sin was a greater evil than our actual ones, not in intension, but in extension, because it infected the whole human race. As for other sins, if they are not actually destroyed, it is not because

Jesus Christ did not come to redeem us from them all, but it is through the fault of those who do not wish to partake of the most precious fruit of his redemption. "The light came into the world, and men loved darkness rather than the light." (John III, 19.) Jesus Christ, the sun of justice, brought light to all, the light of grace for this life, and the light of glory for the next. If however men persist in shutting their eyes to this light, and consequently remain in the darkness of their sins, and fall afterwards into the darkness of eternal perdition, the fault of this is not at all to be attributed to the light, which shone also for them, but to their stolid obstinacy, which refused to see it.

The incarnation not absolutely necessary.

The incarnation, absolutely speaking, was not necessary, since it was not necessary that human nature should be repaired; or even if God willed that it should be raised up from its fall, it was not necessary that he should do it in the present form, for he could have effected it in many other ways: either by condoning sin by the pure effect of his mercy, without requiring any satisfaction, or by being contented with an imperfect satisfaction, such alone as could be given by man. But once that God exacted a perfect satisfaction, such as would be a compensation adequate to the fault, the incarnation was needed for us. For no mere man could ever have rendered such a satisfaction, both for the reason that the good of one, or even of many individuals, cannot equal the evil of the

5

whole nature, and also because sin has a certain infinity, by being an offence against the infinite majesty of God. Consequently, it was necessary that the satisfaction should be offered by a person, who should be at the same time man, since it had to be offered for the sin of man, and also God, so that his satisfaction might have an infinite value, and thus be tantamount to the offence. Now this is the same as to say that the incarnation was necessary, by which the Divine Person would assume human nature and become God-Man.

Chapter X.

Fitness of the Incarnation on the part of God.

To take human flesh was not in the least unsuitable to God, but rather most becoming. For is it not exceedingly befitting to God to manifest externally the immense riches of his invisible perfections? This is the end to which all creation was directed. "For the invisible things of God are clearly seen, being understood by the things that are made." (Rom. I, 20.) And again, "The heavens declare the glory of God." (Ps. XVIII.) All creatures are as a book, in which are written the grandeurs of God; or rather they are, as it were, so many words which proclaim and exalt the wonders of their Creator; and because they are finite and imperfect, they strive in many ways to say what God says by his unique, infinite, and eternal word which is his Word. Now in the mystery of the incarnation the divine perfections are manifested in the most excellent manner, especially his mercy, his justice, his wisdom and power. His mercy, because his heart could not bear to see the ruin into which his creatures were fallen, and therefore he wished to extend his hand to relieve them. His justice, because man having been overcome and made a slave of the infernal tyrant, he wished that he should be set at liberty not by any other than by man; in such a manner, however, that the rigor of justice should be firmly maintained. His wisdom, because he knew how to devise a way the best adapted to cancel a debt which was most difficult to pay. His power, because there is no greater nor more wonderful work than that God should be made man.

A second reason for the fitness of the Incarnation.

Consider a second reason why it appears evident, how much it was becoming to God to become incarnate. In general, that is fitting to a thing, which is suitable to it according to the proper condition of its nature. Thus, for example, it is fitting to man to reason, because that is conformable to the rational nature which he has. In like manner it is fitting to a flower to spread its perfumes around; it is fitting to the sun to diffuse its rays, because all this is according to their natural character. Now the nature of God is to be good, nay, he is the very essence of goodness; and it is entirely according to the proper nature of goodness to communicate itself to another. It is, therefore, befitting to God, the supreme good, to communicate himself to the creature, and in a supreme manner; and this is just what he did in the incarnation by uniting the created nature to himself, and himself to it by the most intimate kind of union that can be formed between the infinite and the finite.

Reasons why it was most fitting that the second Person should become incarnate.

Although any of the three divine Persons might have become incarnate, it was however most befitting for several reasons, that the second Person, that is, the Son, should become incarnate. First, because as human nature had been created by the power of the Father through the Word, as everything else, so it was also proper that it should be re-created by the power of the Father through the Word, so that the regeneration might correspond to the first generation. Secondly, because those things which are alike to each other, are suitably associated together. Now all creatures are made after the likeness of the Word of God, since the Word is the exemplary idea of all that is created. Thirdly, because as the artist, for example, the painter or the sculptor, in order to restore a picture or a statue from the damages which it may have sustained, makes use of that very same exemplary idea which regulated the first formation of the work; so in the same manner, it was proper that human nature, having degenerated from its primitive perfection, should be repaired by its same divine archetype. Fourthly, because although all creatures resemble the Word, yet human nature enjoys such resemblance in a most particular way by the reason with which it is endowed, and notably by the elevation to the supernatural order of grace and of glory.

Accordingly, we find in the holy scripture the same name 'image of God' given both to the Word and to man. Of the Word the Apostle says, that he is 'the image of the invisible God.' (Colos. I, 15.) And the same Apostle says of man, that 'he is the image and glory of God.' (1. Cor. XI,

7.) It is true that of the Word it must be understood, that he is the perfect image, and for that reason in the same divine nature as the Father; of man, that he is the imperfect image, and for that reason in a nature different, and participated from the divine. But for this very reason as this imperfect image of God became deformed, since it was impressed on a frail and changeable nature, it was fitting that it should be reformed by him who is the perfect and unchangeable image of God; just as when the image of the king, stamped on wax, becomes disfigured, it is renewed by means of the firm and solid image of the king's seal. Fifthly, because the proper perfection of man as such, namely as rational, is wisdom; and the Word of God is eternal wisdom, and the fountain of all wisdom: "The Word of God on high is the fountain of wisdom." (Eccl. I, 5.) Werefore it was fitting that from this fountain man should obtain his perfection. Sixthly, because the end of the incarnation was, that men should become worthy of the heavenly inheritance which is due to sons only: "If sons also heirs." (Rom. VIII, 17.) It was proper, therefore, that through this same natural Son of God they also should acquire a like sonship in the way in which they are capable, that is, by adoption: "Those whom he foreknew he also predestinated to be conformable to the image of his Son." (Rom. VIII, 29.) Seventhly, because as man had estranged himself from God by an inordinate desire of knowledge, it was proper, on that account, that he should return to God by means of the true wisdom.

CHAPTER XI.

Fitness of the Incarnation on our part.

If the proper condition of human nature be attentively examined, there appears in it a special fitness to be assumed by the Son of God. And, indeed, in human nature there is linked together a twofold congruity for such an assumption, namely, dignity and necessity. Dignity, because it is intellectual, and, therefore, suitable and naturally inclined to be united to the Word in some manner by its operation in knowing and loving it. Necessity also, because subject to original sin, and consequently in need of reparation. Now these two congruities were found united in no other nature; for in the irrational nature dignity was wanting, and in the angelic nature necessity was wanting. It might be objected that necessity was wanting indeed in the good angels, because sin was wanting, but not wanting in the rebels. I answer that it was wanting in the rebels, because their sin was not remediable, in the same way as the sin of man is not remediable after death. "Death is to men what the fall was to the angels." (St. John of Damascus.) As by death the state of trial ceases in man, and the state of final destination begins, where there is no longer place for amendment and remission, so also it happened in the wicked angeis through their prevarication. To understand this point well, we must remember that the state of trial for the angels was all confined to a single instant in which, by corresponding to grace, they should have merited happiness, and could also by rejecting grace merit damnation. The reason of this is, because grace accommodates itself to nature, and it is proper of the nature of the angels not to proceed gradually, and by way of reasoning in the acquisition of knowledge, and in general of their connatural perfection, but to attain at once all the perfection to which they are naturally ordained. Now as by nature they are ordained to natural perfection, so by the first meritorious act they found themselves ordained to the supernatural perfection of glory; and, consequently, as they obtained at once their natural perfection, so likewise immediately after that first act, the good angels attained the full possession of their supernatural perfection, and were happy; and, on the contrary, the angels who prevaricated, having in that first act gone astray, lost it without remedy and were condemned.

The Incarnation the most useful means for us.

Although the Incarnation of the Word was not a necessary means for healing human nature, yet it was the most useful for us, because it was the most adapted to promote our good. First in regard to faith, which is better certified, since we believe God himself, who speaks directly; for as St. Augustine says: "The Son of God, who is truth itself, having become man, constituted and established faith, in order that man might with greater confidence advance to truth." Secondly, in regard to hope; because nothing was so necessary to raise our hope, as to make us know how much God loved us. Now what proof of this could there be more evident, than that the Son of God should deign to become partaker of our nature? Thirdly, in regard to charity, which is most greatly inflamed at seeing the wonderful love of God towards us. Fourthly, as to the practice of virtue, to which the words and example of the Word incarnate are the most powerful incentive; for as St. Augustine remarks: "Man who could be seen, was not to be followed; God who could not be seen, was to be followed. In order, therefore, that one might be shown to man, who could be seen by man, and followed by man, God was made man." Fifthly, as to the full participation of the divinity, which is man's true beatitude, and our last end; for in Christ the fulness of the divinity was communicated substantially to the humanity; whence we also draw confidence of being able to become partakers of the divine nature by grace and by the beatific vision.

The Incarnation the means of freeing us from every evil.

The incarnation was also the most efficacious means of removing from us every evil. First, because by it man is instructed not to prefer the demon to himself, nor to make much account of

him for being entirely spirit, whilst he sees human
nature so much elevated by union with the divine
Person.   Secondly, that by understanding better
how great is the dignity of his own nature, he may
render himself even more solicitous not to debase
it by sin.   Hear St. Leo: "Recognize, O Christian,
your dignity; and having been made partaker of
the divine nature, do not return to your former
vileness by a degenerate way of living."   Thirdly,
it contributes greatly to keep down our presump-
tion, whilst we see how great is the necessity of
satisfaction and merits for obtaining pardon and
salvation.   Fourthly, because it helps, moreover,
to crush and confound our pride, the root of all
our evils, by placing under our eyes the examples
of a God so exceedingly humbled.   Fifthly, in
order to effect condignly our deliverance from the
slavery of sin, for which neither man alone, nor
any other mere creature was sufficient.   "Weakness", as St. Leo says, "is assumed by power,
lowliness by majesty, mortality by eternity; in order
that, as it was suitable for our remedy, one and the
same mediator between God and men could die as
man, and rise again as God.   For unless he were
true God, he could not afford the remedy; and unless he were true man, he could not furnish the
example."

Chapter XII.

Fitness of the Incarnation as to the Time.

Consider that God sent his divine Son in the fulness of time; that is, in the time which, according to his infinite wisdom and most beneficent charity, he had ordained, so that his coming might turn to our greater profit: "But when the fulness of time came, God sent his Son . . . that he might redeem those who were under the law, that we might receive the adoption of sons." (Gal. IV, 4, 5.)

First of all reflect how very justly this time is called full time. For in it were fulfilled the figures of the law, as Jesus himself testified, saying: "Think not that I am come to destroy the law or the prophets, but to fulfil." (Matth. V, 17.) Because in it were accomplished the promises made in so many ways and so often by God to the ancient fathers concerning the future Messiah. But above all by the fulness of grace which the divine Redeemer came to bring into the world. For Jesus Christ was truly that 'river of God full of waters' mentioned in the psalms. He was the river of God, because proceeding from God, and sent by God: he was full of the living waters of grace, of those waters which spring up to eternal life: and he came among us to inundate our souls abun-

(75)

dantly with his waters, so that we too might partake of his plenitude to such a degree that our very hearts might become sources of like waters and of like rivers. "And of his fulness we have all received." (John I, 16.) "The water that I will give, shall become in him a fountain of water springing up unto life everlasting." (John IV, 14.) "Jesus stood, and cried out, saying: 'If any man thirst, let him come to me and drink. He that believeth in me, as the Scripture saith, out of his belly, shall flow rivers of water.'" (John VII, 37, 38.)

Why the Incarnation did not take place in the beginning.

No doubt some will ask, why the eternal Father did not send his Son at the beginning of the world, or immediately after the fall of Adam. He did not send him at the beginning of the world, for the reason that the work of the incarnation was particularly directed as a remedy of human nature; and medicine is given only to those who are already sick: "They that are in health need not a physician, but they that are sick. . . . For I am not come to call the just, but sinners." (Matt. IX, 12, 13.) Nor did he send him immediately after the fall of Adam, chiefly because this required the very quality of human prevarication which had sprung from pride. It was therefore necessary that man should be delivered in such a manner, that he should first humble himself by recognizing his own misery and the necessity he had of a deliverer. On this account God left him in the first place under the natural law alone, in order that he might experience the strength, or rather the weakness, of his nature. Afterwards he added the written law, and permitted the malady still to increase, not through the fault of the law, but through the human frailty, to the end that man, always feeling his infirmity more and more, might more earnestly invoke the physician, and seek the aid of grace. In the next place, this was in accordance with the orderly progress in good, according to which it is required to begin with the imperfect and then advance to the perfect. Hence the apostle says: "Not first that which is spiritual, but that which is animal. The first man was of the earth, earthly; the second man from heaven, heavenly. . . Therefore, as we have borne the image of the earthly, let us bear also the image of the heavenly." (1. Cor. XV, 46, 47, 49.)

The animal and earthly man was to precede, and afterwards the spiritual and heavenly man was to follow; first we were to bear the image of the earthly Adam by being subject with him to the death of sin, and afterwards to bear the image of the heavenly Adam by rising with him and by him to the life of grace and glory. In the third place, as the coming of a great monarch is accustomed to be announced a long time beforehand, so that the subjects may prepare themselves to receive him with more honor, so also it was even far more becoming the dignity of the Word incarnate, that his coming should be signified beforehand, and promised in many ways, in order that men might conceive a greater desire and expectation of him, and receive him with more faith.

The Incarnation came neither too early nor too late.

As it was not expedient that the incarnation should take place at the beginning of the world, so also for several reasons it was not expedient that it should be delayed to the end. First, in order that human nature might be able to enjoy longer and more abundantly the precious fruit of the redemption. In the next place, in order that the remedy might not come too late; for if it had been deferred so long, the perversion of the human race, which under the natural and under the written law went on always increasing, would have come to such a pass that all knowledge and reverence of God, and all regard for morality, would have disappeared from the face of the earth. Finally, in order that the extent of the divine power might be shown, which in many different ways worked out the salvation of men; first by faith in the future, and then by faith in the present and the past.

Chapter XIII.

The Quality of the Human Nature assumed by Christ.

The Son of God, through his inexplicable charity and most tender mercy towards men, being in the form, that is, in the nature of God, and therefore true God, abased himself not by losing the plenitude of his divine nature, but by taking the form, that is, the true and real nature of a servant, and becoming man like us. "Who being in the form of God . . . . abased himself and took the form of a servant, being made to the likeness of men." The most sacred body of Christ is therefore in the first place a true and real body, and in every respect like ours, being composed of flesh, of bones and blood, and in a word of all the various parts which are required for the constitution and integrity of the human body. "Feel and see," said Christ to the disciples, "for a spirit hath not flesh and bones, as you see me to have." (Luke XXIV, 39.) And if Christ is called by the apostle a heavenly man, and one come down from heaven, it is not because his body was not truly terrestrial and human; but he is said to have descended from heaven, first on account of his divinity which, without ceasing to be in heaven, began to be here on earth in a new manner, that is, according to human nature; and again, because the body of Christ was formed by heavenly power, that is, by the operation of the Holy Ghost.

The soul of Christ truly and really a human soul.

In like manner the most holy soul of Christ is truly and really a human soul, that is, a rational soul endowed with all and the same faculties as our souls, and is substantially united to the body as its form, vivifying it and constituting together with it a true and perfect human nature, that is, of the same kind as our own. The only difference is, that in us the compound nature which results from the union of the soul with the body, subsists in itself and by itself, and is therefore a person also; whereas in Christ the human nature is joined to the pre-existent Person of the Word, which subsists in it, and not it in itself, and therefore in Christ it is not a person. So if it be said in the Scripture that the Word was made flesh, it is not meant by that to exclude the soul, but because in scriptural language the word flesh often implies the whole man. Thus, for example, it is said in Isaias: "And all flesh together shall see that the mouth of the Lord hath spoken." (Isaias XL, 5.) Thus too in several other places. To say, then, that the Word was made flesh, is equivalent to saying, the Word was made man.

Again in regard to the Word humanified, there were other special reasons why the entire man was called flesh. First, because by the flesh the Son of God appeared visible to us. Secondly, because by taking flesh, the abasement of the Word is much better seen, and consequently his love for us. Thirdly, because the flesh owing to its imperfection, being further from the infinite dignity of the Word, it might seem less capable of being assumed by him; hence it was the more necessary that explicit mention should be made of it.

It was fitting for Christ to take a human nature from the race of Adam.

Although the Son of God could have assumed a human nature which was not of the generation of Adam, still it was most fitting that he should take it from the race of Adam, as he did; and chiefly for three reasons. First, in order that every regard for justice might be observed, which seemed to require that he who had sinned, should himself also make satisfaction. It was fitting, therefore, that that nature for which satisfaction was to be made for the sin, with which the race of Adam was defiled, should belong to the same race. Secondly, because in this way the dignity of man was better saved and restored, since the conqueror of the devil sprang from the same race which had been enslaved by the devil. Thirdly, because in this way the power of divine omnipotence was better manifested, seeing that from a corrupt mass of sin, weak and fallen into extreme vileness, it was able to draw out the humanity of Christ most pure from every blemish, and raised to such a height of power and honor.

6

CHAPTER XIV.

Grace of Union in Christ.

In Christ we have to distinguish a threefold grace. The first is called the grace of union, and is the identical hypostatic union of his human nature with the divine person. The second is the habitual grace by which the soul of Christ is sanctified and replenished above all others. The third is the grace which he has as head of the Church, in as much as he is the source of grace to others. These three graces are pointed out in order by St. John, the evangelist. The grace of union by the words, 'and the Word was made flesh.' The habitual grace by the words, 'full of grace and truth.' And the grace of head of the Church by the following words, 'and of his fulness we have all received.' For the present we shall consider only the first grace, that of union.

This is placed, as we have already said, in the same most wonderful ingrafting, if it can be so called, of the human nature in the divine person; and is called grace, because it was a gratuitous gift which, without any precedent merit, was given by God to Christ's humanity. Observe, then, that this grace is doubtless infinite, since the person of the Word, which is united to the human nature, is infinite; and that in virtue of such a union, the

(82)

humanity of Christ is rendered holy with substantial, uncreated and infinite sanctity, yea, with the very sanctity of the Word itself. For as by the accidental union of the soul with sanctifying grace, the soul is rendered holy with the accidental, created and finite holiness of grace, so and much more by the union, not accidental but substantial, of the humanity with the Word, which is sanctity by essence, is the humanity rendered holy with the substantial, uncreated and infinite sanctity of the Word. In order to understand this better, let us for a moment imagine that the sanctifying grace of a soul goes on increasing until it becomes infinite. It is plain that as the grace is gradually increasing, the sanctity of the soul is increasing, and when the grace would become infinite, that soul would be infinitely holy; and this on the supposition that grace remains always in its condition of participation and created likeness of the divine essence, and united to the soul accidentally. Now advance a step further; and imagine that this infinite grace be no longer an accidental perfection, but a substance; no longer a participation and created likeness of the essence of God, but God Himself; and that it be united to the soul no longer accidentally, but substantially, in such wise that infinite sanctity forms between this soul and God a most intimate relation, similar to that which exists between our soul and our person. What shall we think of such a soul ? Have we not reason to say that this soul is infinitely holy, and holy with the very sanctity of God ? Now this is just what is verified in the most sacred humanity of Christ by the hypostatic union with the Word. Because in virtue of such union, there are bound together with an ineffable, but most real embrace, the human nature and the divine person, which is essentially infinite sanctity, uncreated and substantial. It may be objected perhaps that, if it be so, then the humanity of Christ will be as holy as the Word itself, since the very sanctity of the Word belongs also to it. I grant that the sanctity of the Word belongs also to it; but not in the same manner, nor by the same title. It belongs to the Word essentially; to the humanity not essentially, but by a mere gratuitous gift, and therefore, in relation to it, is called grace. It belongs to the Word by identity, since the Word of itself is holy and sanctity; it belongs to the humanity not by identity, but by personal union, and is therefore called the grace of union.

Hence we can infer the most singular love of God towards the human nature of Christ. For God, by loving, confers on the object loved the good He wishes it: and, therefore, by the general love which he has towards all creatures, confers on them the natural being which they have; and by the special love which He has for rational creatures, confers on them a supernatural being, that is, a most intimate and gratuitous participation of His divine essence, which is grace, with which He sanctifies them: but to the humanity of Christ, through a most special love of predilection for it, He wished, in addition, to communicate to it His own same personal being, and to anoint it, that is, to sanctify and to deify it with all the plenitude of His divinity: "For in him dwelleth all the fulness of the Godhead corporally." (Colos. II, 9.) And St. Gregory Nazianzen says: "He is called the Christ on account of the divinity; for the divinity is the unction of the humanity, not sanctifying by operation, as in the other christs, but by the full presence of the one who anoints, the result of which is that he who anoints is called man, and that which is anointed becomes God."

Both soul and body of Christ sanctified by the grace of union.

By the grace of union, not only the soul, but also the body of Christ is sanctified, because the whole humanity of Christ was united substantially to the Word — the uncreated sanctity. And for that reason the Apostle said that in Christ the divinity 'dwelleth corporally,' that is to say, in his body also, and not in the soul only, as in the other saints, in whom God dwells by habitual grace, which is in the essence of the soul and by the knowledge and love, which are acts of the soul's faculties. Consequently, the flesh also of Jesus Christ partakes, as far as it is capable, of the substantial sanctity of the divine person to which it is united. The consequence is, first, that it also is rendered worthy of supreme worship. Secondly, it is rendered most pure and spotless, incapable of any stain of sin, or even of incentive to sin, and of any disorder or defect which might include the least impropriety. Thirdly, it is consecrated to

God in the most singular manner, or rather it is most verily made God's own. Fourthly, in virtue of such union it has a right to be conjoined with the holy and blessed soul of Christ, and to enjoy also the happiness proportioned to it; and if for some time it did not enjoy this, it was through a special miracle, in order that the work of man's redemption might be accomplished in the manner preordained by God. Lastly, it is not only holy, but it is moreover sanctifying and vivifying.

How in Christ the grace of union precedes habitual grace.

In Christ the grace of union precedes habitual grace, not in time, but in concept, for three reasons. First by reason of the sources of these two graces. The source of the grace of union is the person of the Son, who is said to be sent into the world, in as much as he assumed human nature. The source of habitual grace is the Holy Ghost, who is said to be sent, in as much as he dwells in the soul by sanctifying grace. Now the mission of the Son, according to the order of thought, is anterior to the mission of the Holy Ghost, because the Holy Ghost proceeds from the Son. Wherefore the personal union of the Son with the human nature, in which the grace of union consists, is anterior in idea to the dwelling of the Holy Ghost in the soul of Christ by habitual grace. Secondly, the same is deduced from the relation which habitual grace has to the grace of union, that of effect to the cause; for the reason that habitual grace in man is caused by the presence of the divinity, as light in the atmosphere is caused by the presence of the sun. Now in Christ the presence of the divinity is by the union of the divine person with the human nature; habitual grace, therefore, is to be conceived as the effect, and consequently as subsequent to such union, just as brightness follows the sun from which it emanates. The third reason is drawn from the end of habitual grace. Habitual grace is ordained for operating aright; it therefore presupposes the person, since to operate is the property of a person. Now in the human nature of Christ there is not, and cannot be conceived a person without the hypostatic union: but precisely, in virtue of such union, this nature, which has no personality of its own, becomes the nature of the person of the Word, which acts in it and by it. Hence habitual grace is posterior in idea to the hypostatic union or grace of union. And this same truth is pointed out in those words of Isaias (XLII, 1): "Behold my servant, I will receive him. . . I have given my spirit upon him;" which words (as appears in St. Matthew XII, 18) are to be understood of Christ. First it is said, 'I will receive him,' to signify the grace of union, and then it is added, 'I have given my spirit upon him,' to express habitual grace, which came after the union, as light after the sun, according to what has just been indicated.

Chapter XV.

Habitual Grace.

Let us first consider what is meant by habitual grace. It is a supernatural and permanent quality, which is infused by God into the soul of the just, to be an intrinsic and connatural principle of supernatural operations, as, for example, our intellect is the intrinsic and connatural principle of the concepts, judgments and reasonings, which we are continually forming. Yet we must not confound grace with the infused virtues, such as faith, hope and the rest, but it is distinct from these, as the root from the trunk, or as the rational nature from the natural virtues which perfect it. As, then, the natural light of reason is distinct from the acquired virtues which are named after it, so the light of grace is distinct from the infused virtues which in like manner are named after it, presuppose it, and are derived from it. Hence the Apostle says to the Ephesians (V, 8): "You were heretofore darkness," because without the light of grace, "but now light in the Lord;" in other words, you are now light not by essence, but by participation, that is, by the light of grace. He then adds: "Walk ye as the children of light," that is, so walk hereafter by acts of the infused virtues, as becomes those who have been regenerated

(88)

by the light of grace. For as the acquired virtues, such as justice, natural temperance, and the like, dispose a man to walk conformably to the natural light of reason, so the infused virtues dispose a man to walk conformably to the light of grace. Consequently, grace does not reside in the powers, but in the essence of the soul, since every perfection of the powers has the nature of virtue. Now grace, as has been said, is anterior to the virtues and their roots. It should reside, therefore, in a subject which is anterior to the powers and their roots; and such precisely is the essence of the soul.

Habitual grace in Christ.

Besides the grace of union in Christ, we must admit also habitual grace by which his soul was intrinsically and formally sanctified and deified, as is the case with the other just; in a manner, however, incomparably more eminent, and proportioned to the most sublime dignity of a soul which was substantially united to the Word of God. And the most evident proof of this is deduced precisely from the hypostatic union of the soul of Christ with the divine person, and this in three ways. First, by the closest proximity which the soul of Christ, in consequence of such union, has with God, the author of grace. For the nearer a thing is to the influencing cause, the more it partakes of the influence, provided it be fit to receive it. Now the nearness of the soul of Christ to the divinity, which is the source of grace, is the greatest that can be: and, on the other hand, it is the very best disposed to receive the precious influence, having no impediment, as being most free from all demerit, nay, being most deserving of every most singular gift of God. In the second place, by the most sublime dignity to which the soul of Christ was exalted. For is it not proper that the spouse of a king, simply because she is such, no matter of how low a condition she may be, should be endowed and adorned according to royalty, as becomes the supreme dignity of the spouse, who has chosen her? Now the soul of Christ is espoused to the divine Word, nay, united to him in a manner much more intimate and close than is any spouse to her husband, so that it really becomes all his own. How much more proper then, that it should be endowed and adorned as becomes the dignity of the divine person, who has assumed it, that is, endowed and adorned in a divine manner. Now the divine vesture and ornaments are habitual grace, and the other supernatural gifts, which follow it. In the third place, from the hypostatic union it comes to pass, that the humanity of Christ becomes the most special object of God's love and complacency. Yea, this same union is an act of God's most singular predilection towards it. Now, love wishes a correspondence equal, as far as possible, to itself. Imagine a mother that loves her babe, the fruit of her womb, with the greatest tenderness. See with what affection she kisses it, caresses it and presses it to her bosom. But she is not satisfied with all this; she desires that the little one should also on its part kiss, caress and embrace her, and show by

such acts how much it loves her. And if, perchance, the babe should be unable to show such
affection towards her, what would she not do to
render it capable of a correspondence of its love
with her's? Apply then this example to our case.
By the hypostatic union God loved, and in an ineffable manner pressed to his bosom Christ's human
nature. But this was not sufficient for his love.
Doubtless he wishes the humanity of Christ also
on its part to be pressed to him with the operations
of knowledge and of love, in the most perfect and
intimate manner possible to a human nature in the
present state of supernatural elevation; that is, to
cling to him with the most perfect vision and
affection and beatific fruition. For this reason,
since the humanity of Christ is naturally incapable
of producing such acts, God infused into it the
supernatural habit of grace, which is the proportionate root thereof. From the arguments hitherto
adduced, we see here a confirmation of what was
said in another place, that the habitual grace in
Christ comes after the grace of union, as brightness
comes after the sun. Hence this grace in the
humanity of Christ is not the fruit and reward of
merits, but is an embellishment connatural to the
dignity and requirement of a nature assumed by
the Son of God.

The fulness of grace in Christ.

In Christ there was not only grace, but even the
fulness of grace: "Full of grace and of truth."
(John I, 14.) Grace is said to be full when it is

the greatest both as to essence and efficacy; that is to say, when grace is possessed both in the greatest excellence possible, and in the greatest extension to all the effects of grace: As for example, in a monarchy the authority of the king is full, for the reason that it is supreme, and because it embraces all the powers that regard the authority of perfect civil society.   Now Christ from the first had grace in the most perfect degree possible in the present order established by divine wisdom.   This is evident, whether we regard the soul of Christ in relation to God, or in relation to ourselves. In relation to God, because his nearness to God, the source of all grace, is so great, that greater cannot be imagined between the creature and the Creator. Therefore, the grace which flows into it from such a source must also be the very greatest.   In relation to ourselves, because the soul of Christ received grace not for itself alone, but that it might be transfused into us all, so that in its turn it also might become a fountain of grace for us.   Therefore, as in that body which would be the cause of light or heat to all other bodies, there ought to be the greatest light, the greatest heat, so also in the soul of Christ, which is the cause of grace for us all, there should be the greatest grace.

Moreover, the grace of Christ was full as to efficacy; for it extended without exception to all the effects of grace, such as virtues, and the supernatural gifts which spring from habitual grace, as from the root. The reason of this is, because grace was conferred on Christ as on the first and universal principle in the class of those who are endowed with grace. Now the efficacy of the first and universal principle in any class should extend to all the effects which are contained in that class. So to return to the example adduced, the power of a prince in a monarchy extends to all the effects of authority that belong to civil society. But this is to be understood in the sense, that in Christ there is contained whatever perfection there is in all the effects of grace, but without the defects which perchance may be found in them. So, in like manner, the prince has whatever authority there is in the subordinate officials, but without the dependence and restrictions which are in them.

It is true that not only Christ, but others also were said to be full of grace; but they were not styled full of grace after the same manner as Christ. Reflect, therefore, that the plenitude of grace may be considered either absolutely or relatively. Absolutely, that is on the part of grace itself; relatively, that is on the part of the subject invested with it. Absolute plenitude is that which we have described, and is proper only of Christ. Relative plenitude is when one has grace in that degree of perfection and virtue which becomes his condition, and this plenitude of grace is not *the proper* of Christ, but is communicated to others through him. Thus the Bl. Virgin was full of grace, for she had the grace corresponding to that state to which she was chosen by God, of being the mother of his only begotten Son. St. Stephen also was full of grace, because he had the grace proportionate to the state to which he was chosen by God, of being a minister and martyr of Christ. Hence we see that such a plenitude can be greater or less, according as one is called by God to a higher or lower state.

The habitual grace in Christ in some sense infinite.

Although the habitual grace in Christ according to its essence be finite, since it is a created entity, and resides in a created and finite subject, as the soul of Christ is, yet in some sense it may be said to be infinite, because without limitation, whether in respect to the gift conferred, or in respect to him who received it, or in respect to the end for which it was ordained. In respect to the gift conferred, for the reason, as we have seen, that grace was given to Christ in all the plenitude and perfection to which it could extend, as became him who should be not only supremely sanctified in himself, but also the principle of sanctification to the whole human race. In respect to the nature which received grace, because it received of it as much as a created nature is capable of in the order now determined by God in the degrees of elevation of the creatures, of which without exception Christ is the head. In respect to the end for which grace was ordained, since it was ordained to a union with God, much greater and more perfect than that to which grace is ordained in all the other saints, even to the greatest union that can exist between the soul and God, that is, to personal union. Wherefore the divine omnipotence could indeed make a grace greater and better in itself than the habitual grace of Christ, but he could not cause it to be directed to a more perfect union with God than the hypostatic union with the person of the only begotten Son of the Father. We must be on our guard, however, against mistake, when we hear that habitual grace in Christ was ordained to the union of human nature with the Word, by thinking that grace was a quasi disposition previous to such a union. No, grace was not a disposition, but on the contrary was a consequence of the hypostatic union, and therefore it is said to be ordained to this, in the same way as the royal crown may be said to be designed for the royal dignity, by way of symbol and ornament proper to such dignity.

In Christ grace was not capable of increase during his passible life on this earth. But in us it can increase as long as we are in this life. First on the part of grace, which is never in the highest degree, and can therefore always advance. Secondly on the part of the subject, since we have not yet arrived at the term, as have those in bliss, but we are still on the way to our heavenly country. Now neither of these things was verified in Christ, for in him grace was most full from the beginning, because from the first instant it attained its end fully, which was union with God in the most perfect manner imaginable. Besides, Christ as man enjoyed most truly from the first moment of his conception the beatific vision. But if such be the case, how could it be said that 'he advanced in wisdom, in age and in grace before God and before men' ?   (Luke II, 52.)   It could be said with all truth, for although the habit of wisdom and of grace remained always the same in him, for the reason that it was always most perfect, yet in the effects or works which he produced in virtue of these habits, the perfection of wisdom and of virtue always was, and always appeared greater.   He advanced therefore, as he increased in years, in as much as he performed with the same habits, actions always more perfect.   Such would be the advancement of a plant, in which the vital vigor would be very perfect and always the same, and in virtue of this would go on, as the seasons succeed each other, adorning itself first with leaves, then with blossoms, and afterwards with fruit.   Such too would be the advancement of a very skilful musician, who possessing the same art in perfection, would go on drawing from his instrument melodies always sweeter and sweeter.

Chapter XVI.

The Virtues in Christ.

In Christ there was whatever is contained in the infused virtues, and that in the most singular degree. Nor could it be otherwise. For as the faculties of the soul spring from its essence, so the supernatural virtues, which perfect the faculties, proceed from habitual grace, which perfects the essence; and the choicer the grace from which they spring, the more excellent they are. Now the grace in Christ was most full and most perfect. It follows, therefore, that there sprang from it all the virtues in the highest degree, to perfect each faculty and each act of his soul.

No defects in the virtues of Christ.

As has been said, the virtues in Christ contained whatever perfection they could have, and therefore all those defects were excluded which by chance they could suppose or contain, and which were unbecoming the dignity and high state of his soul. From this we can infer that in him there was charity, and that it was most consummate; for the reason that charity is love, and love does not admit in its conception any imperfection. Hence even in heaven it is not destroyed, but reigns and glows more than ever. But in him there could not be faith and hope, just as these virtues are not in those who possess the vision and fruition of God. Not faith, since it is the property of faith to believe divine things without seeing them. But the soul of Christ from the first moment of its existence clearly beheld the essence of God. Not hope, because it is the property of hope to expect the fruition of God not yet obtained; but the soul of Christ possessed it always and fully from the beginning. Observe, however, that faith was entirely excluded in Christ, because his knowledge was most full. But hope was excluded only in as much as it is a theological virtue, for his soul always possessed that good which is the principal object of this virtue, namely God. But it was not excluded entirely, for he did not always possess all those other goods, which belonged to the complete perfection of his human nature, such, for example, as the immortality and glory of the body. Hence he expected and hoped for these goods.

All the infused cardinal virtues were in Christ.

In a similar way all the infused cardinal virtues were in Christ, and consequently all the others which are included in them or connected with them. His reason, therefore, was perfected with the most perfect prudence; his will with the most perfect justice; the irascible part of his sensitive appetite with the most perfect fortitude, and the concupiscible part with the most perfect temperance. This however is always to be understood, by leaving out the imperfections with which these virtues in us are connected. Thus, for instance, in Christ there were no depraved desires whatever. But that did not preclude temperance in him, which is rather the more excellent, the freer a man is from those disorderly appetites. As to continence, if by that is meant a resistance to the disorderly motions of concupiscence, it is not a perfect virtue, but less than a virtue, because it does not purport an entire subjection of the sensitive appetite to reason, and on this very account could not be found in Christ.

Finally, if so great and so splendid were the supernatural virtues with which the soul of Christ was endowed, we may judge what also must have been the natural virtues, which combined with the others to adorn it. These virtues are known as intellectual or moral, according as they perfect the reason or the appetite, and they are called acquired virtues, since they are given to us by nature only in germ, and the perfection of them must be acquired by us gradually by a repetition of acts. Now all the habits of the natural virtues, supposing their imperfections eliminated, concurred undoubtedly to embellish the soul of Jesus Christ; and all without comparison exceedingly more perfect than they were ever in any man. Nor was it gradually, as in us, but in the plenitude of their perfection from the first instant, when that most noble soul was at the same time created and united to the Word. And this, because it thus certainly became the incomparable dignity of a soul, that was raised by God to an eminence so sublime.

Chapter XVII.

The Gifts of the Holy Ghost.

By gift is meant here a supernatural habit infused by God, by which a man is disposed to
follow promptly the impulse of the Holy Ghost;
and it is different from virtue which disposes him
to follow with promptness the rule and movement
of reason. The gifts of the Holy Ghost are necessary for man to attain his supernatural end, for
which the influence of reason is not sufficient,
although it be informed with the theological virtues; but in addition to this, the movement of the
Holy Ghost is also required. Let us represent to
ourselves a ship built with consummate skill, and
furnished with everything necessary to have it
obedient to the rudder. Let us suppose, too, that
a most skilful pilote has charge of the rudder to
guide it. All this is not sufficient to reach the
desired port, but it is necessary, also, that a favorable wind should blow, and that the vessel with its
sails spread, should receive its impulse. Now a
similar thing happens to man. In order that he
may be able to tend to and reach the right land,
the land which is the inheritance of the children
of God, reason, however elevated and perfected by
supernatural virtues, is not sufficient, but the
breath of the Holy Ghost is also required; and

therefore it is necessary that the soul be furnished with the gifts by which, as the vessel by its sails, it be rendered capable of receiving and seconding the impulse of the Holy Ghost which moves and guides it. "Thy good Spirit shall lead me into the right land." (Ps. CXLII, 10.) "Whosoever are led by the Spirit of God, they are the sons of God . . . and if sons of God, heirs also." (Rom. VIII, 14, 17.)

These gifts are seven, four of which perfect a man in his reason: wisdom and intellect in speculative reason; counsel and knowledge in practical reason; and the other three perfect him in the appetite regarding himself and others: and these are fortitude, piety and fear. Hence they are coextensive with the intellectual and moral virtues jointly, that is, they extend to all the faculties which can be the principles of human acts, since they can all be moved by God. As the moral virtues all unite in prudence, because by prudence, the reason by which they are governed is perfected; so the gifts of the Holy Ghost are mutually bound in charity, by which the Holy Ghost dwells and reigns in our hearts: "The charity of God is poured out into our hearts by the Holy Ghost, who is given to us." (Rom. V, 5.) He, therefore, who has charity has every gift, and he who has it not, has not any. Lastly observe that the gifts will remain in heaven as to their essence, for there man will be entirely subject to God, because God will 'be all in all.' (1. Cor. XV, 28.) They will cease, however, to operate in those matters which

belong to the present life, such as the evils we have
to avoid, the dangers we meet, the difficulties to
overcome, and other such things as cannot take
place in the state of bliss.

All the gifts above mentioned were in Christ.

In Christ there were without doubt, and in the
most admirable manner, all the gifts above mentioned, being that his soul, much more than any
other, 'was led by the Spirit,' yea, moved most
perfectly by the Holy Ghost. "But Jesus full of
the Holy Ghost returned from the Jordan, and was
led by the Spirit into the desert." (Luke IV, 1.)
We must not think that by this we diminish in any
way the highest perfection of his virtues, for the
reason, as we have seen before, that however eminent the virtues may be, they always have need of
being assisted by the gifts, which perfect the powers
of the soul in relation to the movement of the Holy
Ghost. Nor is it any objection to this, that the
soul of Christ always enjoyed the contemplation
of the heavenly abode, for, as has been said, the
gifts remain even in heaven; and besides, Jesus
Christ was, it is true, in possession of the beatific
vision, but he was at the same time a wayfarer.
From this we may conclude how it may be said of
Christ with the strictest truth, that he both received
the gifts of the Holy Ghost, and at the same time
bestows them. He received them as man, and he
bestows them as God, for the reason that from him
as God, proceeds the same Giver of divine gifts.

In Christ there was also the fear of God.

In Christ there was also the fear of God. Concerning this there may be some reason for doubting, for it is written that perfect charity casts out fear: "Perfect charity casteth out fear." (1. John IV, 18.) And the charity of Christ was perfect beyond measure. Observe, then, that the fear of God may be either servile or filial. Servile fear shrinks from the evil of pain. It is a good fear, and comes from the Holy Ghost, but is not among the gifts of the Holy Ghost, because the fear of God, which is a gift of the Holy Ghost, is necessarily joined with charity, like the other gifts, and the more charity is inflamed, the more it increases; whilst, on the contrary, servile fear is just that fear which charity casts out; and the more perfect this is, the further it drives it away. Filial fear, which is also called chaste fear, recoils chiefly from the evil of guilt. It is called filial, because it is proper of a son to fear offending his father; and it is called chaste, because it is proper of the wife to fear offending her husband; and so the one and the other fear because they love. We see, then, that the soul which has this fear, fears through the love it bears to God its father and its spouse. And therefore this fear, so far from being expelled by charity, is even begotten by it, and advances in growth equally with it. Now this is exactly that fear which is numbered among the gifts of the Holy Ghost.

Moreover, fear is referred at the same time to a twofold object, that is, to evil and to good. To the evil from which it shrinks; to the good to which he that fears acknowledges his dependence. Thus, for instance, in servile fear the evil is the pain, and the good is the power and the right which the superior has of inflicting chastisement. In filial and chaste fear, the evil is the offence, and the good is the preeminence and dignity that the father or husband has, on account of which love and submission are due to them, and not offence. Consequently, in fear there is included a twofold tendency, one of flight in respect to evil, the other of subjection and reverence in respect to good. These premises being laid down, it is easy to understand in what manner the fear of God could be in Christ. It was not servile fear, but was filial and chaste fear. And this same fear was not in regard to evil, for he was impeccable, and therefore he could not fear separation from God by offence; but it was in regard to good, in as much as his soul being moved by the Holy Ghost, humbled itself to God with feelings of reverence proportionate to his supreme dominion. And the soul of Christ was full of this most perfect fear, as it was full of charity. Hence it is written of him: "He shall be filled with the spirit of the fear of the Lord." (Isa. XI, 3.)

In Christ there were also the twelve fruits of the Holy Ghost.

In Christ there were also, in their highest perfection, the twelve fruits of the Holy Ghost, enumerated by St. Paul in his letter to the Galatians, chap. V; and the eight beatitudes, announced by Jesus himself in the sermon which he made on the Mount. This follows manifestly from what has been said regarding the virtues and the gifts of the Holy Ghost. For the fruits and the beatitudes do not differ from the virtues and from the gifts as different habits, but only as the acts of the habits from which they proceed. Fruits of the Holy Ghost are called the operations which a man performs by virtue of the Holy Ghost, which is in him like a divine seed, and therefore renders him capable of bearing divine fruits: "Every one that is born of God, doth not commit sin, for his seed remaineth in him." (1. John III, 9.) We call beatitudes certain acts of higher perfection, by which man advances and approaches with great strides to the attainment of his last end, which is the true beatitude; and on this account these same acts are called beatitudes, because he that perseveres in them is sure of arriving at glory, and even in this life already enjoys a foretaste of it. Therefore, the difference between the beatitudes and the fruits is the same as exists between the more and the less perfect. That an act of a man be fruit, it is enough that there be contained in it the properties that correspond to material fruits. These properties are two. The first is, that the fruits are the last term to which the power of the plant reaches; the second is a certain sweetness by which they become agreeable to the palate. And thus a human act, to become fruit, ought to be the last act of the faculty, that is, it ought to be the second or ultimate act; and besides it should be accompanied by a certain delight, which happens every time the operation is congenial to the one who operates. Moreover, to be the fruit of the Holy Ghost, it is necessary that the act proceed from a man, not according to his natural virtue, but according to the superior virtue which comes from the Holy Ghost. From this we see that every virtuous, supernatural act is the fruit of the Holy Ghost, whereas by beatitudes are meant only some of the more remarkable supernatural works, which therefore are ascribed rather to the gifts of the Holy Ghost, than to the virtues. Hence it is, that all the beatitudes are fruits; but all the fruits are not beatitudes.

This being so, it is most certain that, as in Christ the virtues were most perfect, and the gifts most perfect, so likewise the fruits of the Holy Ghost were most perfect, and the beatitudes most perfect. As regards the rewards which correspond to the merits of the various beatitudes, and they are all reduced primarily to the perfect felicity of heaven, and secondarily to the imperfect felicity which the just enjoy even on earth, Jesus by his most holy operations merited them all for us, as the head for his members, and he also merited them for himself in that respect in which they were still wanting to him, so that his glory and exaltation as man might be complete.

Chapter XVIII.

The Gratuitous Graces.

Grace is divided into sanctifying grace, which is called *gratum faciens*, that is, making acceptable, by which man is united with God; and into grace *gratis data*, that is, gratuitously given, by which man cooperates in the salvation of his neighbor. Of these two, the first is the more noble, as it disposes man immediately to union with his last end; the second is less noble, as it adapts him immediately to that which is a means and disposition for attaining such a union. This last is called *gratis data*, because it is not owed, but is granted gratuitously, and not *gratum faciens*, since it is not conferred, that the recipient may be justified by it, but rather that he may contribute to the justification of others. The various kinds of gratuitous graces are enumerated by St. Paul in his first epistle to the Corinthians (XIII, 8, 9, 10), and are reduced to three classes. Some are required for the full knowledge of divine things, and these are faith, wisdom and knowledge; some for the confirmation of doctrine, and such are the virtue of healing and of working other prodigies, prophecy and the discernment of spirits; others for announcing becomingly the revealed truths, such too are the gifts of languages, of interpretation, and of

explaining rightly the divine word. Notice, however, that by faith there is not meant the theological virtue, which should be common to all
those who are members of Christ, but a peculiar
understanding and certitude concerning the truths
of faith, whether it be joined with obscurity, as in
us, or with perfect clearness, as in Christ. In like
manner wisdom and knowledge are numbered here
among the gratuitous graces, not in as far as they
are gifts of the Holy Ghost, and consequently are
found in all those who have charity, but in as far
as they imply a special abundance of knowledge,
either of divine things which is wisdom, or of
human things which is science, by which, he who
possesses them, may easily instruct others, convince and confute his opponents; and as such they
are found only in those to whom the Holy Ghost
wishes to impart them: "But all these things one
and the same Spirit worketh, dividing to every
one according as he wills." (1. Cor. XII, 11.)

The gratuitous graces also were in Christ.

As in Christ there was sanctifying grace, so
also there were the gratuitous graces. This is
beyond all doubt, since these graces are ordained
to bring men back to God by instructing them in
the truths of faith, and generally in the truths
which concern human salvation. Now of such
truths Christ is the first and principal master, since
he was the first who announced them, and from
him the apostles and their successors received
them. Hence the Apostle said: "How shall we

escape, if we neglect so great salvation, which having begun to be declared by the Lord, was declared to us by them that heard him." (Hebr. II, 3.)

These graces, then, were in Christ, and they were commensurate with his quality of supreme and universal doctor and head of the whole Church, and with the dignity and virtue which redounded in his human nature from union with the Word. They were therefore most signal, and above all conception more admirable than in any other; and not only one or another, some or many, but all were united together in him, so that also in regard to these graces it was verified that Jesus 'was full of grace,' and that God the Father 'doth not give the spirit by measure' (John III, 34) to his Son, but gave it to him beyond all measure. They were not for a time, and in the manner of a transient act, as is the light in the air, and as they are wont to be granted to the other saints, but perpetual, and in the manner of permanent habits, as is the light in the sun, so that he could use them when he wished, according to his good pleasure. And for this reason it was said of him that the spirit of God was to repose and dwell in him: "The spirit of the Lord shall rest in him." (Is. XI, 2.) "He upon whom thou shalt see the Spirit descending and remaining on him, he it is that baptizeth with the Holy Ghost." John I, 33.) Lastly, they were united in him as in the first source from which they were to be conveyed to others, according as should be determined by him, because it belongs to Christ to distribute also these graces to the members of his mystical body: "To every one of us is given grace according to the gift of Christ. . . . And some indeed he gave to be apostles, and some prophets, and others evangelists, and others pastors and teachers." (Ephes. IV, 7. 11.)

In Christ there was the gift of prophecy.

Consider particularly how prophecy was in Christ, regarding which some doubt may perhaps occur. Observe then, in the first place, that prophecy does not necessarily imply an obscure and imperfect knowledge, which certainly could not be admitted in Christ; but it means only a supernatural knowledge of those things which are remote from the senses of men, and from the ordinary knowledge of those who are found in the state of wayfarers. Notice, in the second place, that he cannot be called a prophet, who knows and announces those things that are distant in regard to others, with whom he is not; or, in other words, that a man be called a prophet, it is necessary that he be with those, in regard to whom the things which he sees and announces are distant. This is evident as to place and time. Thus, for example, he will be a prophet who, being in Rome, knows and announces what is taking place in Paris; but he would not be a prophet, who would know this and announce it whilst in Paris. In a like manner, he would have been a prophet who in the last century had foreseen and predicted the events of the present century. But he is not a prophet, who knows and relates them whilst living in this age, whilst they are taking place.   It follows from this that neither God, nor the angels, nor the blessed can be called prophets, although they know and announce those things that are far from our know-ledge; for the reason that they are not together with us, that is, they do not share with us our same state.   But Christ, before his death, was not only a possessor of the beatific vision, but also a wayfarer, and therefore as a wayfarer he was most truly a prophet, because as such he communicated in the same state with us, that is, with those from whose knowledge the things, which he knew and announced, were remote.

Chapter XIX.

Christ the Head of the Church.

Jesus Christ is most truly the Head of the Church: "He hath made him head over all the church, which is his body." (Ephes. XXII, 23.) And surely it is the prerogative of the head to be above all the other members, because it is more eminent; and because it is more perfect, as it collects in itself all the senses, whilst in the other parts there is only the sense of touch; also because it belongs to it, to govern externally the other members of the body, and to convey its influence to them interiorly. Now these three things belong spiritually to Christ as man, regarding the mystical body of the Church, since he is the highest and first of all, not in time, but in dignity; hence he is called 'the first-born among many brethren,' and has the fulness of all graces within him, and therefore is said to be 'full of grace and of truth,' and because the external government belongs to him, and from him the internal influence of grace is diffused upon all the members of the Church, all of whom receive of his fulness. Here we must observe two things. The first is, that the grace which Christ has as head of the Church, does not differ from habitual grace, by which his soul is sanctified, except in the concept; but in the essence is the same grace which is personal to Christ, in as much as it justifies his soul, and is the grace of the Church's head, and in as much as it is the source of justification for others. The second thing is, that although the heart be the primary and most vital part of the human body, yet Jesus Christ is not called the heart of the Church, but the head. The reason for this is, because the head is a visible part, and in a like manner its dominion over its members is visible, whereas the heart is an unseen part, and exercises its influence in the body without being seen. For that reason the Holy Ghost, who invisibly vivifies and unites the various members of the Church, is compared to the heart; and Jesus Christ is compared to the head, according to his visible nature, in which and by which he presides over his Church.

Christ is the head of men both as to their souls and bodies.

Christ is the head of men according to his whole humanity, not as regards their souls only, but also as to their bodies. He is head according to his entire humanity, because the divinity is united to his soul and body, and therefore both, that is, his whole and entire humanity, influences men as an instrument of the divinity. And he is head not only of the souls, but of the bodies also, since he transfuses his virtue both into the souls and the bodies, primarily into the souls by vivifying them with grace and with glory, secondarily into the bodies, in as much as the members of the

8

body become instruments and arms of justice, which, through the merits and efficacy of Christ, reigns in the soul, and furthermore, because the life of glory shall be communicated from the soul also to the body. The body, therefore, partakes of the spiritual influence of Christ in two ways, as an instrument of grace, and as a partner of glory.

Christ is the head of all men without exception.

Christ is the head of all men without exception, because all men who have been since the beginning of the world, and shall be to the end, belong in some way to the mystical body of the Church; and because Jesus is the fountain of salvation and propitiation for all: "He is the Savior of all men, and especially of the faithful." (Tim. IV, 10.) "He is the propitiation for our sins, and not for ours only, but also for those of the whole world." (1. John XI, 2.)

Christ then is the head of all, but according to different degrees. First and principally, he is the head of those who are united to him actually by glory; next of those who are united to him actually by charity; then of those who are actually united to him by faith only; then of those who are united to him only in potency, not yet reduced to act, but which is to be reduced to act, according to the divine predestination; and lastly of those who are united to him in potency, which shall never be in act. But the damned and the demons have ceased entirely to be members of Christ, since they are no longer united with Christ even in potency. But they shall not cease, on this account, to be subject to his power: "For he hath put all things under his feet." (1. Cor. XV, 26.) All however are under him, not as members of his body, but as his foot-stool. "The Lord said to my Lord: Sit at my right hand until I make thy enemies thy foot-stool." (Ps. CIX, 1. 2.)

It may be asked, how it can be said that those are of the Church who have not even faith. They are of the Church, not in act, but in potency, which potency is founded on two things; first of all, and above all, on the merits of Jesus Christ, which are most sufficient to effect the salvation of the whole human race ; and next on free will. Nor should we wonder at hearing that the Church has members in potency; for this is exactly the difference there is between a man's natural body and the mystical body of the Church, that the members of the natural body exist all at the same time, but the members of the mystical body are not all actually at one time, either as to their natural existence, for men of all times belong to the Church, or as to their being in the state of grace, since even those belong to the Church who are without grace, but can have it.

To Christ alone belongs the internal communication of grace as the head of the Church.

As regards the internal communication of grace, it belongs only to Christ to be head of the Church; but as to the external government, it may belong also to others, but not in the same manner as to

Christ, because, in the first place, he is the head of all those that belong to the Church in whatsoever place or time or state they are found. But others are called heads either in respect to some particular places, as bishops who are heads of their dioceses, or if they have no limitation in place, still they have it in time, as the Pope, who is head of the whole Church, but only during the time of his pontificate. Besides this, the bishops as well as the Pope are heads of men considered only in the state of wayfarers. In the second place, Jesus Christ is head of the Church by virtue and authority of his own, whereas others are styled heads in as much as they take the place of Christ, and hence they are secondary heads and subordinate to Christ the supreme head: "For what I forgave, if I have forgiven anything, for your sakes have I done it in the person of Christ. — We are ambassadors for Christ, God as it were exhorting by us." (2. Cor. II, 10; V, 20.) And, in the same way, as others are called heads of the Church, they take also the name of foundation and of pastors, being always understood as foundation and pastors of the second order, and dependent on Christ, the primary foundation and pastor. As St. Augustin says, 'to his members he granted to be pastors, but none of us says of himself, he is a door; this he has reserved as proper to himself.' The name of door is proper only to Christ. Because it is not as those other names, which may refer as much to the principal as to the secondary authority. The door always signifies the principal authority, because through it, and through it alone, everyone enters the house. Hence Christ alone is the door, and therefore of him alone it is said, that he is the one: "By whom also we have access through faith into this grace, wherein we stand." (Rom. V, 2.) And he himself clearly affirmed, 'that no man cometh to the Father, but by me.' (John XIV, 6.) So no one can have ingress into the Father's house, whether the earthly one by grace, or the heavenly one by glory, except through this only door, which is Christ.

CHAPTER XX.

Christ the Head of Angels.

Christ, according to the human nature, is head not only of men, but likewise of the angels, for as St. Paul expressly testifies of him, 'God the Father has set him at his right hand in the heavenly places, above all principality and power and virtue and dominion, and every name that is named, not only in this world, but also in that which is to come.' (Ephes. I, 20. 21.) And of this there can be no doubt, for there should be one and the same head of one and the same body. Now angels and men, wayfarers and the possessors of bliss, all compose one sole mystical body of the Church, since they are all ordained to one sole end, that is, eternal happiness; and from the unity of the end, there comes the unity of the social body. Christ, therefore, according to his humanity, is the head of all, both of angels and of men. And indeed, these three prerogatives by which he is called and is the head of men, belong to Jesus Christ also in regard to the angels, for without doubt, even in regard to the angels he is above them by dignity, by the most perfect participation of divine gifts, and by the dominion and influence which he exercises over them.

The relations of Christ's humanity with angels and men are not equal.

Although Christ is also the head of the angels, it does not follow from this that the relations of his humanity with men and angels are altogether equal. There is a difference in two things. In the first place, as to his conformity, which is greater with men, since these agree with the humanity of Christ in the same species. With the angels it is less, since they correspond with it only in the genus of intellective nature. In the second place, as to the influence which his humanity exercises on both. For the influence of Christ's human nature on men is the end to which it is itself ordained, as the divine Word assumed our nature to become for us in it, and by it, the spring of supernatural life; whereas its influence on the angels is not the end, but the consequence of the Incarnation, for it is true, or at least more probable, that the Word did not become incarnate to communicate its influence to the angels as the head does to the members; but the Incarnation being accomplished, and human nature being thereby raised to the most exalted dignity, it follows that it has the right and efficacy of dominating and influencing also the angels.

In what the influence of Christ's humanity on the angels consists.

Let us consider in what the influence, which the humanity of Christ exercises on the angels, precisely consists. It does not act on them, as on us, by removing sin and punishment which is the impediment to supernatural life and glory, because such an impediment cannot exist in them at present, since they are already beatified; and when it could have existed, which was during their transitory state, it did not at all take place. Nor does it even exercise an influence by meriting for them grace and substantial glory, for by what we can gather from the holy scriptures, which are the only means by which we are given to know what depends on the mere will of God above all claim of the creature, the Incarnation of the Word was effected not to merit the sanctification and glorification of the angels, but to accomplish the redemption of the human race.

In order, then, to understand well in what the influence of Christ's humanity on the angels consists, it will be well to presuppose two things. The first is that the angels are all indeed most noble and most perfect spirits, and all enjoy the beatific vision; still they have not all the same degree of perfection, whether in the natural or supernatural order. On this account they are divided according to the different excellence which they have, both natural and supernatural, into three hierarchies, or sacred principalities, subordinate one to the other; and besides, each hierarchy is subdivided into three orders or choirs, which take different names corresponding to the various properties and various offices that belong to each. And in the same way, as the degree of perfection of nature and grace is not equal in all, neither is the degree of knowledge which they have naturally or supernaturally, but this also is greater or less, according as they are found more or less elevated in the various choirs and various hierarchies. It is true, that in the angels there is not and cannot be ignorance properly so called, that is, a privation of due knowledge, but only nescience, or an absence of knowledge relating to those things appertaining to the state of nature, or of grace or of glory, the knowledge of which is not their due either by the condition of their nature, or by the condition of their beatitude. This nescience, as is clear, is more extended in the lower, and more restricted in the higer angels; still it is found in some manner in all, because the knowledge even of the most perfect is finite. It is true, they all enjoy the beatific vision, but they do not see God as much as he is knowable. This would be to comprehend the divine essence, and is proper to God alone.

The second thing to premise is, that the angels of the second hierarchy are purified and enlightened and perfected by the angels of the first hierarchy, and in like manner the angels of the third hierarchy by those of the second, and in general the lower by the higher; and these are called the hierarchical acts, which the angels exercise one upon another. The first act is to purify the subordinate angels by removing from their intellects the defect, if it may be called so, of nescience. The second act is to enlighten them, which they do in two ways, by strengthening the intellective power of the less perfect, just as a warmer body by its presence increases the warmth of a body less warm;

and also by proposing to them the truth in a manner proportioned to the capacity of their intelligence. The third act consequently perfects them by the apprehension of the truth made known, which is the end and perfection of the intellect. And these three, as is plain, are not properly distinct acts, but rather than three different acts, they are three several respects of the same act, by which they manifest the truth, and therefore diminish the nescience, and increase the perfection of the intellect. The sun does something like this for us. It purifies us by dispelling the obscurity of the night, it enlightens us by clarifying us with its rays, and by rendering bodies visible to our eyes, it perfects us by making our visual faculty pass from potentiality to act, and perceive its proper object. We have another example also in what the master does with his scholar. He purifies him from the darkness of ignorance, he enlightens him by proposing to him, in a form best suited to his capacity, the truth which he wishes to teach him, and so perfects him by new informations by which he enriches and adorns his mind.

After this it will certainly not be hard to understand in what the influence, which the humanity of Jesus Christ exercises on the angels, consists. As the more elevated angels purify, enlighten and perfect the less elevated, so also the humanity of Christ, but in a manner incomparably more eminent and more divine, performs these same acts towards all the angels, even the highest and nearest to the throne of God; towards these immediately,

and in others by means of these, since the human
nature of Christ in heaven is placed above all the
blessed, and is seated even at the right hand of
God. And this perhaps is what St. John wished
to signify, when he affirmed in the Apocalypse
(XVI, 23), that the heavenly Jerusalem has no
need of the sun, or of the moon: "For the glory
of God hath enlightened it, and the Lamb is the
lamp thereof." He said, 'the glory of God,' to
denote the brightness of the substantial glory or
the divine essence, which is openly manifested,
and he added 'the Lamb is the lamp thereof,' to
indicate the light of accidental glory, which proceeds from the Lamb of God, that is, from Christ
according to his human nature, in which the Son
of God was slain and immolated for us. For the
most sacred humanity of Jesus is a fountain of
light in heaven, and not only of a most vivid and
delightful corporeal light, but also a fountain of
spiritual light for all the heavenly spirits in the
manner described.

CHAPTER XXI.

Christ the Spouse of the Church.

The word Church may have two meanings; the one more restricted, the other more ample. In the more restricted sense it means the mystical body of Christ, as distinct from its head; in the more ample sense it comprehends the body and head united together. When it is affirmed, that Christ is the spouse of the Church, the Church is spoken of in the first meaning, and not in the second. In the second meaning the Church includes the spouse and the bride, as being united together spiritually, they constitute but one person morally. And according to this second meaning, Christ may in some wise be said to be a member of the Church, since he has an office of his own different from that of the other members, which is to transfuse supernatural life into all the others. Whereas Christ cannot in any wise be called a member of his spouse. Observe, moreover, that only the first person of the B. Trinity is the father of the spouse, but all the three divine persons are really the father of the bride. However, by appropriation also we may attribute paternity to the Father in relation to the bride.

How Christ is the spouse of the Church.

Let us consider how Christ is shown to be the spouse of the Church. If we notice what are the relations which exist between husband and wife, we shall see the very same existing between Christ and his Church. The husband is the head of the wife, and Christ is the head of the Church: "The man is the head of the woman, as Christ is the head of the Church." (Ephes. V, 23.) The husband governs the wife, not as a slave, but as free, that is, not having his own, but her utility in view. Christ is also the savior of the Church, that is, he from whom the Church has all her good: "He is the savior of his body." (Eph. V, 23.) The wife should consequently be in thorough submission to the husband, and the Church in like manner is subject in all to Christ: "As the Church is subject to Christ, so let the wives be to their husbands in all things." (Eph. V, 24.) The husband should love his wife from his heart; thus too did Christ love the Church: "Men love your wives, as Christ also loved the Church." (Eph. V, 25.) But notice here the difference between the love of any other spouse and that of Christ. The love of every other spouse presupposes the spouse already existing, and possessed of those advantages of beauty, talent, riches and the like, which render her estimable and amiable to him. In Christ it is not so. The existence of the Church and of its prerogatives is not the cause, but the effect of Christ's love. Because he loved it, he formed it, and formed it worthy of himself. He cleansed and sanctified it in the laver of baptism, which has the efficacy of his blood. He has made it holy and immaculate by the communication of his grace in the present life; and by the communication of his glory in the future life, he will render it all glorious without spot or wrinkle, or any other thing that might tarnish or cloud its whiteness and splendor: "Christ loved the Church . . . . that he might sanctify it, cleansing it in the laver of water in the word of life, that he might present it to himself a glorious Church, not having spot or wrinkle, nor any such thing, but that it should be holy and without blemish." (Eph. V, 25. 26. 27.) "The marriage of the Lamb is come, and his wife hath prepared herself. And to her it hath been granted that she should clothe herself with fine linen glittering and white. For the fine linen are the justifications of the saints." (Apoc. XIX, 7. 8.) The husband should love his wife as himself : "Let every one of you in particular love his wife as himself." (Eph. V, 33.) But Christ loved the Church to such a degree, that he went so far as to immolate himself for it: "Christ loved the Church and delivered himself up for it." (Eph. V, 25.) The husband abandons his father and mother, to be united with his wife: "For this cause shall a man leave his father and mother, and shall adhere to his wife." (Eph. V, 31.) Christ too left his Father, in as much as he came into this world, and assumed our flesh: "I came forth from the Father, and am come into the world." (John XVI, 28.) He abandoned his mother, that is, the Synagogue, to be united continually with his Church until the end of ages: "Behold I am with you all days even to the consummation of the world." (Mat. XXVIII, 20.) The union of the husband and wife is not only moral, but also physical: "And they shall be two in one flesh." (Eph. V, 31.) The union likewise between Christ and the Church is also physical. First by the hypostatic union of the Word with a nature of our species, for in that nature assumed by the Word, the whole mass, as St. Gregory of Nissa remarks, is virtually blended with him. That nature was, as it were, the choicest first-fruit of the Church, and in it and by it the whole Church came to be united with the divine person of the Word in an ineffable manner. In the second place by the sacrament of the Eucharist, by which Christ, God and man, is truly, really and substantially present in his Church; and not only this, but he comes also to communicate and unite himself in the most intimate way with all and each of its members, by feeding them with his very body and blood. Lastly the fruit of matrimony is the fecundity of the wife; and the fruit of the spiritual marriage between Christ and the Church is the fecundity of the Church, by which she becomes the mother of all who are regenerated to the supernatural life of grace and glory. Thus we see how between the union of Christ with his Church, and the matrimonial union of the man with the woman, there is the greatest resemblance, and that the one is the representation of the other. But which of these two is the exemplar, and which the image? According to the doctrine explained by St. Paul in his letter to the Ephesians, the exemplar is the union of Christ with his Church, and the image is the nuptial union of the man with the woman; which, that it might be more like its prototype, was raised by Christ to the supernatural order, and to the dignity and holiness of a sacrament. For this reason also Christian matrimony is styled by the Apostle a great sacrament, just because it is a sign and a copy of that most admirable union which exists between Christ and his Church. "This is a great sacrament, but I speak in Christ and in the Church." (Eph. V, 32.) There are three sacraments called great in a particular manner: baptism, for the greatness of the effect it produces, which is to open the gates of heaven; the eucharist, for the greatness of what it contains, which is Christ the very fountain of grace; matrimony, for the greatness of the thing it signifies, which is the mystical nuptials of Christ with his Church.

The Church has the fecundity of a mother and the integrity of a virgin.

The Church, the spouse of Christ, in addition to the fecundity of a mother joins the integrity of a virgin, and of a virgin the more chaste, as her spouse is more pure and inviolate. This the Apostle meant to signify when, writing to the faithful of Corinth, he said: "For I have espoused you to one husband, that I may present you as a chaste virgin to Christ." (2. Cor. XI, 2.) I have espoused you, he says, not to myself, nor to many, but to one man alone, who is Christ. How had he espoused them to Christ? By converting them to the faith, and incorporating them with him in baptism.   He adds also, I have espoused you, that you may be a chaste virgin to Christ.   Take notice how from the plural he passes to the singular: I have espoused you . . . as a chaste virgin.   Why so?   To show that of all the faithful there is formed but one Church, one only spouse of Christ, and virgin spouse, nor virgin only, but chaste also. What difference is there between virgin and chaste? Virginity means integrity of the body; chastity means integrity of the spirit.   The meaning then is, that the Church should be incorrupt both in soul and in body, and for this reason we say 'chaste virgin'.

To understand this, it is well to know that in the Church we distinguish a two-fold element, an external and visible element which is called the body of the Church, and an internal and invisible element which is called the soul of the Church. The body of the Church is made up of the society of those who are bound together with the triple, external and visible bond of the profession of one same faith, of the communion of the same sacraments, and of submission to the same pastors, especially to the Roman Pontiff.   The soul of the Church consists in the internal and invisible principle of its life, that is to say, in what renders it living and life-giving supernaturally.   Hence to the soul of the Church belong sanctifying grace, the infused virtues, actual grace, the gifts of the Holy Ghost, the graces called *gratis datae*, and in short all those supernatural gifts which have for their end the conservation and advancement of the life and holiness of the Church.

9

Now if the Church be considered in itself, that is, in its constitution, in its end and its means, it is plain that it is free from every contamination, both in body and in soul. If again it be viewed in its members, the Church which is already made glorious in heaven in all and each of its members, has no spot nor wrinkle, but is altogether immaculate and holy. But the same cannot be said of the Church still militant here upon earth. It happens sometimes, that some of its members break those ties which hold them united to the others, and thus they come to break the integrity of the body of the Church; or to speak more accurately, the Church itself always maintains in reality the unity and integrity of its body inviolate, and therefore remains always a virgin, but those who separate from it, become thereby broken and corrupt members. From this it is evident that schismatical and heretical churches are no longer virgins or spouses of Christ, but fornicators and adulterers. In like manner in respect to the soul of the Church, not all its members are always vivified, nor always in the same manner. It has members that are weak, and members already dead. In such members the spiritual integrity, and therefore the chastity of the Church fails; not indeed because the soul of the Church is, or ever can be less pure in itself, but because such members are no longer worthy of being informed by it, or at least are not worthy of partaking of all its efficacy.

From what has hitherto been said we may infer that even in Christian matrimony the bride represents the Church but imperfectly, since she represents it only as to fecundity, not as to virginity. There was but one matrimony, in which the bride was a perfect figure of the Church, the spouse of Christ, and that was the matrimony between Joseph and Mary; seeing that Mary was at the same time a virgin and a mother, and thereby symbolized both prerogatives of the Church, that of a fruitful mother and that of a chaste virgin.

The Church is both a spouse and a queen.

Reflect that the Church, the spouse of Christ, is not only a most chaste virgin, but she is also a most august queen, because she is the spouse of Christ the king, and by being the spouse of the king, she is thereby queen, and a queen so much the more august, according as the royal dignity of her spouse is greater. For this reason the sacred interpreters apply to her those words of the psalm: "The queen stood on thy right hand in gilded clothing, surrounded with variety." (Ps. XLIV, 9.) In these words four most signal prerogatives of this royal spouse are pointed out. The first is of standing continually in the presence, and at the side of her spouse, all intent on observing and seconding his intimations. This is the meaning of 'stood'. The second is a most singular participation in the most excellent gifts of her spouse, and this is what is signified by the words 'on thy right hand.' Hence it is said also of Christ, that as man he is seated at the right hand of God, to signify, that his human nature does not partake infinitely, but in a more excellent manner than any other creature, in the divine goods of the Father. The third prerogative is the most precious gold which is lavished on her garments: 'In gilded clothing.' By the garments of the Church the holy doctors understand two things, doctrine and good works. Both these garments are glittering with gold: doctrine is glittering with the gold of divine wisdom; and good works are glittering with the gold of charity. Nor is it to be wondered that so great an abundance of such choice gold be poured out in the Church, since she has with her the living source of this double gold. She has with her the source of the gold of wisdom, for her head is Christ, who is divine wisdom itself, and the fountain of all wisdom. She has with her the source of the gold of charity, for her heart is the Holy Ghost, who is divine love itself, and the fountain of all holy love. The fourth prerogative is the variety with which she is surrounded, without any detriment, but rather with the greatest enhancement to her beauty; variety of virtues and of their degrees and of their acts, variety of sacred gifts, of offices and of dignities in her members, variety of nations that she has gathered to her bosom, by regenerating them to Christ, variety of times, of places, of vicissitudes, of war and of peace, of humiliations and of honors, of persecutions and of triumphs; varieties that surround her on every side, but do not change her in the least. She remains always equal to herself, always the beloved, the invincible, the faithful, the chaste and august spouse of Christ.

Chapter XXII.

Beatific Knowledge of Christ's Soul.

Besides the uncreated knowledge belonging to the divine nature, there was also in Christ the created knowledge belonging to creatures. For certainly it was not becoming the Son of God to take an imperfect human nature, as by it he should bring the whole human race to perfection; and therefore, although he already knew all things perfectly by divine knowledge, still the human soul assumed by him should also have its own proper knowledge to perfect it. Otherwise the soul of Christ would have been most imperfect, more so than the soul of any other man whatever. Nay, it would have been assumed by the Word uselessly, for every thing is called useless which fails to produce its proper operation. The fire is useless which does not heat, the medicine is useless which does not cure, the plant is useless which does not fructify. So in like manner, if the intellective soul of Christ had not had the operation suitable to it as to its intellectivity, or in other words, if it had not had the knowledge proper to it, it would have been like that unfruitful tree, of which it was said: "Why doth it take up the ground?" (Luke XIII, 7.)

In what this knowledge of Christ's soul particularly consists.

Let us consider in particular what this knowledge was, with which the soul of Christ was enriched. It was before all the beatific knowledge belonging to those in glory, which consists in the intuitive vision of the divine essence. Of this there can be no doubt. For when a soul is raised by God to a dignity, such as that of the soul of Christ, there is no prerogative however extraordinary, which does not become it, and which is not, as it were, a natural consequence of that first and most extraordinary of all, namely, of being united personally to the Word. Besides, is it not true that, as the earth owes its light to the sun, so we too owe to Christ, as man, the supernatural light of glory? Reflect then how proper it is that the soul of Christ should be illustrated with such a light to the highest degree. For what doubt is there, that light should be in the sun, and more vivid than on earth; and, in general, that the perfection of every effect must be found in the cause, and in a manner more excellent than in the effect?

How great the perfection of this knowledge was.

We shall now examine how great the perfection of this knowledge precisely was. First it is certain that the soul of Christ could not adequately comprehend the divine essence by it, that is, know it with a knowledge so vast and so clear, as to be able to measure its whole immensity, sublimity and profundity, and take in all that was knowable.

This is not possible, except by an infinite mind, which is the mind alone of God himself. Yet if it was not infinite, oh! how great was its extension and how great its clearness!

With regard to extension, could we say in some sense that the soul of Christ knew all things in the Word? If by all things is understood every thing that comes into existence, whenever it may be, we must affirm that it knew them all, that is, that it saw in God all that is, all that has been or will be, whether done or said or thought by any one at whatever time. The reason is because every one of the blessed certainly discovers more or less truth in the divine essence, according as he contemplates it more or less perfectly; each one however sees in it all those things that belong to himself. Now to Christ belong all things existing at whatsoever time, since all are subject to him, he being the supreme judge and head of all, not only as God, but also as man. Wherefore there is no doubt that his soul beholds them every one in the Word, and even the most secret thoughts, for he is the judge also of these. And, therefore, what was said of him that "He knew what was in man" (John II, 25), may be referred not merely to divine knowledge, but also to the knowledge which his soul had by the beatific vision. On the other hand, if by 'all things' we wish to denote not only those which are at some time in act, but those also which are in potentiality, but never reduced to act, it cannot be said in general, that the soul of Christ knew them all, but it is necessary to distinguish between those that are possible in regard to the divine power only, and those that are possible also to the power of creatures. As to the first of these, the soul of Christ did not know them all, for that would be to comprehend all that God can do, which is the same as to comprehend the divine omnipotence, and consequently the divine essence. But as to those things that regard the power of creatures, the soul of Christ had a perfect knowledge of them all, because in the Word it fully comprehended the essence of created things, and therefore their power, and all the effects which can result from this power.

So much then regarding the extension of the beatific knowledge of Christ. But what was the perfection of its clearness? Certainly it was not so great as to equal the infinite claritude of God's knowledge, but such doubtless as to far surpass that of all other creatures, however high they are, either in the order of nature or of glory. Nor could it be otherwise, for the reason that the most sacred soul of Christ is the nearest to the very fountain of the light of glory, which is the Word of God: "The Word of God on high is the fountain of wisdom." (Eccl. I, 5.) Hence from it that soul should, more than any other creature, partake in great abundance of the divine influx, by which it was rendered fit to contemplate more perfectly than any other creature truth itself, which is the essence of God. On this account Christ was called full, not of grace only, but of truth also: "Full of grace and of truth" (John I, 14), to denote that, as grace was most full in Christ, so likewise the beatific vision of divine truth was most full in him.

What follows from this reasoning.

Two things follow as a consequence from the previous reasoning. The first is that the beatific knowledge of Christ agrees in great part as to the object with God's knowledge, which we call vision, and which is the very knowledge by which God sees as present to him in his eternity all things that are to exist at any time. Notice well, however, that if these two knowledges agree as to the object known, they do not agree also in the claritude of cognition, as was said a little before; but the claritude of divine knowledge as far transcends the claritude of the knowledge of Christ's soul, as the uncreated light of the divine intellect surpasses the created, supernatural and most vivid light of Christ's soul, that is infinitely.

The second thing is, that when our Lord in discoursing on the day of judgment, said to his disciples: "Of that day or hour no man knoweth, neither the angels in heaven, nor the Son, but the Father" (Mark XIII, 32), he did not wish to signify, that even he as man did not know the time. For as St. Chrysostom justly reasons, if it was given to Christ as man to have authority and knowledge of universal judge, which is much more, how then was he not given to know the time of the judgment, which is much less? He said therefore, '*Neque filius scit*,' — Neither does the Son know, that is, '*Non facit scire*,' — He does not make known. As God had already said to Abraham: "Now I know that thou fearest God" (Gen. XXII, 12), not because God did not know it from the first; but 'now I know,' meaning now I have made thee know.

Chapter XXIII.

Infused Knowledge.

Here we shall consider what this infused knowledge is, of which we treat. It is well to presuppose with St. Augustine, that in the angels there is a twofold knowledge. The matutine knowledge, by which they know things in the Word; and the vespertine knowledge, by which they know things in themselves in their proper nature. The first is called matutine, because as the morning is the beginning of the day, so the Word, and the being which things have in the Word, is the beginning of the being which they have in themselves. The second is called vespertine, because as the day terminates in the evening, so the production of creatures terminates in that being which they receive and possess in themselves. Neither of them is called meridian, because both are imperfect and mixed with some obscurity, like the morning and evening twilight. In God alone the light of the intellect is in its fulness, and therefore only the knowledge of God can be compared to the meridian. Matutine knowledge belongs to the good angels only, because they alone deserved to be admitted to the intuitive vision of the Word and of the other things in him. The vespertine knowledge at the beginning was common to all the angels, by which each one knew himself. But after this first operation, some rose to the praise of the Creator by acknowledging him for their first beginning and last end, and thus from the vespertine they passed to the matutine knowledge; whilst others on the contrary stopped in the contemplation of their own perfections, taking pride in them, and placing their end in themselves, and thus became most dark, and eternal night. Hence the present knowledge of the reprobate angels cannot be termed even vespertine, since this is related and ordained to the matutine, but it should rather be called nocturnal, and therefore the demons are styled spirits and powers of darkness.

But how does this knowledge of things in themselves, which is termed vespertine, arise in the angels? It is certain that the angelic intellect, as well as that of any other creature, is not by its own sole essence sufficiently determined to understand all things. That belongs to the intellect of God only, who being a most pure and infinite act, in virtue of his essence, comprehends himself and every other truth. The created intellect is like a virgin soil, which is well adapted to bear any kind of fruit, but has need of being fecundated with seeds which have to complete and determine its generative power: and if it is not seeded, it will remain unfruitful. In a like manner the intellect of the creature, to be able to conceive and generate its word, which is its fruit, has need also to be fecundated by an intelligible species, which is its seed that completes and determines its intellective power. In this respect the human and the angelic intellect agree, as both have need of such species or seeds of knowledge to understand. But the difference is in this, that the human intellect needs to borrow its intelligible species from material objects; and on that account is furnished with an activity of its own, which is called active intellect. This, after the sensible images have been collected by the senses, and joined together in the fantasy, separates them from the grossness of the material conditions which they have, and by this means makes them seeds fit to be inserted in the immaterial faculty of the intellect. Hence it is that human knowledge is called acquired, since it is acquired successively, little by little. But it is not so in the angels. Their intellect has from the first instant all its seeds implanted in it by God himself, that is to say, all the intelligible species, which are, as it were, a precious store due to the perfection of their nature. And hence the knowledge of angels is called innate or infused as it is not gained gradually by begging the species from objects, but is infused into them all at once, and perfect in the very act of their creation.

After what has been said, it will be easy to understand what is meant by saying that the soul of Christ had infused knowledge. The meaning is, that as in the angels, besides the matutine knowledge by which they see the divine essence and the other objects in it, there was another called vespertine, by which they know things in their proper nature through innate species; so also in the soul of Christ, besides the beatific knowledge by which it contemplates God immediately and things in God, another knowledge must be admitted, by which it comprehends things in themselves by means of intelligible species infused into it by God, and proportionate to the human mind. This, therefore, is called human knowledge and corresponds to the vespertine knowledge of the angels.

Why the soul of Christ was endowed with infused knowledge.

If we inquire why the soul of Christ was endowed also with this knowledge, the reason is because, as was intimated before, it was not becoming that the human nature assumed by the Word of God should be imperfect. Now it would have been imperfect, if the capacity of its intelligence had not been altogether and in every way reduced to the act, but had remained at least in part in potentiality, like a soil that can, but does not produce, for the reason that it is not cultivated. It was necessary, then, that it should have been actuated and determined to understand all those things in regard to which it was potential. On this account the human intellect of Christ, as well as that of the angels, might with reason be compared to the terrestrial paradise, of which it is written that it was planted by God himself from the beginning: "And the Lord God had planted a paradise of pleasure from the beginning." (Gen. II, 8.) Or it might be likened also to a living harp, which without need of being touched by hand, would be already disposed of itself to form all the harmonies that its strings can produce; or to a very bright and living mirror which would have in itself the power of forming all the images it wished, so that it could at every moment represent by itself whatever kind and as many as it would.

The properties of this knowledge.

You wish to know perhaps more particularly what are the properties of this knowledge. First of all, it was as ample as is the power of the human soul to understand, that is, as ample as are the truths which the human soul can learn either by the natural light of the intellect, or also by revelation, whether they appertain to the gift of wisdom or of prophecy, or to any other gift of the Holy Ghost. The soul of Christ then knew all these truths fully by infused knowledge, yet by this he did not see the essence of God immediately, for that is the property only of the beatific knowledge.

In the second place, Christ was able to use the infused knowledge without the aid of fantasms. For it is true that in the present state our intellect is so weak, that it cannot make a step without the support of the imagination, but the same does not occur to the souls in bliss, which even after the resurrection of the body, will not be at all subject to this, but will master it fully, and hence also they will then be able to understand with complete independence of the sensitive faculties. Now Jesus Christ was not a wayfarer only, but at the same time he possessed the beatific vision, and he had

the conditions of a wayfarer, especially as to the
body, and those of a possessor of bliss especially as
to the soul. Therefore he had not the least need
of fantasms, to understand, although he was able
to make use of them, if he wished.

The third property is that this knowledge was
not discursive as to its origin, although it might
have been so as to its use. It was not as to origin,
because it was not obtained by Christ by deducing
one cognition from another, as happens in us, but
it was impressed in his mind by divine operation,
and not produced by the investigation of reason.
It might have been discursive in use, for Christ, if
he wished, could have concluded one thing from
another, just as when he asked Peter, whether the
kings of the earth exact tribute from their own
children or from strangers, and being answered,
'from strangers,' he added: "Then the children
are free." (Mat. XVII, 25.)

The fourth property is that this knowledge in
Christ was habitual, that is, it was not all and
always in act, but after the manner of a habit, which
he could use when and in what way he pleased.
This was because it had been infused by God into
his soul in a manner conformable to the nature of
the subject that received it. Now the manner connatural to the human soul is to receive and retain
knowledge in the mode of a habit, which means,
not in the manner of an apple that hangs already
ripe from the tree, but in the manner of a seed
which could however without difficulty or delay
produce its fruits when desired. Hence we see

also in this the difference there is between the beatific knowledge and the infused knowledge. The former was not habitual, but always actual, and actual in respect to all the things to which it extended; the latter was in a mode proportioned to human nature, and therefore was not always in act, but in habit. Both were most perfect; the former most perfect absolutely; the latter not absolutely most perfect, but only in the genus of human knowledge.

Was this knowledge of Christ greater or less than in the angels?

We shall consider now whether this knowledge of Christ was greater or less than that of the angels. As to the multitude of the objects known, and as to the certitude and claritude of the cognition, it is without doubt far superior to the vespertine cognition of the angels, even the highest, for the reason that the light infused into the soul of Christ is beyond measure more excellent than that which may appertain to the angelic nature. It is, however, inferior as to the mode of knowing, which is proportioned to the subject in which it resides, that is, to the human soul; and therefore it is such that although it does not require, still it does not exclude the mixing of reasoning and of fantasms, as has been said.

Chapter XXIV.

Acquired Knowledge.

Let us study well the nature of this knowledge called acquired, and which is properly the knowledge connatural to man. Whence does intellective operation arise in us? Not from innate species, as in the angels, but from species drawn from sensible objects. These impress their images in our senses and in our imagination. But these corporeal images, invested as they are with conditions belonging to matter, cannot influence the intelligence, which is an immaterial faculty. On that account it is needed that they be stripped of their materiality by the action of that power of the soul which is called the active intellect. This being effected, they are then already proportioned to the intellect, and capable of determining its operations.

To explain this process better, we may make use of the following comparison, remembering however that similitudes are never so perfect as not to be lame in some respect. Imagine you have a piano-forte with its key-board outside and its musical chords inside. What is required in order to have sound ? You will say that a hand is required to touch the key; then the chord with its note will respond to the movement of the key. Very true. But how is it that at the movement of the key the chord responds with sound, whilst

(146)

the stroke on the key does not touch the chord immediately? You will answer, that this happens through the action of an intermediate mechanism, which conveys and transforms the movement of the key, and thus fits it to make the due impression on the chord, to form the note desired. Very well. Now apply all this to our case. The keys will represent the senses and the imagination; the musical chords the intelligence; the intermediate mechanism the active intellect. The corporeal objects move the keys, that is, the senses and the imagination. The acting intellect transforms and transports this movement; it transforms it by freeing the fantasms from the adherence of matter; it transports it by transferring them from the sensible to the intelligible order. In this way the sensible impression comes as far as to strike the intellect, which then too renders its sound. And what is the sound belonging to the intellect? It is its word or inward speech, by which the mind expresses ideally in itself and to itself the object, and of which the external speech, whether oral or written, is the sign. We think this sufficient for explaining the meaning of acquired knowledge and the way in which it is produced.

Christ had this acquired knowledge also.

This knowledge also was found in Christ. In fact, nothing which regards human nature was wanting in him, and nothing useless. Nothing was wanting, because the Word assumed the human nature perfect; nothing was useless, because, if

God never does anything in vain, much less can it be believed that he did so in the humanity of Christ. Now among the various things that belong to human nature, there is the faculty of abstracting intelligible species from fantasms, which is called the acting intellect. But what doubt is there, that such a faculty would have been useless in the soul of Christ, if it had to remain always idle ? It had therefore its own operation; and consequently there were in him intelligible species through the action of the acting intellect, and this is equivalent to saying, that in him there was acquired knowledge.

Let us examine more minutely the qualities of this acquired knowledge. First in regard to extension, what things did Christ know by it? Every thing that man can know by the operation of his acting intellect. Therefore he did not know by it all things absolutely, nor even all those things which he knew by infused knowledge. For example, the essence of spiritual substances in itself, because this cannot be known by the mere light of the acting intellect. You may say, perhaps, that not even all the sensible objects came under the senses of Christ; so that it cannot be said also of these, that he had an acquired knowledge of them all, as this knowledge is acquired through the senses. I answer, that at least some were perceived by his senses, and that sufficed for him to have a knowledge of all the others, since man, through the medium of the light of the acting intellect, can proceed to understand the effects from the causes, the causes from the effects, similars from similars, contraries from contraries, and in this way pass over from one knowledge to another; and this can be done the better, according as the force of reason is stronger, which in Christ was without doubt the most powerful.

The other property of this knowledge is, that Christ advanced in it not only according to the effect, but also according to the essence of the knowledge. The advancement, according to the effect, is in the works, which show a knowledge always greater: the advancement, according to the essence, is when the very habit of knowledge is increased. In the infused and much more in the beatific knowledge, the progress of Christ was as to the effect, not as to the essence, for both were perfect from the beginning, for the reason that both were generated in Christ by a cause of infinite efficacy, which therefore does not need time to produce its complete effect. But acquired knowledge has for its cause the acting intellect, which does not work its effect all at once, but successively. Hence it is that, according to this knowledge, Christ did not know in the beginning every thing that can be known by it, but little by little; and thus he went on, really advancing in it by degrees, as he advanced in years. In what sense, then, can it be said that such knowledge was always perfect in Christ? It was always perfect relatively, that is, according to that grade of perfection which suited his age, but it was not absolutely perfect, except when he reached mature age. In the same

way as his body was, it is true, perfect, but first as
that of an infant, then as that of a child, and so
on until it became simply perfect on reaching
manhood.

From this it can be understood also how admiration could take place in Christ: "And Jesus
hearing this wondered." (Mat. VIII, 10.) Admiration arises from the knowledge of something
new and unusual. According to the beatific and
the infused knowledge, nothing new and unusual
could ever reach him, but something could, according to acquired knowledge, especially as to ex-
perimental information, which is obtained through
the experience of the thing itself. So according
to this there could be and really was admiration in
Christ, for he wished to assume also this feeling
for our instruction, and to teach us that what he
admired is worthy of admiration.

Some deductions or corollaries.

Here are some conclusions that may be drawn
concerning the knowledge of Christ, from what
has been said in the present and in the other considerations. The first is, that in Christ not only
according to the divine nature, but likewise according to the human nature, 'are hidden all the
treasures of wisdom and knowledge' (Colos. II, 3);
all the treasures of wisdom, which is the knowledge
of divine things, all the treasures of knowledge,
which is the cognition of created things. In fact,
by acquired knowledge there were in him all the
treasures of wisdom and knowledge connatural to

the human soul; by infused knowledge all the treasures of wisdom and knowledge connatural to the angels. Moreover, by the same infused knowledge he had also in him all those treasures of wisdom and knowledge, that can be communicated to angels or to men by divine revelation. Lastly, by the beatific knowledge there were in him, although in a participated and finite, yet most singular and full mode, the treasures of wisdom and of knowledge, solely connatural to God.

The second consequence is, that Christ did not at all owe his knowledge either to men or to angels. He did not owe it to men, for, on the contrary, it belongs to him to be the head and teacher of all men, so that as all receive grace through him, so through him also they receive the doctrine of truth: "For this was I born, and for this came I into the world, that I should give testimony to the truth." (John XVIII, 37.) If, therefore, he interrogated the doctors, it was not to be taught by them, but to teach them. Our Lord, says Origen, asked questions, not that he might learn something, but that he might teach by asking questions; for questioning and answering wisely proceed from one fountain of doctrine. And indeed it is added in the gospel, 'that all who heard him were astonished at his wisdom and his answers.' (Luke II, 47.) Neither did he owe his knowledge to the angels, for it belongs to him to instruct the angels themselves, whose head also he is. So in this we are not to judge of the soul of Christ from what happens to the souls of others.

These, besides the knowledge which they derive naturally from sensible things, can be, and sometimes are, supernaturally enlightened through the intervening operation of angels. But the soul of Christ having been united in a most extraordinary manner to God, was also in a more than ordinary way enlightened by God, so that in addition to the acquired knowledge which it obtained from sensible objects, it was overflowing with knowledge and grace immediately from the divine Word, from which the angels themselves had all their knowledge.

Lastly, from what has been said, it will be easy to understand how in Christ there could be combined two different series of acts of the will, not only according to the twofold nature divine and human, but in the human nature itself, since in the same human will there were found together fruition, joy, and the other acts proper to the beatified on the one side, and on the other, fear, sadness, sorrow, free obedience, and the like, which regard the state of wayfaring and of merit. The reason is, because the will follows the apprehension of the intellect, which in Christ was manifold, and therefore the acts of the will were also manifold, some corresponding to the beatific knowledge and to the condition of the blessed, others corresponding only to the knowledge either infused or acquired, and to the condition of wayfarer.

CHAPTER XXV.

The active Power of Christ's Soul.

There can be no doubt that omnipotence belonged to Christ, as regards his divinity, but not also as regards his humanity, for the reason that the active power should be proportioned to the perfection of the nature which acts. Therefore an infinite power should correspond to the divine nature, which is infinitely perfect; which is the same as to say, a power that should be omnipotent, that is, a power to do all that does not involve a contradiction in itself. But the perfection of Christ's human nature is finite; therefore its power also is necessarily finite, and consequently not such as to extend to all that can be, but limited to a determinate order of possible things. This same reason too, as is evident, holds with even more force in regard to the soul of Christ, which is a part of human nature.

The soul of Christ viewed in two aspects in the exercise of its power.

The soul of Christ may be viewed in two aspects in the exercise of its power, either as it operates of itself by the natural or supernatural virtue existing in it, or as it operates as the instrument of the Word, which is personally conjoined to it. If viewed in the first manner, the soul of

Christ had the efficacy to cause all those effects which befit a rational soul, such as governing the body, regulating human acts and like things, and, owing to the fulness of grace and knowledge with which it was replete, to enlighten all other rational creatures, even the angelic spirits of the highest choirs. But if it be considered as an instrument of the Word united to it, it could effectuate works much more excellent and truly divine, just as the iron, red-hot from the intensity of the fire with which it is penetrated, heats and burns and causes other like effects proper to fire, which the iron of itself could not produce.

Therefore, the soul of Christ had from the Word the instrumental efficacy to perform all the miraculous works that might be conducive to the end of the incarnation, which is of restoring all things, whether in heaven or on earth: "That he might make known to us the mystery of his will. . . to establish all things in Christ which are in heaven and on earth, in him." (Eph. I, 9. 10.) And it had this efficacy in the most sublime and fullest manner, so that Jesus Christ could not only perform prodigies himself, but also transfer a like power to others. In fact, it is stated in the gospel that, having called to him his twelve disciples, he gave them power over unclean spirits, to cast them out, and to cure all kinds of diseases and maladies: "And when he had called his twelve disciples together, he gave them power over unclean spirits, to cast them out, and to heal all manner of diseases and all manner of sicknesses." (Mat. X, 1.)

Yet even as an instrument of the Word, the soul of Christ could neither create nor annihilate anything; for to draw things out of nothing, or to reduce them to nothing, as well as to conserve them in being, is an action proper of God alone, to which no creature can concur, even in quality of instrumental cause.

How the soul of Christ had the power of doing what it wished.

We shall now consider in what sense it may be affirmed that the soul of Christ had in it the power of doing what it wished. In two ways it wished the execution of a thing. Some things it wished, as feasible by the power of God, such for example as the resurrection of a body, and similar miraculous works, which it could not effect, except as an instrument of the divinity. And as to such effects, it could not of itself do all it might wish, nor did it even wish to do them of itself, that is, of its own power. Other things it wished, as feasible by its own power, either natural or gratuitous; and of these we must say, it could do what it wished, for it is most certain that, through the highest wisdom and rectitude with which it was adorned, it never wished to do of itself anything above its ability.

CHAPTER XXVI.

Human Defects assumed by Christ.

The Son of God wished not only to assume a body truly human, but he wished it also to be subject to suffering and death like ours. First, for the end of the incarnation, which was to satisfy for the sin of the human race; since he satisfies for the sin of another, who takes upon himself the punishment due to the sin of another. Now the defects to which our flesh is subject, such as death, sorrows, hunger, thirst, fatigue, and the like, are the punishment of sin, which was introduced into the world by Adam: "By one man sin entered into the world, and by sin death." (Rom. V, 12.) On that account, then, our most amiable Redeemer wished to take upon himself our infirmities: "Surely he hath borne our infirmities." (Is. LIII, 4.) This too is what the Apostle signified, when he said that God sent his Son 'in the likeness of sinful flesh,' that is clothed with a flesh corresponding to that of us sinners, passible and mortal. Secondly, to confirm the faith in the incarnation, for if the body of Jesus Christ had been exempt from those infirmities, which are inherent to every human body, it might seem that it was not a reality, but merely the semblance of a human body. Thirdly, to give us an example of patience, by bearing and bravely encountering difficulties, toils, labors, sorrows, and the weakness of the flesh, even to the most painful death on the cross. Fourthly, that we might have a stronger and livelier hope of immortal life, even for our flesh, while knowing that his flesh, passible and mortal like ours, was raised to a state of impassibility and immortality.

Christ's bodily imperfections.

Christ made himself like us only as to the quality of the bodily imperfections to which he wished to be subject, but not as to their cause. In us the cause of such imperfections was sin, which infected our nature, for 'by sin death entered into the world.' But the human nature in Christ was free from every blemish and had the purity in which ours was in the state of primitive innocence, and even much more. Wherefore, it was not for the debt of sin, but by his own free will, that Christ took on himself such defects, and by an impulse of the most tender affection towards us, loaded himself with our infirmities, to relieve us from them, since by his sufferings and death he merited for us impassibility and immortality, even for our bodies in the life of glory.

Not all the human defects took place in Christ.

Not all the human defects, however, could have place in Christ. For the reason that some such defects, like ignorance, propensity to evil, repugnance to good, are opposed to that perfection of knowledge and grace, which became the dignity of the divine person, and was required for the accomplishment of our redemption. Hence these defects did not exist in Christ. There are other defects peculiar only to some men, and for particular causes, such as the various maladies which have their origin either from some personal fault, or from the imperfection of the generative power. Certainly none of these were found in Christ, for there was never any disorder in the life that he led, and his flesh was conceived by the action of the Holy Ghost, whose wisdom and efficacy is infinite, and therefore could not err nor fail. Still there remains a third kind of defects, which is derived commonly in all men from the sin of our first parent, such as hunger, thirst, and the like, but especially death. All these Jesus Christ took upon himself voluntarily, as these were not opposed to, but rather contributed to the end for which he came into the world, which was to satisfy for the common prevarication of our whole nature. And although by these defects the divinity became more concealed, yet the humanity, which is the way to reach the divinity, was manifested.

Chapter XXVII.

Impeccability of Christ.

Christ wished to take on himself our defects, for three reasons especially. To make satisfaction for us; to confirm the reality of human nature; and to become for us a model of virtue. Now sin would not have helped at all for this threefold purpose, but would rather have been quite prejudicial, as being contrary to the example of virtue, and to the value of satisfaction, for 'the Most High approveth not the gifts of the wicked' (Eccli. XXXIV, 23.); and contrary even to human nature, for sin of itself does not belong to man's nature, of which God is the cause, but has been over-sown by the demon, who is the capital enemy of our nature, and is therefore called 'the enemy' and 'a homicide from the beginning.' In Christ, then, there was no sin either original or actual. If sometimes it appears in the Scriptures that sin is attributed to Christ, it is to be understood either as said, not in the name of him our head, but of us his members, or because Jesus Christ was 'a victim for sin,' offered in sacrifice for our sin, or because he assumed a passible and mortal body 'in the likeness of sinful flesh,' of flesh infected with sin.

In Christ there was no sin whatever.

In Christ there not only was not, but could not be any sin whatever, principally for two reasons.

(159)

On account of the beatific vision, which his soul enjoyed from the first instant of its existence, as that vision fixes the will immovably in the love of God above all things, and consequently renders it incapable of doing wrong. In the next place, and chiefly, on account of the hypostatic union of Christ's humanity with the Word, as by this union the humanity became sanctified, not merely with the fulness of every created grace, but with the very fulness of the divinity itself; thus becoming truly holy with the uncreated holiness of the Word. Now every defilement of sin is infinitely repugnant to such sanctity, just as a light essentially infinite would be infinitely repugnant to every shadow of darkness.

In Christ there was no 'fomes peccati' or propensity to sin.

The inclination of the sensitive appetite to that which is contrary to reason, is what is called 'fomes peccati'. In Christ no such defect existed, nor could exist. First, because it would have been of no advantage, but rather an obstacle to the work of redemption. Again, because it belongs to the moral virtues, to subject the inferior part of the soul to reason, and the more perfect they are, the more they do so. Hence it is clear that the greater the force of virtue will be, the more will that of the 'fomes' be weakened, and where virtue is consummate, the 'fomes' will be completely extinguished. But in Christ all the moral virtues existed in a most perfect degree, and therefore the sensitive appetite was entirely subject to reason, so that in him there could be no 'fomes peccati'.

Chapter XXVIII.

The Passions in Christ.

By the passions of the soul are understood properly the various affections of the sensitive appetite towards sensible good or evil; as love, hatred, desire, abhorrence, and the like. That such passions existed in Christ, we cannot doubt; for the Son of God took human nature with all that belonged to its integrity and perfection. Now in human nature the animal nature is included, as the genus in the species; and the sensitive appetite with its various affections or passions, belongs to the animal nature. These, therefore, were also assumed by the Word in becoming incarnate. There is, however, a threefold difference between Christ's passions and ours. The first difference regards the object; for in us such passions tend most frequently to illicit things, and this was not so in Christ. The second difference regards the principle or source; because in us the passions often go before the judgment of reason; but not so in Christ. In him all the acts of the sensitive appetite sprang dependently from reason. The third difference regards the effect, for in us such movements are often not confined to the sensitive appetite, but mount up to reason and master it. Whereas in Christ those movements which sprang up naturally in the sensitive part, remained there,

11

so that reason was not hindered in the least by them from doing what was becoming.

What those passions in Christ were in particular.

We shall here consider in particular what those passions are, which onr Lord wished to experience in himself for our comfort and example. There are two parts in the sensitive appetite: the concupiscible part, which has for its object a sensible good or evil regarded simply as such, that is, in as far as it is convenient or hurtful; and the irascible part, that has for its object a sensible good or evil, in as far as it is arduous, or difficult to be obtained or avoided. To the concupiscible part belong six different passions or affections of the sensitive appetite: love and hatred, which are a certain agreement or disagreement of the appetite with what is apprehended as convenient or repugnant; desire and escape, or abhorrence, in regard to a good or evil absent; delight and sadness in regard to a good or evil present. To the irascible part belong five other passions: hope and despair concerning a future good; fear and daring regarding a future evil; and anger as to a present evil, which arises from sadness, and is a desire to avenge an injury done us. To anger there is no other contrary passion corresponding in the irascible, for the reason that a present good is not arduous, and is the object of delight; and as to a present evil, either the appetite succumbs, and sadness takes place, which belongs to the concupiscible, or it rises up, and anger ensues. The different kinds of passions, therefore, are reduced to these eleven, and they were all in Christ, excepting of course the imperfections with which they are found in us; and they were most sensitive, just as in any other true man, nay more so, owing to the perfection of the inferior powers of his soul, and of the organs of his body. Thus, for example, Jesus loved his life, his most blessed mother and his disciples sensibly; he desired and hoped sensibly for the resurrection and glory of his body, when it was still to be, and when it took place, he sensibly delighted in it; he had a sensible hatred and abhorrence for his sufferings and death; also fear, in as much as the sensitive appetite naturally shrank from them; and since he was certain that infallibly they were to happen, he also felt sensibly the dread of despair concerning the good of preserving his life, which he naturally loved. He showed daring by waiting for and going to meet his persecutors, and anger by driving out the profaners from the temple.

What passions remain in Christ now in glory.

Consider what are the passions which exist in Christ even at present in the heavenly glory. But first it will be well to ponder in general which are the passions that are found in the blessed. We do not refer here, as is plain, either to God or to the angels, for in them there are not and cannot be passions of any kind, since in them there is no sensitive appetite. Nor do we even refer to the beatified souls, as long as they are separated from their bodies; for it is evident that also in these the passions cannot have place, since the sensitive powers are the property, not of the soul alone, but of the compound, soul and body. Consequently, these powers do not remain in disembodied souls in act, but only virtually and, as it were, in root. We treat therefore only of men in glory, after the resurrection, in whom consequently both soul and body partake of the state of bliss. Now what are the passions that can be found in men in that glorified state? First of all, not all the passions are compatible with that state, which are named in regard to that which is apprehended as evil and hurtful, for nothing can be, or appear to be, evil and hurtful to the blessed. From this it follows, that in the blessed there can be neither hatred, nor abhorrence, nor sadness, nor fear, nor daring, nor anger, seeing that all these passions relate to evil. Among the passions that are named in relation to good, not even those that belong to the irascible are attributable to the blessed, for the good, that is the object of the irascible, is not a good simply, but an arduous good. Now there cannot be any arduous good for the blessed, for the reason that such arduousness to attain what they apprehend as suitable for them, would already have the nature of evil. Thus then even the two passions of hope and despair are excluded. There remain, therefore, the three passions of the concupiscible, which relate to good, and these are love, desire, and joy. As to love and joy, it is evident that they have no repugnance whatever, but rather the greatest conformity to the glorified state, for love implies an inclination to good whether present or not; and joy means quiet in a good already present and possessed. These two passions therefore remain, even in the blessed, and in a most perfect manner. As to desire, some doubt might arise, since desire signifies a tendency to an absent good; and for the blessed it seems that there cannot be any absent good. Notwithstanding this, if we consider attentively, we shall see that this passion also may be found in the blessed, provided, however, it be understood in the proper manner. It should be understood, then, not in relation to those goods that appertain to the essential beatitude, for these are not absent, but are necessarily present and possessed, but in relation to those goods which appertain to the accidental beatitude. Besides it is to be understood of desire that is felt, indeed, but not connected with any uneasiness, solicitude or need. It cannot be denied that desire, understood in this way, can take place in the blessed; for it is certain that they have accidental joys. Now those same goods, which are an object of joy when present, may be an object of desire before being present. For example, the conversion of sinners is an object of joy for the blessed when it happens; and before it happens, it will be an object of desire. The most glorious triumph of Christ the judge will be an object of the greatest joy for all the blessed on the last day. Why then should it not be said that it is the object of their desire now, and even sensible in those already risen, as in the mother of God?

We see now what the passions are, which even

at present remain in Christ.   They are those three alone which can be found in glory, namely, love, joy, and desire in the manner just explained.   And in truth, who will deny that Christ now loves his mother sensibly, and rejoices sensibly in her exaltation in heaven, and desired sensibly this exaltation before it was effected?   We may say the same also in regard to ourselves wayfarers, and to you, the reader.   The heart of Jesus glorious in heaven bears a sensible love for us, and has a desire for, and a sensible joy at our good; and this love, this desire and joy of his is most lively, and the greatest in its kind, because it is such as becomes the most perfect and benevolent heart that ever existed, or ever shall exist.

Chapter XXIX.

Christ was at the same time a Wayfarer and a Possessor of Bliss.

The wayfarer is one still on the way, tending to bliss; the possessor of bliss is one that has already reached it, and has possession of it. Now the perfect beatitude of man consists in both soul and body together. In the soul, by the beatific vision and fruition of God; in the body, by its being glorified, for as the Apostle says, after it is sown in corruption, in dishonor and weakness, an animal body, it shall rise in incorruption, in glory and power, a spiritual body. (1 Cor. XV, 42–44.)

The beatitude of Christ while on earth.

Although Jesus Christ, while mortal here on earth, had beatitude as far as what belongs to the soul, since his intellect beheld the divine essence fully and immediately, and his will loved and enjoyed it, still he did not possess it as to the rest, because his soul was subject to suffering in the inferior part, and his body was passible and mortal, for glory did not pass from the superior to the inferior part, nor from the soul into the body. Therefore he was at the same time possessor of the beatific vision, for the reason that he already possessed the beatitude proper of the soul. And at the same time a wayfarer, because he was still tending to the beatitude in what was yet wanting, so that the happiness of his human nature might be perfect. Nor is there any incongruity in this, for he tended, it is true, to the end and possessed it at the same time, not however according to the same things, but according to different things, as we have already shown.

A difference.

There is a twofold difference between the state in which the saints now in heaven are, and the state in which Christ's human nature was while on earth. This being taken into account, we can understand how those, although at present blissful only in soul, must be considered nevertheless as simply possessors of bliss, and not wayfarers also, as Christ was. The first difference is that the souls of the saints are not in any way passible, as the soul of Christ was. The second is that their bodies are not glorified, it is true, but they no longer take even a step towards beatitude, having already terminated their course, and are now waiting in the grave until the day of retribution shall come for them also, whereas the body of Jesus Christ by what it suffered was tending also to its own proper glory.

Chapter XXX.

The Two Wills in Christ.

In Christ there are two wills, one human and the other divine, because he has two natures, the divine and human, both perfect, and the will belongs to the perfection of nature. Moreover, it is certain that the human nature of Christ was endowed with free will, for this also is a property necessary for the perfection of human nature. It is true that the will of Christ was confirmed in good, or in other words, unalterably set on wishing that alone which was good. But it was not unalterably set on wishing this or that good in particular, and therefore it belonged to him to choose among the various goods with free will. It is thus that the blessed are free, and thus much more is God free with the most perfect freedom.

The human will in Christ only one as a faculty.

The human will in Christ is only one, considered as a faculty or power, but there are two different acts or movements to be distinguished in it, just as in every other human will. The one is according to the natural inclination, the other is according to the deliberation of reason. The one is called the natural, the other the rational will. The one tends to that which agrees naturally with the will, and also that which agrees naturally with the other powers, and with human nature in general, because by the will we desire not only those things that regard the power of the will, but those also which regard all and each of the other powers, and the whole man.   Thus for example with this will we desire the knowledge of truth, which is a good of the intellect, so also existence and life, which are goods of the whole human nature.   The other can tend to that which of itself would be an evil in regard to nature, such as burnings, cuts, and death itself, but in as much as they are means of obtaining what reason apprehends as a good, for instance, health of the body, or the salvation of the soul.   The one is not absolute, because it has the condition implied, viz. provided nothing be determined by the deliberation of reason against it.   The other is an absolute and true will, and is properly and simply styled the will of man.

Again, besides the intellective appetite in Christ, there was also the sensitive appetite, which is improperly called the will also, for although it is not rational by essence, yet it is rational by participation, in as much as the light of reason is reflected in it, since it is of its nature subject to reason, and governed by it.

The human will of Christ conformable in everything to God's will.

The human will of Christ was conformed to the will of God in every thing and for every thing. In fact, conformity of the human with the divine will belongs to the rational, or deliberate and absolute will, for it belongs to this to regard the object wished for, as it relates to the divine will. Now the rational will of Christ was conformed always and in every thing to the will of God. This is manifest from the words in the gospel: "Not as I wish, but as thou." By these words he shows that he wished with his deliberate and absolute will, that which pleased God should be done, and not that to which his sensitive appetite and his natural will naturally inclined. Nor is it any wonder that the sensibility and the natural will of Christ recoiled from suffering and dying, although such was the will of God. Nay, so it had to be, and not otherwise, for during his mortal life he wished to allow his flesh to do and to suffer that which was proper to it, and likewise all the other powers of his soul, in order that each of them might operate in a manner connatural to itself. Now sensibility naturally abhors sensible pain, and the natural will refuses those things that are contrary to nature, and are evils in themselves, such as dishonor, death, and the like. For this reason, with a little reflection, we shall see that these same repugnances were really not opposed to the will of God, but rather wished for by it, because it was his will that in the human nature of Christ every faculty should do that which was in accordance with its natural condition.

No contrariety of will in Christ.

We cannot admit that in Christ there was any contrariety of will. Two things would be required for such a contrariety: first, that the diversity refer to the same object under the same aspect. For instance, if a judge desired the death of a criminal on account of the public good of society, and the parents of the criminal desired that he should live on account of the private good of the family, there would be no contrariety of will, because although they view the same object, yet it is under a different aspect. It was just so in Christ: his sensitive appetite rejected his passion as painful and hurtful; his natural will as an evil of nature; whereas the divine and deliberate human will desired it, not as a good in itself, but as a means ordained for the end of the salvation of mankind. In the second place, in order to have contrariety of will, it is required that opposition be found in the will itself. If then the rational will desires one thing, and the sensuality or natural will another, there is no contrariety, unless the sensitive appetite or natural will prevail so far as to change or lessen the movement of the rational will, for in such case the contrary movement of the sensitive appetite, or of the natural will, would be communicated also to the rational will. In Christ there was nothing of this, since in him neither the divine will nor the rational was hindered or retarded in the least by the natural will, or by the sensitive appetite; as, on the other hand, neither the divine will, nor the rational will, repressed or lessened the movement of the natural will and sensitive appetite. Hence in Christ there was no conflict of will.

But it is said that Christ was in agony: "Being in agony" (Luke XXII, 43); and agony would

seem to imply a struggle of the mind. Very true;
but in Christ there was no agony as to the rational
will, as happens to a man who first wishes one
thing, and then wishes the contrary, according as
he considers now one motive and now another.
This proceeds from the weakness of reason, which
cannot discern what course is absolutely the best.
But Christ saw most clearly and most certainly,
that it was absolutely the best that by his passion
the divine will should be fulfilled concerning the
salvation of the human race. The agony, therefore, of Christ is to be understood respecting the
sensitive appetite and natural will, in as much as
it signifies horror and dread of an evil that was
impending.

Chapter XXXI.

The Operations of Christ.

As in Christ there are two wills according to the two natures divine and human, so also there are two operations corresponding to the double nature divine and human. Nor could it be otherwise, since both natures in Christ are perfect; and though they are united together in the same person, yet they are distinct, and not confused into one. Now if in Christ there were but one sole operation, we should have to say, either that one of the two natures is imperfect, because wanting in its operative power, or that the divine and human power are confused, and form but one sole operating efficacy, which would imply a confusion of the two natures. Sometimes however the operations of the two natures in Christ combine to produce the same effect, yet without being confused, but by being united together, as the operation of the sculptor and of the chisel are united to form the same statue, or as that of the painter and his brush, to form the same picture; and in general, as the operations of a principal cause and an instrumental cause concur in accomplishing the same thing. In the production, therefore, of such effects the two natures act together, the divine making use of the human as an instrument, and the human partaking the efficacy of the divine, as the instrument partakes the efficacy of the principal agent. In the same manner as the instrument, acting as such, produces an effect, which is in proportion to the efficacy of the principal cause, and superior to its own, so Christ's human nature, in as much as it is moved by the divine nature, causes effects proportioned to the efficacy of the divine nature, and superior to its own, as when with a simple touch he cures the lepers, or with the sound of his voice he calms the storm, and resuscitates the dead. In a similar way an iron hammer, when red-hot, strikes and burns; it strikes as iron, and burns in virtue of the fire with which it is heated.

Besides these operations of Christ, which might be called mixed, as in them the two natures concur together in the manner explained, there are others also that are proper, either of the divine nature alone, or of the human nature alone. Of the divine nature alone, such as creation, preservation, concurrence with the actions of creatures; of the human nature alone, such as to eat, to sleep, to walk, to suffer, to die. On this account it is necessary to distinguish three classes of operations in Christ: some divine, some human, and others divine and human at the same time. But in all these various operations, the operator is always one and the same, that is, the divine person of the incarnate Word, who operates sometimes by the divine nature, sometimes by the human nature, and sometimes by both natures, as has been pointed out.

All this being so, it may be asked what then

are those operations of Christ, called theandric or human-divine.   All indeed may be styled so, although in a more or less proper sense.   The operations of the divine nature in Christ may be called theandric for the reason that the person, who performs them, is at the same time God and man.   The operations of his human nature may be called theandric for two reasons, and consequently in the strictest sense.   First on account of the person operating, who is a divine person, from whom even in such operation an infinite value and an infinite dignity are derived.   Secondly, because no human operation of Christ was unaccompanied by the divine operation, not only because the divine concurrence was needed, as well as in any other operation of creatures, but also because all the actions and passions of human nature were in a special way ordained or permitted by Christ, as considered in his divine nature.   In fine, the operations in which the two natures divine and human concurred, can with all rigor be termed theandric, since they are most truly human-divine, not only because the person to whom they belong is Man-God, but also because they proceed from him according to his two-fold nature human and divine, as has been explained.

How the human operations of Christ were meritorious for himself.

The human operations of Christ were meritorious in regard to himself.   The Apostle declares that Christ was exalted through the merit of his obedience: "He humbled himself, becoming obedient unto death . . . . wherefore God also hath exalted him." But how could he merit? For merit two conditions are required: the state of the one who merits, and the faculty of meriting. The state of him who merits, namely, that he should lack the thing which he gains by merit, since no one can merit what he already possesses. The faculty of meriting which embraces two things: the one is natural, and is the free will, for no one can merit by his own act, unless he is master of his act, which he gives as the price, as it were, for the reward. Now the dominion of the act is had by the free will. The other thing is supernatural, and is grace, for the reward of beatitude is supernatural, and therefore the sole forces of nature are not sufficient to merit it. Now all these conditions were fulfilled in Christ. As long as he was mortal on this earth, he lacked some of those goods that are required for perfect beatitude, namely, impassibility of the soul and the glory of the body. In regard to these he was still a wayfarer. He had too the faculty of meriting, both on the part of nature by free will, and on the part of grace, by the plenitude of all graces. Consequently, there is no doubt that he was capable of meriting.

That he did in fact merit, is clearly inferred from the very dignity of Christ, for it is certainly more honorable to possess a good thing through our own merit, than to possess it without merit, merely as a gratuitous gift, because he that possesses by his own merit, is in some way the very

12

author of the good which he has, whereas he that possesses without his own merit, owes all solely to the munificence of another. Hence it is that we always make more account of those, who by signal works raise themselves to a high rank, than of those who reach a similar grade through the liberality of a prince, or through birth. Now the supereminent dignity of Christ demands that we attribute to it the most estimable thing there is. We must then say that Christ truly merited for himself those goods in regard to which he was as yet in the state of wayfarer. And when did he merit ? During the whole time he was wayfarer, that is to say, from the first moment of the incarnation up to the moment of his death.

But in order to know in particular what the goods were which Christ merited for himself, two things must be borne in mind. The first is that he who merits, as we have already seen, needs to be without the good which he obtains in consequence of merit. The second is, that there are goods in relation to which the imperfection of being without them for some time, is less than the perfection of acquiring them through our own merit ; and there are goods in regard to which the imperfection of being without them for some time, is greater than the perfection of acquiring them by our own merit : such in our case is grace, knowledge, the beatitude of the soul, the divinity. Hence it is evident that all those goods of the second kind were not obtained by Christ by way of merit, having been possessed by him fully from the beginning. There remain therefore the goods of the first kind, which were properly merited by Christ, and are reduced to the following: the beatitude of the body, the impassibility of the soul, his glorious resurrection, the triumph of his ascension to heaven, the exaltation of his name, which includes all that pertains in any way to his external glory, and was besought by Christ himself, especially in that prayer which he addressed to his divine Father: "I have glorified thee on earth . . . and now glorify thou me, O Father" (Jno. XVII, 4, 5), and this prayer was assuredly most efficacious and meritorious. Hence the reward of his merit were those various testimonies of his dignity and majesty, which are related in the holy gospel, and rendered to him at one time by the Father, as in his baptism and in his transfiguration; at another time by the angels, as at his nativity; at another time by the very elements, as a star announced his birth to the Magi, as the sun was darkened at his death, and the whole earth was shaken. And, consequently, the reward of his merit was the supreme power of king and judge over all the universe.

The operations of Christ meritorious for himself and others.

Consider that the operations of Christ were meritorious not only for himself, but likewise for others. And the reason is because to him grace was given not only as to an individual person, but as to the head of the whole Church, in order that it might redound from him to all his members. And, therefore, the operations of Christ as well in relation to himself, as in relation to his members, have that same value as the operations of any other who is in grace have in regard to himself.

Now as the operations of every one, who is in the state of grace, are undoubtedly meritorious for himself, so likewise the operations of Christ are meritorious not merely for himself, but also for all those others who are joined and subordinate to him, as members to the head, and with him form mystically one person, as it were. Hence it is that St. Paul, in comparing the merit of Christ with the demerit of Adam, declares that if the demerit of Adam was transmitted to others for their condemnation, in the same manner and much more is the merit of Christ transmitted to others for their justification: "For if, by the offence of one, many have died, much more the grace of God and the gift in the grace of one man Jesus Christ have abounded unto many. . . . Therefore, as by the offence of one unto all men to condemnation, so also by the justice of one unto all men unto justification of life" (Rom. V, 15, 18). But how is the merit of Christ transfused into others? In a manner analogous to that in which the demerit of Adam is propagated in his descendants. His demerit is propagated by means of carnal generation, and the merit of Christ is propagated by means of spiritual regeneration, which is effected in baptism, by which men are invested with Christ and become members of one body of which he is the head:

"For as many of you as have been baptized in Christ, have put on Christ. . . . For you are all one in Christ Jesus" (Gal. III, 27, 28).

Now what in particular were those goods which Christ merited for us? He merited the remission of both original and all our actual sins : in this sense, however, that the merit of Christ is of itself the universal and sufficient cause of the remission of all sins; but in order that they may be really remitted, it is necessary that such merit be applied to each one in the manner required, just as a medicine, that would have in itself the virtue of curing every disease, would need, in order to cure the diseased, to be applied to each of them in a suitable manner. He merited sanctifying grace together with all the supernatural gifts annexed to it. He merited the eternal and supernatural beatitude corresponding to grace. He merited all the actual graces, which are needed for man that he may dispose himself to justification. He merited all the supernatural aids which are conferred on the just to enable them to persevere and increase in grace, and in the merit of glory. He merited also the remission of temporal punishment by applying to us his own satisfaction, and by rendering our satisfactions acceptable and efficacious in the sight of God. This is to be understood not only of those who are still in life, but also of the dead who are in purgatory, whenever a punishment is remitted to them in virtue of the indulgences and satisfactions of the living, since both have their value from the merits of Christ. In brief,

Christ has merited for us eternal salvation and everything that conduces to it.

Neither does all this derogate in the least from our merits. Quite the contrary; for if our merits have value, they owe it precisely to the merits of Christ, and for two reasons; first, because in virtue of his merits the principle itself of all our merit, which is grace, is conferred upon us; secondly, because in virtue of these same merits our works, done with grace, are ordained and accepted by God for the reward of glory. Hence it is plain that our merits, so far from obscuring the merits of Christ, rather make their efficacy much more manifest, because they let us see how Christ not only merited himself, but obtained also for his members, the virtue of meriting. From this we can understand how eternal life, and the other goods which we can and should merit for ourselves, are at the same time a crown and a grace — a crown in respect to our merits — a grace because these merits themselves are for us gifts of God.

CHAPTER XXXII.

Subjection of Christ to His Father.

Human nature has a triple subjection towards God. The first regards the degree of perfection, as the divine nature is the very essence of goodness, and therefore infinite goodness; and human nature, like every creature, has a finite goodness, which is a participation of the goodness of God. Similar to this is the subjection of the stream to its source. The second regards power, since human nature and every other created nature is in the hands of God, and subject to the disposition and operation of his providence. Similar to this is the subjection of the clay to the potter, who works and fashions it according to his pleasure. The third which belongs to it especially, is the subjection which it has towards God in regard to its own proper act, that is, to obey with its will the ordinances of God. Similar to this is the subjection which a subject has to his sovereign and lawgiver.

The Son of God then having assumed human nature, assumed likewise this triple subjection, which belongs to it. Indeed, as to the first, he himself declared that the Father was greater than he: "The Father is greater than I" (John XIV, 28). Here greater means better, for as St. Augustine says, 'in those things that are not greater in bulk, to be greater or better is the same.' Accordingly, to the one who had called him "Good Master", he replied: "Why askest thou me concerning good? One is good, God" (Mat. XIX, 17). This was to give us to understand that, according to human nature, he was far from the greatness of the divine goodness and perfection, before which all created goodness, however excellent it may be, is as if it were not, for it is as a drop of water in comparison to an ocean, that has no shores. The second kind of subjection is pointed out by St. Paul, when he asserts that the Son of God took the form of a servant, meaning that he took a nature which, like every other creature, is the servant of its Creator, and subject in all things to his ordinations. And, in fact, everything that concerned the humanity of Christ took place by the divine disposition. As to the third manner of subjection, Jesus himself several times protested, that in every thing which he did, he always aimed at doing the will of his Father: "I must be about the things that are my Father's" (Luke II, 49). And again: "I do always the things that please him" (John VIII, 29). This, too, is the subjection of obedience to the Father even unto death, mentioned by St. Paul to the Phillippians (II, 8).

Christ both master and servant of himself.

Moreover, it may be said with truth that Christ is master and servant of himself, greater or less than himself, provided, however, that it be rightly understood. If by this is meant that in Christ there are two persons, one of which is master and the other servant, it is absolutely false, and is the heresy of Nestorius.   But if by this is meant only the diversity of the two natures in one same person, there is no error in it, for it is true that in Christ there are two natures, the divine in which he corresponds to the Father, and rules and ordains together with him, and the human in which he corresponds to us, and is subject and obedient as to the Father, as he is to himself.

Meaning of the Apostle's declaration.

What does the Apostle mean, when he affirms that, 'when all things shall be subdued unto him (the Son), then the Son also shall himself be subject to him (the Father), who subjected all things to himself'?   (1. Cor. XV, 28.)   He wishes to signify that when all things shall be fully subjected to Christ, then shall Christ be fully subject to the Father.   Even at present Jesus Christ has supreme authority over all things, since all power has been given to him by the Father: "All power is given to me in heaven and on earth" (Mat. XXVIII, 18). But in fact all do not recognize him as their Lord, nor do all execute his will.   When the world however shall have an end, and the present state of human generation shall cease, then all shall be totally subject to Christ, and his will entirely fulfilled in all, although in different ways, according to their different merits.   In the just it shall be fulfilled by their full glorification, that is, of all the just, and not in soul only, but likewise in body. In the reprobate it shall be fulfilled by their full punishment, that is, of all the reprobate, both in soul and in body, and all, whether the elect in heaven or the damned in hell, shall experience and confess the sovereign dominion of Christ. Then also shall Christ be fully subject to the Father, for he shall be subject to him not only in his humanity, but also in all his members, who compose the mystic body of the Church, then no longer militant, but all triumphant and glorious, without spot or wrinkle to impair its beauty. Then, indeed, will the triple subjection to God be perfect in all his saints, for the participation of the divine goodness will be perfect in them, not only in the natural order, but also in the supernatural by the beatific vision and fruition; perfect will be the fulfilment of divine providence and predestination, perfect the submission and conformity of their will with that of God.

Chapter XXXIII.

Prayer of Christ.

Let us ponder in what way prayer could take place in Christ. To pray is to declare our will to God, to the end that it be accomplished. If therefore there had been in Christ the divine will only, it certainly would not have behooved him to pray, for the divine will is of itself operative of what it wills. But in Christ besides the divine will there was also the human, which of itself is not competent to effect what it desires. Therefore it behooved Christ to pray as man, and according to the human will.

Christ willed to pray for himself in two ways.

Christ wished to pray for himself in two ways, both being for our instruction. The first was by expressing the feeling of the sensitive appetite, and also the natural movement of his human will, as when he prayed that the chalice of the passion might be removed from him. By this he intended to show principally three things: that he had a true human nature with all the feelings connatural to it; that it was not wrong for a man, according to natural feeling, to wish for that which God does not wish, and to dislike that which God wishes; and that man however should submit his natural feeling to the will of God. The other way was by

(187)

expressing the feeling of his rational and deliberate will, as when he besought the Father for the glory of his resurrection: "Lifting up his eyes to heaven, he said, Father, the hour is come, glorify thy son" (John XVII, 1).

This he did for three reasons. The first was to teach us, that the Father was the principle from which he proceeded eternally as to his divine nature, and by whom he was sent into this world. And, therefore, although he too was God and omnipotent as well as the Father, yet he wished to address his prayer to the Father: "Because of the people who stand about, have I said it, that they may believe that thou hast sent me" (John XI, 42). And St. Hilary says, 'he needed not prayer: he prayed for us, that the Son might not be unknown.' The second reason was to make it known to us, that the Father was the author also of all the goods of his human nature, and that therefore he rendered him thanks for the goods already received in it, and asked of him those which he still expected. The third was to incite us by his example to pray, and to point out to us how we too in our prayer should return thanks for the gifts already granted, and ask for those not yet obtained.

Christ's prayer was always heard.

The prayer of Christ was always heard. Hence St. Paul said of him: "In the days of his flesh, offering up prayers and supplications with a strong cry and tears, he was heard for his reverence" (Heb. V, 7). And Jesus himself affirmed it, saying: "I knew that thou hearest me always" (John XI, 42). And, in fact, when is it that a prayer is said to be heard? It is when the will of the petitioner is fulfilled, because prayer is the interpreter of the will. Note, however, that we treat here of the absolute and deliberate will, which is the one that is properly called the will of man. Now, according to that will Jesus Christ never willed any other thing, except that which he knew to be willed by God. On this account every will of Christ, even human, was executed, and consequently every prayer of his was heard. Nor is there any difficulty in the request which Christ made in the garden to his Father, of removing from him the chalice of his passion: "Take away this chalice from me" (Mark XIV, 36). These words have been understood in different ways by interpreters, but, in whatever way, they are not opposed to what we have said. According to some, Jesus Christ prayed that the fruit of his passion might be communicated to others, or also that the examples of his virtues, especially that of his fortitude, might be imitated by those who after him were to suffer for justice and the faith. According to others, Jesus Christ prayed really that the chalice of his passion might be removed far from him, to let us know the natural repugnance which, as man, he felt at sufferings and death. If then his prayer be taken in the first sense, it was heard in full: if taken in the second, it is true that what he asked for was not done; but in that case it was because his prayer was merely

the expression of the natural inclination of his will
and sensitive appetite, and not of the rational and
deliberate will, which did not even wish that it
should be done.

Chapter XXXIV.

Christ the Mediator between God and Men.

Jesus Christ is mediator between God and men, and the only perfect mediator: "For there is one God and one mediator of God and men, the man Christ Jesus" (1. Tim. II, 5). The proper office of a mediator is to unite those between whom he is mediator, so that extremes may be joined together in the middle. Now Christ did this by reconciling with God men who were separated from him by sin: "For God indeed was in Christ reconciling the world to himself" (2. Cor. V, 19). And he reconciled us with God in the most perfect way, by destroying sin both as to guilt and to punishment, with a satisfaction not barely sufficient, but superabundant beyond measure, and by meriting for us the gifts of grace and of glory with a merit likewise superabundant. Nor was it only some men, but it was the whole human race that he reconciled with God: "Who gave himself a redemption for all" (1. Tim. II, 6). He was therefore a perfect mediator, and as such he was unique, because no other had, or could have, the power of efficaciously and fully effecting our union with God, except him who was at the same time both God and man.

Christ the true and only perfect mediator.

Let us now consider how the title of mediator is to be understood when attributed to others besides Christ. It must be understood that they are secondary and imperfect mediators, that is, in as far as with Christ, and dependent on Christ, they concur in some way, to effect the union of men with God. Thus the prophets and the priests of the Old Testament were called mediators, because they foretold and prefigured Christ, the true and perfect mediator. The priests of the New Testament may also be called mediators, because they are ministers of the true mediator, and in his name, and in his place, and by his power offer to God the victim of peace, and dispense to men the sacraments of salvation. The good angels also are intermediators between God and men; for according to the order of nature they are placed below God, and above men. Hence they too exercise the office of mediators, not however as principal, but as subordinate, for the reason that angels are also the ministers of Christ, the supreme mediator. "And behold, angels came and ministered to him" (Mat. IV, 11).

As for the demons, they are in some sense intermediators between men and God, but their mediation is altogether opposed to that of Christ. Jesus Christ had beatitude in common with God, and mortality in common with men; and he interposed between God and men to make men immortal from being mortal, and to make them happy with him for ever from being miserable. The demon has immortality in common with God, and misery in common with men, and he intrudes himself between men and God to hinder men from arriving at a blissful immortality, and at the same time to drag them with him to endless misery. The demon, therefore, is a malign medium, whose characteristic is to separate friends, whilst Christ, on the contrary, is the good mediator whose property is to reconcile enemies.

Jesus Christ is mediator, not as God, but as man.

In this there is no difficulty, if we understand well the properties of a mediator. They are two, first to be a middle term, and then to join together the two extreme terms. To be a middle term, and therefore to be distant from both the extremes; to join the extremes together, and therefore to communicate to one term what belongs to the other. Now these two things cannot apply to Christ as God, but only as he is man. They cannot apply to him in as much as he is God, for as such he is not at all distant, nor different from the Father and the Holy Ghost in nature and authority; nor have the Father and the Holy Ghost any perfection, which is not in the Son, so that this could communicate to one term, that is to men, what belongs to the Father and Holy Ghost, as a thing not their own, but belonging to the other term. They apply to Christ as man, for as such he is distant from God in nature, and from men in the dignity and fulness of grace and of glory, which come to his human nature from union with the

13

divinity, and unite men with God by communicating the precepts and gifts of God to them, and by offering him satisfaction and intercession for men.

From what has been said, it is plain that the quality of mediator cannot apply either to the Father, or to the Holy Ghost. When, therefore, the Apostle asserts that 'the Spirit himself asketh for us with unspeakable groanings,' he does not mean that he acts the part of mediator for us, nor that he also groans, which would be repugnant to his infinite beatitude, for to groan is the effect and sign of pain. But he 'asketh with groans' in as much as he is the cause, that we entreat and groan. He is the cause that we entreat through the holy and inflamed desires that spring from charity, which is diffused in our hearts by the Holy Ghost: "The charity of God is poured out into our hearts by the Holy Ghost, who is given to us" (Rom. V, 5). For to entreat is to declare one's desires. He is the cause that we entreat with groans, because the livelier the desire is, the greater is the grief we feel, seeing ourselves still far from the heavenly goods for which we sigh. And with 'unspeakable groanings,' because unspeakable are the goods of the country for which we sigh and groan, and unspeakable the affections of our heart, in as much as they proceed from the intimate and hidden impulse of the Holy Ghost.

Chapter XXXV.

Priesthood of Christ

Jesus Christ is most properly the priest and chief of all priests, and therefore the true high-priest: "Having therefore a great high-priest, who hath penetrated the heavens, Jesus the Son of God, let us hold fast our confession" (Heb. IV, 14). In fact, what is the office of a priest? It is to be mediator between God and the people, in such a way that he dispenses to the people the gifts of God, and offers to God the prayers of the people, and renders in some way, especially by the offering of sacrifices, satisfaction for the sins committed by the people: "For every high-priest taken from among men, is appointed for men in the things that appertain to God, that he may offer up gifts and sacrifices for sin" (Heb. V, 1). This is applicable to Christ most principally; because by his means the divine goods have been conferred on men, and the greatest and most precious of them: "By whom he hath given us very great and precious promises, that by these you may be made partakers of the divine nature" (2. Pet. I, 4). He too, by sacrifice offered by him, reconciled the human race with God: "Because in him (Christ) it hath well pleased that all fulness should dwell, and through him to reconcile all things unto himself" (Colos. I, 19, 20). Jesus Christ then is priest

(195)

true, and supreme pontiff, and first not in time, but in dignity and authority.   Nor is this all.   He is, moreover, the source of all priesthood, for the priest of the ancient law was a figure of him, and the priest of the new law acts in his person : "For what I forgave, if I have forgiven any thing, for your sakes have I done it in the person of Christ" (2. Cor. II, 10).   In a word, all the value of the old and new priesthood is derived from his priesthood.

Christ's priesthood effects the expiation of our sins.

The priesthood of Christ has the fullest and most efficacious virtue of effecting the expiation of our sins.   Two things are required to expiate sin: to cancel the stain of the sin, which is done by grace ; and to remove the debt of punishment, which is done by the satisfaction which man offers to God.   Now the priesthood of Christ effects both these things perfectly, because by it grace is given us, by which our hearts are justified: "Being justified gratis by his grace through the redemption that is in Christ Jesus, whom God had set forth to be a propitiation through faith in his blood" (Rom. III, 24, 25); and by it the divine justice is altogether satisfied, since Jesus Christ took upon himself our infirmities and our sorrows: "Surely he hath borne our infirmities and carried our sorrows" (Isaias LIII, 4).   Thus he paid most fully the punishment that was due to our sins.

We see, then, with how much reason the Baptist, on seeing Christ, exclaimed : "Behold the

Lamb of God, behold him who taketh away the sin of the world'' (John I, 29). And how well the Apostle reasoned by comparing the sacrifice of Christ with the sacrifices of the old law: ''If the blood of goats and of oxen and the ashes of a heifer being sprinkled, sanctify such as are defiled, to the cleansing of the flesh, how much more shall the blood of Christ, who through the Holy Ghost offered himself without spot to God, cleanse our conscience from dead works to serve the living God?'' (Heb. IX, 13, 14.) If the shadows could do so much, how much more can the reality? If the blood of irrational victims availed to sanctify and purify bodies, how much more will the immaculate blood of Christ avail to cleanse souls from sins, which are truly dead and death-bearing works, so that we also, by living a divine life ourselves by his grace, may be able to serve God worthily, who is living and is life. But to what limit does the efficacy of Christ's priesthood extend? Beyond all limit. For although Christ is a priest, not as God but as man, yet the person is the same, who at the same time is priest according to human nature, and God according to the divine nature; and on this account in the sacrifice of Christ an infinite value of expiation results from the infinite dignity of the divinity.

Christ's priesthood endures forever.

The priesthood of Christ remains forever: ''Thou art a priest forever'' (Ps. 109, 4). To understand how this is true, we shall distinguish two things that regard the office of priest. The first is the offering of sacrifice. The second is the perfect completion or consummation of the same sacrifice, which consists in this that those, for whom the sacrifice is offered, obtain its end. Accordingly, the offering of Christ's sacrifice ended in his passion and death, but the consummation lasts, and will last forever, because the end of his sacrifice was not the temporal goods of the present life, but the eternal goods of the future: "But Christ being present a high-priest of the good things to come . . . by his own blood entered once into the sanctuary, having obtained eternal redemption" (Heb. IX, 11, 12). And this consummation of Christ's sacrifice was prefigured by what the legal pontiff did, when according to the prescriptions of Leviticus, once in the year, after having immolated a goat and a calf without the sanctuary, he entered with the blood of these victims into the Holy of Holies. Thus too Christ entered into the Holy of Holies, that is into heaven, and opened and prepared for us the way to enter therein, in virtue of his blood, which he shed for us on earth. But the legal sacrifice had not an eternal value, and therefore had to be repeated every year, whereas Jesus Christ with one sole oblation rendered perfect forever those that are sanctified: "By one oblation he hath perfected forever them that are sanctified" (Heb. X, 14).

Why Christ was called priest according to the order of Melchisedech.

Now we shall examine in what sense, and why

Jesus Christ was called priest according to the order of Melchisedech. It certainly was not in the sense, that the priesthood of Melchisedech was superior to the priesthood of Christ, but because in Melchisedech there was a figure more resembling Christ, and the preeminence of his priesthood over the Levitical. For this reason the Apostle said of Melchisedech, that he resembled the Son of God: "But likened unto the Son of God" (Heb. VII, 3), to signify that he was but an image, for it is said of an image that it resembles the prototype, but not of the prototype that it resembles the image.

Melchisedech then was a special image of Christ, and principally for four reasons which are mentioned by St. Paul in his letter to the Hebrews, chapter VII. First in the name, as Melchisedech means king of justice, and he was king of Salem which signifies peace : "Who indeed is king of justice, and then also king of Salem, that is, king of peace" (Heb. VII, 2). Now Jesus Christ is King of kings: "The Lamb shall overcome them, because he is Lord of lords, and King of kings" (Apoc. XVII, 14). Nor is he only a just king, but justice itself : "Who is made to us wisdom from God, and justice" (1. Cor. I, 30). Neither is he only king of peace, but he is our peace, as the Apostle says: "For he is our peace" (Eph. II, 14). Secondly, because 'Melchisedech was without father, without mother, without genealogy, without beginning of days, without end of life,' according to the words of the same Apostle (Heb. VII, 3). This is said, not because he had not

these things, but because they are not mentioned
in the Scripture. But in this very thing he represents Christ, who was born on earth without a
father, and in heaven without a mother, and without genealogy, for his generation is inexpressible.
"Who shall declare his generation?" (Is. LIII, 8.)
As God, he has no beginning of days nor end, and
even as man, he will also live without end, for
"Christ rising from the dead dieth now no more"
(Rom. VI, 9).   In the third place, Melchisedech
was a priest, but not of the Levitic order.   In like
manner Christ did not wish to be born of the race
of Levi, to show that his priesthood was not the
legal, but different from it, as the truth from the
figure.   In short, "Melchisedech received tithes
from Abraham, and blessed him, who had the
promises" (Heb. VII, 6).   In this he showed his
superiority over Abraham; for "without all contradiction, he who is less is blessed by the greater"
(Heb. VII, 7).   In like manner it belongs to the
inferior to offer tithes to the superior; and not only
as regards Abraham, but also as regards Levi and
the Levitical priesthood, for "even Levi who received tithes, paid tithes by Abraham, for he was
yet in the loins of his father when Melchisedech
met him" (Heb. VII, 9, 10).   Through Abraham
and in Abraham even Levi and his tribe paid
tithes to Melchisedech, and were blessed by him;
and therefore also in relation to them the superiority of Melchisedech's priesthood was manifested.

In this Melchisedech was singularly the type of
Christ, that he represented the excellence of Christ's

priesthood over the priesthood of the law.   But in what does this excellence particularly consist ? Above all in this, that the ancient priesthood was not eternal, and had not the power to cleanse from sins, whereas Christ, 'For that he continueth forever, hath an everlasting priesthood, whereby he is able also to save forever them that come unto God by himself, always living to make intercession for us' (Heb. VII, 24, 25).   And as he is 'a high-priest, holy, innocent, undefiled, separated from sinners, and made higher than the heavens' (Heb. VII, 26), so also the ineffable virtue of his priesthood renders like to him, holy, innocent, undefiled, separated from sinners, those who by his means approach God, and whom he raises with him aloft to heaven.

Chapter XXXVI.

Christ a most perfect Victim.

Jesus Christ was at the same time priest and victim, for the victim offered by him in sacrifice was no other than himself: "Christ also hath loved us, and hath delivered himself for us, an oblation and a sacrifice to God for an odor of sweetness" (Eph. V, 2). Even in this there is the greatest difference between the ancient sacrifices and Christ's sacrifice. In the former, irrational victims were offered, which man substituted instead of himself, in order to signify his total dependence on God, and also his guilt, and how by his sins he was deserving of death. On the contrary, Jesus Christ did not substitute other victims in his stead, but instead of that substituted himself as a victim in place of the whole human race, by taking upon him our iniquities, and making himself the price of our redemption. He is, therefore, as man both victim and priest at the same time. He is victim, in as much as he is offered up, and priest, in as much as he offers the sacrifice, which he himself as God receives in common with the Father and the Holy Ghost.

Jesus was a sacrifice the most perfect in every respect.

And, indeed, man needs to have recourse to God with sacrifice to obtain three things principal-

ly.   Above all the remission of his sins, then the
preservation of the state of grace, in which his true
peace and salvation are found, and lastly the perfect union with God, which will be had chiefly in
glory.   This three-fold aim of sacrifice was indicated by the three different kinds of legal victims,
which were offered in the ancient law, called sin-
offering, peace-offering, and holocaust.   These
sacrifices of the law could indeed show our in-
digence, and could cleanse from some bodily defilement or irregularities, but they had not the virtue
of purifying souls and conferring grace, for they
were 'weak and poor elements,' as St. Paul says.
They were poor, because they did not contain the
treasure of grace within them ; and consequently
they were weak, because they had not the power
to justify, only as far as they helped, as figures of
Christ's sacrifice, to uphold and enliven the faith
in the future Messiah, which was what purified
souls from sin.   But that which the ancient sacrifices, although many, could not do, because poor
and weak, was accomplished most perfectly by
Christ's sacrifice on the altar of the cross, although
but one, because most rich and most powerful.   In
virtue of it our sins were blotted out, because 'he
was delivered up for our sins' (Rom. IV, 25); and
grace, the source of peace and eternal salvation,
was given us abundantly: "He became the cause
of eternal salvation to all that obey him" (Heb.
V, 9).   We were given also a strong hope of obtaining the perfection of glory: "Having therefore, brethren, a confidence in entering into the

sanctuary by the blood of Christ"(Heb. X, 19). Thus we see that Jesus Christ, as man, was at the same time the most perfect sin-offering, the most perfect peace-offering, and the most perfect holocaust.

How the title and quality of Redeemer apply to Christ especially.

Although the work of redemption can be attributed to the whole Blessed Trinity, still the title and the quality of our Redeemer regard Christ especially in as much as he is man. Of this there can be no doubt after what has been said. In fact, what is required that one can be truly called a redeemer? Two things. First of all, that he pay the price for recovering the object which he wishes to redeem ; and next, that the price paid be his own, and not another's, for it is evident that, if one gives that which is not his, he cannot be considered the primary redeemer, but rather the other is, to whom the price belongs. Now both these things apply immediately, and with all propriety, to Christ as man, seeing that he paid the price of our ransom. This price too was all his, since it was nothing else than his very blood and life.

Wherefore the B. Trinity brought about our redemption as the first and the remote cause, in as much as it decreed that the redemption of the human race should be effected, and effected in this manner; and the humanity of Christ was from it and of it; and it inspired the man Christ with the will to suffer and die for us. But our Redeemer immediately and properly was Christ as man, for he as priest offered the price, and he as victim was the price itself of our redemption.

Chapter XXXVII.

Predestination of Christ.

Weigh well the import of this word predestination in the language of Scripture and of the Church. To predestine is the same as to destine beforehand; and to destine means to establish, to dispose, to order. To predestine, therefore, signifies to order in our heart beforehand something to be done. But not every such like preordination is called predestination; but only the preordination that exists in the mind of God from eternity, of things that are to be executed in time. Neither is even such a preordination properly called predestination in regard to every thing, but only in regard to those things which have to be effected by grace, and which consequently belong to the supernatural order and end. From this it is clear that predestination, as to its object, is contained in providence, as a part in the whole, for providence is the divine preordination of all things to their end, and especially to the last end, whilst predestination is a preordination not of all things, but simply of those which refer to the end of eternal life, and that is the beatific vision of the essence of God. Hence, as providence includes also the will besides the intellect, so likewise predestination includes and presupposes the act of the will; in other words, the divine dilection by which God wills supernatural good to the predestined, and the election by which he wills to them a preference above others. In like manner, speaking with precision, as providence is not in the things provided, but in him who provides, so predestination is not in the predestined, but in him who predestines; and as the execution of providence, which is called government, is passively in the things governed, and actively in the one governing, so also the execution of predestination is passively in the predestined and actively in God. From what has been said we can see, that predestination is distinct from divine prescience, as prescience means only a knowledge of future things. whereas predestination comprehends moreover some causality regarding them. Therefore, although God has a foreknowledge of sins, yet his predestination extends only to the goods that concern eternal salvation.

How Christ was predestinated.

In what sense is it true that even Christ was predestinated ? We learn from the words of the Apostle that "he was predestinated the Son of God in power" (Rom. I, 4). Predestination, as we have said, is a preordination made by God of those things that are to be effected by grace in time; it will then be well to distinguish between two graces : the common grace, called the grace of adoption, which is that by which rational creatures are made adopted children of God, and the grace proper of Christ, which is called the grace of union, and consists in the hypostatic union of the human nature with the divine person in Christ, by which man became God, and God became man. Therefore, as the works which are done by God through the grace of adoption fall under his predestination, so also this most wonderful work, effected by God in time by the grace of union, was likewise comprehended in the compass of his eternal predestination. Here then is the reason why Christ is said to be predestinated.

However, for a better understanding of this truth, we may examine a little more closely to whom this predestination in Christ is to be attributed. It may seem perhaps, at first thought, that it can be attributed neither to the divine person of the Word nor to the human nature assumed by him. It cannot be attributed to the person, because this is 'the Son of God in power' essentially and from all eternity, and he did not begin to exist in time and by grace. It cannot be attributed to human nature, because it is false to say, that this nature is 'the Son of God in power'. To whom, then, is it to be attributed? To the divine person, not as it subsists in the divine nature, but as it subsists in the human nature, for the reason that, according to the divine nature, the Word is necessarily and eternally the Son of God, but not so according to human nature. According to this nature he began to be such in time and in virtue of that ineffable grace, which is styled the grace of union. The same also is inferred from the words themselves of St. Paul, where he treats of the predestination of Christ, as he says of him first: "Who was made to him of the seed of David according to the flesh" (Rom. I, 3, 4); and then immediately adds: "Who was predestinated the Son of God in power." By this he would have us to understand that Christ 'was predestinated Son of God in power' according to that nature by which he 'was made of the seed of David according to the flesh'; which is the same as to say, according to human nature.

Christ's predestination the cause of our predestination.

Consider in what way the predestination of Christ is the cause of our predestination. Predestination may be regarded as to the act of God predestinating, or as to the term and effect. As to the act, the predestination of Christ could in no wise be the cause of our predestination, for with one and the same act, eternal and indistinct from his essence, God predestinated both Christ and us. As to the term, the predestination of Christ is doubly the cause of our predestination, being the efficient cause and the exemplary cause. It is the efficient cause, since God predestinated from all eternity not only the things that are to be effectuated in time, but also the manner and order in which they are to be effectuated. And between these two terms of his predestination, which are our salvation and the incarnation of Christ, the order established was that the first should be the effect of the second. He is the exemplary cause in two respects. First in regard to the good to which we are predestinated; for Christ was predestinated to be, even as man, the natural Son of God, and we are predestinated to the adoptive filiation of God, which is a participated likeness of natural filiation: "For whom he foreknew, he also predestinated to be made canformable to the image of his Son, that he might be the first-born amongst many brethren" (Rom. VIII, 29). Secondly in regard to the way of attaining this good, which is through the mere gratuitous gift of God, since in Christ, as is most manifest, human nature, without any preceding merit of its own, was joined to the divine person; and in us the total effect of predestination, in as much as it comprehends even the first disposition to grace, is without any previous merit on our part, but purely and simply from the divine favor. What says the Apostle? He says that God predestinated us according to the good pleasure of his will: "Blessed be God . . . . who hath predestinated us unto the adoption of children through Jesus Christ unto himself, according to the purpose of his will" (Eph. I, 3, 5).

Chapter XXXVIII.

Adoration of Christ.

By adoration is meant that act by which we protest our submission in regard to the excellence of another. In adoration, therefore, it is necessary to distinguish a twofold object, that to which the worship is rendered, and this is called the material object; and that which is the motive for which it is rendered, and this is called the formal object. According to the diversity of such objects, there results a triple manner of adoration. Observe, however, that we treat here of adoration in its most proper signification, that is, of religious, not of civil adoration. The first manner of adoration is called *latria*, and has God for its material object, and for its formal object the uncreated and infinite excellence of God. The second is termed *dulia*, and has the saints for its material object, and for its formal object the created, supernatural excellence of holiness and celestial glory, which is found in them. The third is styled *hyperdulia*, and has for its material object the Mother of God, and for its formal object the supernatural excellence belonging to her, which is far superior to that of all other mere creatures.

Besides this, some adoration is absolute and some relative. The absolute refers to that object

which has perfection in itself, which is the motive
of the worship given it. The relative refers to
that object which is worshipful, not for its own
perfection, but for the perfection of another object,
with which it has a special relation or connection.
Relative adoration follows the nature of the absolute. It will be the relative adoration of latria,
or dulia, or hyperdulia, according as the object in
which the excellence is found, and which is the
reason of the worship, requires an absolute adoration of latria, or of dulia, or of hyperdulia. Thus,
for example, to the images of the Most Holy Trinity the relative adoration of latria is due; to the
images of the saints, that of dulia, and to the
images of the B. Virgin, that of hyperdulia. Absolute adoration can be given only to an intellective
nature, as this alone is of itself capable of honor
and veneration, and is properly directed to the
whole person; for no one, indeed, will say that the
hand or the head of a man is honored, but the man.
Or even if it sometimes happens that our homage
regards some portion of the person immediately,
as when we kiss the foot of the sovereign Pontiff,
it is not that we intend by this to do homage to
that member for itself, but in it to honor the whole
person. There is, however, a difference between
the manner in which that can be the object of
worship which is intrinsic, as the part of a person,
and that which is extrinsic, and not connected
with the person by any relationship more or less
close. Neither of them is worshipped for itself,
but for respect to the person. Yet the one is the

partial object of absolute worship, which regards the entire person, the other only of relative worship.

The adoration due to Christ.

We shall here examine what is the adoration proper to Christ. From what has been already discussed, it will be easily determined. In Christ there is one only person, and it is the divine person, that subsists in the two natures divine and human. Therefore the adoration which is due to him will be that which corresponds to the infinite excellence of the divine person, that is, of latria. The total object of this adoration is the divine person itself of Christ, as it includes the two natures which are its own. The humanity then, with all the parts that compose it, is the partial object, and hence it also is adored with the same absolute adoration and of latria, although not for itself, but for the uncreated excellence of the Word to which it is hypostatically united.

And what kind of worship is proper for the images and the cross of Christ? Call to mind what has been said: honor and reverence are due only to an intellective nature. Insensible things are not capable of honor and reverence, except in virtue of a special relation they have to the intellective nature. This can occur in two ways: either as they represent that nature, or are connected with it in some particular manner. For the first reason men are wont to give homage to the image of a king: for the second, they are accustomed also to give it to his purple, to the sceptre, and to the crown. To all these objects they render the same veneration as to the king, because they do not venerate them for themselves, nor in themselves, but in them and by them they intend to venerate the person of the king. This being understood, it will be easy to answer the question above proposed. The images and crosses of Christ are to be adored not in themselves, but in relation to him: The images by one title only, on account of what they represent, the cross by a double title, because it represents to us the figure of Christ himself on it; and by the contact which it had with the sacred flesh and with the precious blood of Christ. Of course we speak here of the true cross on which the divine Redeemer suffered and died. As to other crosses which are likenesses of that, they too are adorable, but only by the first title, whereas the nails, the crown, the lance, and the other instruments of the passion, are worshipful solely by the second title. Hence it is that we would not venerate the likenesses of these images as we do of the cross, for the reason that there would no longer remain in them any title of worship. But what and of what kind then should that adoration be called, which is given to the images and cross of Christ? Of the same kind as beseem Christ himself, that is, of latria, with this difference however that as to Christ the adoration is absolute, as to those other things the adoration is relative.

The kind of adoration due to the B. Virgin and the Saints.

What kind of adoration is due to the Mother of

Christ and to the Saints? Certainly it is not the adoration of latria, for this is reserved to God alone. You will say, perhaps, that in the Saints, and much more in the B. Virgin, there shines the most vivid image of Christ and his virtues; why then can they not be venerated with the homage of latria, as is done with the inanimate images of Christ? They cannot, just for the reason that they are not inanimate images, but animate and intelligent. Inanimate images are not capable of absolute homage, but of relative homage, and therefore, when they are worshipped, it is already known that the honor given them does not remain in them, but goes to their prototype. On the other hand, the rational creature is of itself capable of veneration, and on that account, if it were offered the homage proper to God, it would easily afford an occasion of erring in a matter of extreme importance, as this relative homage might easily be confounded with the absolute, and thus the creature would be adored instead of the Creator. Notwithstanding this, it is certain that some veneration is due to the saints for the supernatural excellence with which they are adorned as members of Christ, children and most dear friends of God, our advocates and protectors; and an absolute veneration, because this excellence is their own and intrinsic; a veneration, too, by which we recognize and testify at the same time their superiority to us, and their inferiority to God. Such precisely is the veneration called dulia, because superior to every veneration purely human, and inferior to the veneration belonging to God. And what kind of homage is due to the most Blessed Virgin? That homage is due which is proportionate to her supreme and most singular excellence among all mere creatures, both for the treasures of grace and glory that were accumulated in her, and for the most sublime dignity of Mother of God. Consequently, there is due to her an homage quite special, exclusively hers alone, which, without being latria, yet transcends simple dulia. This is the homage which the Church gives to her, and is called hyperdulia. With the same homage, then, of hyperdulia or of dulia the images also of the B. Virgin or of the Saints are to be venerated, although not absolutely, but relatively, as we have already seen.

From the arguments which we have advanced regarding images, we may easily infer what is to be held regarding holy relics. There can be no doubt that to these also a relative homage is due on account of the connection more or less intimate which they once had with the Saints themselves, and especially to their bodies, which were the temples and instruments of the Holy Ghost, who dwelt and operated in them, and are to be one day conformed to the brightness of the body of Christ by a glorious resurrection.

Chapter XXXIX.

The Sanctity of Mary.

Sanctity may be regarded in two ways: in respect to the evil which it excludes, and in respect to the good which it includes. In respect to the evil which it excludes, it consists in the exemption from spiritual stains, and the more perfect such exemption, that is, the more universal the exclusion of what can produce any spiritual infection, the more eminent it will be. Now what kind of exemption was that of the B. Virgin? It was the most perfect, as the exclusion from every stain was most universal, so that she was always not only most free from all stain of actual, mortal, or even the least venial sin, but was moreover, by a most singular privilege, exempt also from the stain of original sin. To her, then, with all truth belongs that praise of the canticles: "Thou art all fair, O my love, and there is not a spot in thee" (Cant. IV, 7). And who can doubt it? It is the property of divine wisdom when selecting a person for any office, to confer upon him the gifts which will render him fit for the office to which he is chosen. Now the B. Virgin was chosen to the dignity of Mother of God. There can be no doubt, then, that God by his grace made her qualified for so great an office, and consequently preserved her from every

(216)

defilement whatever of sin. And indeed, if she
had ever contracted any such defilement, she certainly would not have been fit to be the Mother of
God. First, because, as the honor of parents redounds on the offspring, according to that saying
of the Proverbs: "The glory of children are their
fathers" (Prov. XVII, 6), so reversely the disgrace
of the mother would have redounded on the son.
Next, because of the most special affinity, which
was to bind her to Christ, who was to take from
her his flesh. Now how could she be fit for such
affinity, if she had ever been subject to the yoke of
the demon? "And what concord hath Christ with
Belial?" (2 Cor. VI, 15.) Finally, because
"Wisdom will not enter into a malicious soul, nor
dwell in a body subject to sins" (Wisd. I, 4). The
Son of God, who is the Wisdom of God, was to
dwell in a most singular manner, and altogether
his own, not only in her soul, but also in her body.
But how could this be done, if her soul had not
been in a most singular manner free from all malice, and her body in a most singular manner free
from all slavery of sin? It must be said therefore
absolutely and without limitation, that Mary was
all beautiful, all without spot, because there was
no part of an instant in her life in which the
brightness of her beauty was obscured by the darkness of sin. For that reason Mary, elected to be
the living tabernacle of God, was justly compared
to the sun: "He placed his tabernacle in the sun"
(Ps. XVIII, 5), because the sun from its first
appearance shines with light, and dispels the dark-

ness. This same also was foreshown by what took place in the tabernacle of alliance, which was a figure of the Mother of God. Scarcely was the tabernacle finished, when it was covered with a cloud and filled with the glory of the Lord: "A cloud covered the tabernacle of the testimony, and the glory of the Lord filled it" (Exod. XL, 32). In a similar way with Mary; scarcely had her soul been created and infused into her body, when at that same instant the Lord took possession of her, and protected her from all harm of the enemy, and filled her with his grace.

We must not, however, conclude from this that Mary was not redeemed by Christ. Nay, she too was redeemed by Christ, and in a much more excellent way than others, a way belonging solely to her. Yes, even Mary was redeemed, for although exempt from original sin, it was in view of the merits of Christ the Redeemer. She was redeemed in a more excellent manner, for all others have been freed from sin after having contracted it, whilst Mary was preserved even from contracting it. Thus her redemption was not simply a liberation, as is that of all other men, but a preservation, a grace far more signal, and granted to no other but to her alone.

The B. Virgin was free from all sin and from all propensity to sin.

Mary was not only free from all sin, but also from all fomes or propensity to sin. By the fomes of sin is meant that inordinate inclination of the sensitive appetite, by which it opposes reason in two ways; by inciting to evil, and resisting good. It is called so because it is at the same time the effect and cause of sin; the effect of original and the cause of actual sin. It is also called the law of sin: "But I see another law in my members fighting against the law of my mind, and captivating me in the law of sin, that is, in my members" (Rom. VII, 23). It is called thus for two reasons: First, in relation to God; because man was subjected to this rebellion of the inferior to the superior faculty by the law of divine justice in punishment of his sin; secondly, in relation to sin itself, which having vanquished man the sinner, imposed on him its hard law, as a victor on the vanquished, and as a master on the slave.

This being understood, it will be easy to understand, that as the B. Virgin in view of the merits of Christ was preserved from original sin, so in view of the same merits she was preserved likewise from all propensity to sin. And why not? Can we believe that God, after granting what is greater, would withhold what is less? And that after having by a privilege so extraordinary removed from her the infection of the cause, that is to say sin, would then permit that she should be contaminated with the infection of the effect, that is, the propensity to sin? Let us say rather that from the first instant of her immaculate conception, the most abundant grace, which she received, extinguished in her all propensity to sin, or better, prevented its existence, so that from that first moment her inferior faculties in all their movements were most obedient to reason, just as were those of Adam in the state of original justice.

In this way it was most fully verified that Mary had no stain, for she had not the stain of sin, which is the taint of the spirit, nor had she even the stain of propensity to sin, which is the taint of the flesh.

Sanctity of Mary continued.

Sanctity, besides the exclusion of evil, implies the good of grace, for we treat here of the sanctity that belongs to a rational creature in the present state of supernatural elevation.   Now who can express in words, or even picture in thought, the abundance of grace which was bestowed on Mary? There is no doubt that it far surpassed the amount of grace of any other mere creature, for in every order the nearer a thing is to its principle, the more it experiences its power and partakes of its effects.   Observe those planets which are nearer the sun, how they receive from it more vivid splendors.   So too among the angels; those who belong to the highest choirs, because nearer to God, are much more enlightened with divine light than those of the lower choirs.   Now Christ is the fountain of grace as the principal cause according to the divinity, and as the instrumental cause according to the humanity: ''Grace and truth came by Jesus Christ'' (John I, 17).   And Mary, his true mother according to the flesh, just because his mother, was the nearest to him of any other.   She was then to receive from him a greater copiousness of grace than any other, and that the most like to the grace which is peculiar to Christ. From this we can see with what reason she was styled 'Full of grace'.

But at what time did the B. Virgin obtain such plenitude of grace? Was it at the moment of her conception, or when she became Mother of God, or when she was assumed to the glory of heaven? It can be said with all truth, that in all three of these circumstances she was full of grace. We must however distinguish between three different degrees in the perfection of such fulness, as generally happens in all those things that do not possess all their greatest perfection from the beginning. In a tree, for instance, one is its perfection when it shoots forth its first buds; another when it is decked with blossoms, and another when it is loaded with fruit; although it can be said that each of these different perfections is full, as far as it is complete in its grade. So also with the sun; it sends forth one light before it rises, another when rising, another when it sheds its torrents at midday; and yet each of these three lights can be said to be full in its degree. One will be the full light of the dawn, the other the full light of the rising sun, and the other the full light of midday. A similar thing occurred in Mary. She too was full of the light of grace in her conception, full in the annunciation, and full in the assumption. But in the conception this fulness was such as was required as a first disposition for the future dignity of Mother of God. In the annunciation it was such as became the presence of the Son of God, the sun of justice and splendor of the Father's glory, who actually entered her bosom. Then also was verified what Ezechiel had foretold: "And behold the majesty of the Lord went into the temple by the way of the gate that looked to the east . . . and the house was filled with the glory of the Lord" (Ezech. XLIII, 4, 5). How much more perfect, therefore, was this second fulness of grace with which the Virgin was enriched! In the assumption, finally, the fulness of the light of grace was consummated and crowned with the fulness of the light of glory, such as became her who was the Mother of the King of Glory, and consequently the Queen of heaven and of earth. Then for her began the midday splendors that shall never cease for all eternity.

The B. Virgin had the fulness of sanctifying grace and of all the other supernatural gifts.

As the B. Virgin had the fulness of sanctifying grace, so she had also the fulness of all the other supernatural gifts; and therefore there were in her all the gifts of the Holy Ghost, and all the graces called gratis data, in a most perfect manner. But in order not to mistake, we must distinguish in such gifts and graces the habit from the act. As to the habit, there can be no doubt that Mary possessed all the gifts and all the gratuitous graces in the highest degree, next to Christ. But as to the act, that is, the use of the habit, she did not have it to the same extent, but only as accorded with her condition and the accomplishment of the designs of divine providence. Thus she had the use of the gift of wisdom for contemplation: "But Mary kept all these words, pondering them in her heart" (Luke II, 19). She did not have it for teaching in public, for that did not become her sex, according to the saying of the Apostle: "But I permit not a woman to teach" (1 Tim. II, 12). In like manner she did not use the power of working miracles, whilst she lived here on earth, because at that time it was necessary to confirm the doctrine of Christ with miracles, and therefore it was incumbent only on Christ and his disciples, who were the heralds of his doctrine, that they should perform miracles: hence also of the Baptist we read, that 'he did no sign' (John X, 41). As for prophecy, she made use of it, and in the most sublime manner, as appears from that most wonderful canticle which she addressed to her God, magnifying his mercies, and the great favors conferred on her: "And Mary said, My soul doth magnify the Lord" (Luke I, 46).

Chapter XL.

The Virginity of Mary.

The Mother of Christ was a virgin before giving birth, that is, in the conception of her divine Son, as had been foretold by the prophet Isaias: "Behold a virgin shall conceive" (Is. VII, 14).

The dignity of the three divine persons required this: On the part of the Father, because Christ being the true and natural Son of God, it was not meet that he should have another father besides him. On the part of the Son, because the Son is the Word of God. Now it is the property of a word that it be conceived without any detriment of the mind, which of itself and in itself produces it; nay, the more incorrupt and pure the mind is, the more perfect also is the word. It was meet, therefore, that also the flesh of the Word of God should be conceived without the least detriment of the maternal bosom that begot him. On the part of the Holy Ghost, who is the spirit of all holiness, and sanctity itself, and could not, therefore, whilst he was operating the ineffable mystery of the incarnation in the bosom of the B. Virgin, permit that anything should even only materially lessen the value and dim the brightness of her virginity.

In the second place the dignity of Christ's human nature required this, for by that nature the

(224)

sins of the world had to be taken away: "Behold the Lamb of God, who taketh away the sin of the world" (John I, 29). Wherefore it was proper that he should indeed be in 'the likeness of sinful flesh', that is, similar to our flesh, but not 'sinful flesh', that is, a flesh infected too with original sin, and consequently in need also of redemption. Now how is original sin propagated? It is propagated from the first man, as from a prolific root of sin, to all his descendants, by means of natural generation, which is effected by the 'will of man and the will of the flesh'. It was necessary, therefore, that the humanity of Christ should be conceived, not by the will of man and the will of the flesh, but by God, the same as to say, by a virgin become a mother solely by the supernatural power of God. From this we can understand what a difference there is, even for this reason, between the conception of Christ and that of Mary. Both were immaculate, it is true; but that of the Son was so by the very manner of his generation; that of the mother was different, and was owing to a singular privilege granted her in view of the merits of Christ, the Saviour, who wished to redeem her with a ransom more abundant and more noble.

In the third place Christ wished that his conception according to the flesh should typify our regeneration according to the spirit. On this account, he wished to be conceived of a virgin, so that we might know, that if we wish to be incorporated in him, and become his members, and be partakers of his divine sonship and heavenly in-

15

heritance, we must be born spiritually of his virgin
spouse, the Church.   For as St. Augustin says, 'it
behooved our head, by a remarkable miracle to be
born of a virgin, according to the flesh, by which
he might signify that his members are to be born
of the virgin Church according to the spirit.'

The Mother of Christ was a virgin also at giving birth.

The prophet not only said, 'Behold a virgin
shall conceive', but added, 'and bring forth a son'.
And it was to be so for several reasons.   1st. To
express the peculiarity of him that was born, who
was the Word of God.   For a word not only brings
no corruption to the intellect when it is conceived
internally, but not even when it is uttered externally: rather it increases or manifests the perfection of the mind that brings it forth.   In a similar way, therefore, it was becoming that the body
of the same divine Word should be ushered into
light without at all injuring the virginal enclosure
of the mother.   2nd. Because the effect of the incarnation had to be not to ruin and corrupt what
was sound, but, on the contrary, to heal what was
ruined and corrupted.   But if this be so, who then
can believe that the Word incarnate wished, by
being born, to cause any injury to the virginal integrity of Mary.   3rd. Because he that was born
was the very same, who had so much inculcated
the honor of parents.   How then can we suppose
that in being born he had so little courtesy towards
his virgin mother, that instead of imparting to her

new honors, he would have allowed her in any way
to be a loser in what was so dear to her, her virginity?   4th. Christ in his nativity wished to
appear at the same time both true man and true
God, and therefore united together glories and
humiliations, miracles and abasements.   He wished
accordingly to be born of a woman, to show that
he was man, and of a virgin, to show that he was
God, since there was no other birth more befitting
to God, supposing that God was to be born, than
birth from a virgin.

Mary was a virgin also after giving birth.

The Mother of Christ was a virgin also after
giving birth; so that in her were fully verified those
words which the Lord had already spoken to the
prophet Ezechiel: "This gate shall be shut: it shall
not be opened; and no man shall pass through it,
because the Lord, the God of Israel, hath entered
in by it" (Ezech. XLIV, 2).   And, indeed, any
one that would even suspect the contrary would do
the greatest injury to Christ, to the Holy Ghost, to
Mary, and to Joseph.   He would do an injury to
Christ who, as he is according to the divine nature
the only-begotten Son of the Father, and because
he was an infinitely perfect son, so also it was
befitting that according to human nature he should
be the only-begotten son of the mother, as the most
perfect germ of her bosom, who could not, therefore, and should not have others like him.   He
would do an injury to the Holy Ghost, the divine
spouse of the virgin, who formed in her womb the

pure flesh of Christ.   How then could he have permitted his most holy temple to be ever profaned? He would do an injury to Mary, who would appear very ungrateful if she had not been satisfied with so great a son, and had spontaneously thrown away that virginity to preserve which God had wrought so great and so new prodigies.   He would do an injury to Joseph, whose temerity would have been inconceivable if, after having known by the revelation of an angel that Mary's pregnancy was by the Holy Ghost, he would still not have respected the virginal chastity of his spouse, to which the past mysteries had added so much beauty and splendor. We must then declare absolutely that the Mother of God conceived as a virgin, and afterwards remained always a virgin.

Mary added a vow to her virginity.

So much did Mary esteem and love her virginity that, to render it more precious and more sacred, she wished to dedicate it to God with a vow.   This is the common opinion of the Fathers and doctors of the Church, and it is evidently inferred from the question which the Virgin asked the angel, as St. Augustine argues: "To the angel making the announcement Mary replied: How shall this be done, for I know not man?   This she certainly would not say, had she not previously vowed herself a virgin to God."   Those words 'I know not man' serve to indicate not her present state of virginity only, for this did not prevent her from becoming a mother in the future; they signify in addition the firm will and obligation which she had contracted by vow of keeping unsullied that same virginity in the future. It was for this reason, that she asked how, notwithstanding this, could the announcement of the angel be verified: 'How shall this be done?'

But for what motive did she wish to be bound by such a vow? In order that the fair flower of her virginity might be more acceptable and more fragrant in the sight of God. For such is the virtue which a vow has, that it enhances the worth of the work to which it is joined, and enhances it inexpressibly. It is a bond, it is true, but a golden bond, which gives lustre and wonderful value to that which it binds, and for three reasons. First, because a vow is an act of religion, which is the queen of moral virtues; and all the works which are done in force of it, belong also to this virtue, and partake in its excellence and merit. Secondly, because by a vow a man renders to God an homage much more perfect and agreeable, for he subjects himself to him not only as to the act, but also as to the potency of the act, doing in this as the man who presents his friend not only with the fruit, but at the same time together with the fruit gives him the whole tree. Thirdly, in fine, a vow has this property that it fixes the will immovably in good. Now to operate with the will solidly established in good, increases the perfection of a virtuous act, in the same way as, on the contrary, to sin with the will obstinate in evil, aggravates the malice of sin.

Chapter XLI.

Mary's Espousals with Joseph.

Christ did not wish to be born of one who was a virgin only, but of a virgin who was also a spouse: "When Mary his Mother was espoused to Joseph" (Mat. I, 18). He had several reasons for this, some of which refer to himself, others to his mother, others to us. We shall first consider those which regard him. Thus then he disposed: first, that he might not be rejected by unbelievers as an illegitimate offspring; secondly, that his generation might be described in the usual manner, that is, by paternal ascent; thirdly, that he might be supported by St. Joseph, who on that account was called his foster-father — not that the Lord of heaven and earth needed the means to provide himself otherwise with food or any other thing that he required, but that he might conform himself even in this to the manner of life common to every other man; fourthly, as St. Ignatius the martyr observes, that the conception and the miraculous delivery of the Virgin might remain concealed from the devil, and thus that he might not stir up too much violence against the child when born. But could the devil not perceive whether Christ's mother was a virgin or not? And did he not later on know and confess that

Christ was the Son of God ?   I answer that the
devil can do many things by his natural powers,
from which however he is restrained by the divine
power; and so we must say that this happened in
the present case.   If afterwards he came in any
way to know that Christ was truly the Son of God,
that happened when the time had already come
when Christ would manifest his power against the
princes and powers of darkness, and bear the per-
secution stirred up by them.   But during infancy,
according to the counsels of divine wisdom, he was
not to suffer extraordinary vexations from hell, nor
to manifest his divine power, but was to deport
himself entirely as others of his age; and therefore
it was necessary that the malice of the enemy
should be restrained, so that it might not rage
against him more than was then permissible.

Why Christ was born of a virgin spouse.

Here we shall ponder the reasons why Christ
had to be born of a virgin spouse, both in regard
to the mother herself, and in regard to us.   In regard to the mother: first, that she might not be
held by the Jews in the light of a virgin seduced,
and be punished as such; secondly, that she might
not in the least incur any injury to her reputation;
thirdly, that she might have in Joseph one to afford
her assistance and consolation.

In regard to us: first, that our faith might be
more firm in the birth of Christ from a virgin,
whilst to prove it, were united the testimony of
Joseph, who being a just man would not have kept

Mary with him, if he had not been most sure of her chastity, and the testimony of the Virgin herself, who being also a spouse could have no motive for lying, since pregnancy and birth are the most honorable fruit of marriage; secondly, that those uncautious virgins might have no excuse, who do not with all care avoid any shadow of disgrace, while they see God so careful to keep from his virgin mother the very least shadow of the kind; thirdly, that Mary might be, as it were, a symbol of the Church, which is at the same time a virgin and the spouse of Christ; fourthly, that in the Mother of Christ, virgin and spouse, might be honored at the same time both the state of virginity and the state of matrimony, and that the heretics, who condemned both, might be confuted in advance.

Mary and Joseph had a most true matrimony.

Between Mary and Joseph there was a most true matrimony. Matrimony like every other thing is called true when it attains its own perfection. Now there is a twofold perfection of every object, the first and the second. The first perfection is in the essence itself, by which the thing has its species, for example of a mineral, of a plant, of an animal, etc. The second perfection consists in the operation which presupposes the essence already constituted, and by which the thing attains its end. By this we can understand in what the proper perfection of matrimony consists. The first perfection consists in the mutual and indivisible union of

minds, by which each of the consorts is indis-
solubly bound to keep inviolate fidelity with the
other. The second perfection consists in those
acts by which the end of matrimony is obtained,
which is the generation and education of the offspring. Observe too that the first perfection is
required, and is sufficient, that the thing may be
said to be absolutely true. Thus, for instance, a
child scarcely born, or even before it is born, provided only that the fetus be already informed with
an intellective soul, is a true man, although it is
not capable either of reasoning, or of willing, or of
performing other like acts belonging to a man.
Again in the supernatural order likewise, an infant just baptized is a true Christian, without any
doubt, although it does not perform, and is not in
a condition to perform, any act of a Christian.
All this being established, it is certain that the
matrimony between Mary and Joseph had the first
perfection, because both consented to the conjugal
union of minds. Wherefore it cannot be denied
that theirs was a most true matrimony. Notice,
then, how on this account the angel called Mary:
he called her wife of Joseph: "Joseph, son of
David, fear not to take unto thee Mary thy wife"
(Mat. I, 20).

As to the second perfection, this was wanting
in part, but it was found also in part in a most
signal manner. It was wanting in respect to the
act which has for its end the generation of offspring, for here the offspring was all the fruit of
the most pure bowels of Mary, a virgin soil and

fecundated by no other than by the divine power of the Holy Ghost. It was not wanting in respect to the other acts, which have for end the education of the offspring, which in this case were rather more perfect beyond measure than in any other, commensurate with the condition of such parents and of such a Son. We see, then, with how much reason St. Augustine affirmed, that 'in the parents of Christ the whole good of marriage was complete, offspring, fidelity, and the sacrament. We recognize the Lord as the offspring; fidelity in there being no adultery; and the sacrament, because there was no divorce. The nuptial embrace was the only thing absent.'

Chapter XLII.

The Announcement of the Angel to the Virgin.

Let us weigh the reasons for this annunciation. The first reason was, that due order should be observed in the descent which the Son of God would make upon the Virgin, namely, that she should first conceive him spiritually in her mind, and afterwards bodily in her bosom. For as St. Augustine observes, "The maternal relationship would have profited Mary nothing, if she had not borne him more happily in the heart than in the flesh." The second reason was, that she might give testimony of this mystery with more certainty after she herself had been divinely instructed. The third reason was, that she might willingly render an homage to God by offering herself ready to execute all his intimations, as when she said: "Behold the handmaid of the Lord, be it done to me according to thy word." Lastly, the fourth reason was, to show us that there was to be, as it were, a spiritual marriage between the Son of God and our nature. It was required, therefore, that the Virgin should give her consent in the name of the whole human nature, whose place she held at that time.

The announcement was made by the Archangel Gabriel.

What kind of messenger was sent by God to the Virgin? It was the Archangel Gabriel: "The angel Gabriel was sent by God." Why was an angel chosen to announce the mystery of the divine incarnation? Above all, that even in this case the generally established rule should be maintained, that divine things come down to us from God by means of the angels, just as our supplications ascend to God by means of the angels. Besides, it was conformable to the work of human reparation, which had to be accomplished by Christ, that this should have its beginning with the ministry of an angel sent by God to Mary, the second Eve, as human perdition had its beginning from a wicked angel sent by the prince of demons to the first Eve. In fine, it thus became the virginal purity of the Mother of God, which was not a human thing and earthly, but even angelic and heavenly. But why among all the angels was Gabriel chosen? Because this great archangel is the power of God, as his name signifies, and therefore the best adapted for the office of announcing the coming of Him, who is the Power of the Most High, and who came on earth to overthrow and scatter the powers of darkness.

The angel appeared to Mary in a visible form.

The angel in the annunciation presented himself to the Virgin in a visible form, for the reason that he came to announce the mystery of the incarnation by which the invisible God would make himself visible. It was proper, therefore, for the better announcement of this mystery, that he also should appear visibly. Such too, indeed, were all the apparitions of the ancient Testament, for the same reason, since they were all pre-ordained for this most solemn apparition, in which the Word of God would put on not simply the appearances, but the reality of our flesh, and dwell visible among us. But besides this, the sensible vision of the angel was at once of more consolation and certainty to the Virgin: of more consolation, because it strengthened her not only in spirit, but also in the senses of her body, as was necessary for one who was to receive the Son of God in her immaculate mind and body: of more certainty, because things that fall under the senses are apprehended with more vividness and tenacity, than those which are represented to us only by the understanding or by the imagination.

But if this be true, how can it be said that Mary was troubled? She was troubled by reason of her virginal modesty; but above all on account of her humility, at hearing such great encomiums of herself. But her perturbation very soon ceased, when the angel reassured her by saying: "Fear not, Mary." And this is precisely the difference there is between the apparitions of good spirits and those of infernal spirits. In the beginning both are wont to excite some fear, for the reason that they are unusual, and above the simple powers of visible nature. But in the former the fear does not last long, and soon gives way to joy and peace. In the latter, on the contrary, the fear does not cease, but rather increases, and always tends the more to throw the mind into dismay and desperation.

The order observed by the angel in his embassy.

Consider the wonderful order which the angel kept in performing his embassy, and all adapted to his purpose. He had three things in view. First, to attract the attention of the Virgin, then to explain to her the mystery of the incarnation, and afterwards to induce her to give her consent. And these things he executed perfectly. To win the attention of Mary, he hailed her with a new and unusual salutation, in which he gave her three most singular praises. First, he intimated her fitness to conceive the Word Incarnate, because favored with grace: "Full of grace." Secondly, he expressed the same divine conception by which it would with all strictness be verified, that God would be with her: "The Lord is with thee." In the third place he foretold the honors and blessings which would accrue to her: "Blessed art thou among women." With these praises he held her attentive, because there is nothing that so much excites the wonder of an humble mind, as to hear its own excellences recounted; and from wonder there naturally comes attention. After that the angel proposed the object of his message by announcing the near conception, the birth and the name of the offspring of which Mary was to be the mother: "Behold thou shalt conceive in thy womb, and shalt bring forth a son, and thou shalt call his name Jesus" (Luke I, 31); and by showing his most high dignity, he adds: "He shall be great, and shall be called the Son of the Most High, and the Lord God shall give unto him the throne of

David his father, and he shall reign in the house of Jacob forever; and of his kingdom there shall be no end" (Luke I, 32, 33). Moreover, by declaring in what way the conception would take place: "The Holy Ghost shall come upon thee, and the power of the Most High shall overshadow thee" (Luke I, 35). Lastly, he incited the Virgin to give her consent, by adducing the example of Elizabeth : "And behold, thy cousin Elizabeth, she hath also conceived a son in her old age" (Luke I, 36), and by representing to her the greatness of the divine power, which has no limits: "Because no word shall be impossible with God" (Luke I, 37).

Chapter XLIII.

Christ's Conception.

Whence came the matter from which the most sacred body of Christ was conceived? From Adam, the first father of the whole human race. For the Son of God assumed our human nature to cure it of corruption, and for that reason wished to take it from that stock in which it had been vitiated by the sin of the first parent, which was propagated in all his posterity, so as to apply the remedy where the wound was. But be careful not to argue from this that Christ also contracted original sin. In what manner is original sin transmitted from Adam to his posterity? It is transmitted through the means of the generative power, which transfuses human nature into them, and transfuses it infected with that stain with which the first man had sullied it. In the same way as a broken seal, through the impression which is made of it on wax, stamps there at once both its character and its defect; or else in the way in which actual sin passes from the will to the various members of the body, as for example to the hand, according as these are moved by the will. Now, although the body of Christ received indeed its matter originally from Adam, yet it was not formed by the generative power derived from Adam, but by the supernatural power of God. Hence the infection which contaminates the other descendants of Adam, was not transmitted to him. In like manner as in the wax the impress will be without deformity, if it come from the impression not of a broken, but of a perfect seal; or as the external action of the hand, or of any other member, will not share the internal malice of the will, as long as it is not determined by the will itself, but by some other extrinsic cause.

From this we see that the conception of Christ was partly above the condition of nature, and partly according to it. It was above the condition of nature as to its active principle, which was not the generative power of any man, but the divine power of the Holy Ghost. It was according to the condition of nature as to the matter, which corresponded to that which is found in the conception of every other human child on the part of the mother, and was supplied by the most chaste and pure body of the Virgin.

Why Christ is styled the Son of David and of Abraham.

For what reason is Christ called particularly the Son of David and of Abraham?: "The book of the generation of Jesus Christ, the Son of David, the Son of Abraham" (Mat. I, 1). First, because these two had very special promises of the future Messiah. To Abraham it was said: "And in thy seed all the nations of the earth shall be blessed" (Gen. XXII, 18), which words the Apostle himself interprets as referring to Christ: "To Abra-

16

ham were the promises made, and to his seed. He saith not: and to his seeds as of many, but as of one; and to thy seed, who is Christ" (Gal. III, 16). To David afterwards it was said and sworn by God, that from him would descend the one who would be seated to reign upon his throne: "The Lord hath sworn truth, and he will not make it void: of the fruit of thy womb I will set upon thy throne" (Ps. CXXXI, 11). Hence it is that when the Jews wished to do honor to Jesus, and to receive him after the manner of a king, they cried out: "Hosanna to the Son of David" (Mat. XXI, 9). In the second place, because Christ was to be priest, prophet and king. Now Abraham was a priest, as appears from those words which God spoke to him: "Take me a cow of three years old, etc." (Gen. XV, 9), by which he enjoined him to offer him sacrifice, which is the proper function of a priest. He was also a prophet, as God himself attested to Abimelech, saying: "Now, therefore, restore the man his wife, for he is a prophet" (Gen. XX, 7). Again David, as is well known, was both prophet and king. Lastly, because circumcision had its beginning in Abraham, and the divine election was shown in a most singular way in David, as he was chosen by God to take the place of Saul: "The Lord has sought a man according to his own heart" (1 Kings XIII, 14). Christ, therefore, was especially called the son of both, to signify that he came to bring salvation both to the circumcision and to the election, that is to say, to the circumcised Jews, and also to the

gentiles elected and called to enter the fold of
Christ, and even to hold in it the first place instead
of the Jews, who by their own fault became unworthy of it: "And they shall come from the east
and the west and the north and the south, and shall
sit down in the kingdom of God. And behold,
they are last, who shall be first, and they are first,
who shall be last" (Luke XIII, 29, 30).

The work of Christ's conception common to the whole Trinity.

The work of Christ's conception was common
to the whole Trinity, and therefore the angel, in
announcing it to Mary, expressed all the three persons: the Holy Ghost, by saying 'The Holy Ghost
shall come upon thee': the Son and the Father,
when he said: 'The power of the Most High shall
overshadow thee'; for by the Most High the Father
is understood, and therefore Christ is called the
Son of the Most High; and the power of God the
Father is the Son. "But we preach Christ . . . .
the power of God and the wisdom of God" (1 Cor.
23, 24). Nevertheless, the conception of Christ
is attributed in particular to the Holy Ghost,
and this for three reasons. The first regards the
cause of the incarnation on the part of God. For
the Holy Ghost is the love of the Father, and of
the Son. Now it was out of God's very great love
for us, that the divine Son put on our flesh in the
virginal bosom of Mary: "For God so loved the
world as to give his only-begotten Son" (John
III, 16). The second regards the cause of the incarnation on the part of the nature assumed,

because from that it is understood, that if the Son of God united himself to human nature with so close a tie, it was not for the merits which that nature had, but through grace alone, of which the Holy Ghost is the giver and distributor. The third regards the term of the incarnation, which was that the man conceived should be holy and the Son of God. Now both these things are ascribed to the Holy Ghost, since by him men become sons of God: "And because you are sons, God hath sent the Spirit of his Son into your hearts, crying, Abba, Father" (Gal. IV, 6). He too is the Spirit of sanctification: "Who was predestinated the Son of God in power according to the Spirit of sanctication" (Rom. I, 4). Wherefore, as others are sanctified by the Holy Ghost, that they may be adopted Sons of God, so Christ was conceived by the power of the Holy Ghost in the fulness of all sanctity, that he might be the natural Son of God. Hence it is that after the archangel Gabriel had foretold to the Virgin, that the Holy Ghost would descend upon her: "The Holy Ghost shall come upon thee", he concluded, by saying, "and therefore also the Holy, which shall be born of thee, shall be called the Son of God" (Luke I, 35).

We must be careful, however, not to mistake by thinking that, whilst it can be said that Christ was conceived by the work of the Holy Ghost, it can be equally affirmed that he was the Son of the Holy Ghost according to the flesh. This cannot at all be said. It is true that the Holy Ghost produced the human nature of Christ as the efficient cause, but did not beget it as a father, for he produced it by operating solely in the manner of an acting principle, not originating it from his own substance, and to his own likeness, a thing which is required in generation properly so called.

Three truths in relation to Christ's conception.

In relation to the manner and order of the conception of Christ three truths principally are to be held. First, that this conception was accomplished in an instant; for by the infinite power of the Holy Ghost, the body of Christ was at once formed perfect. Secondly, that therefore in the same instant there was infused into it a rational soul, because it was then already fully disposed to receive its perfect form, which is the intellective soul. Thirdly, that in that same moment also the Word of God assumed it and united it to himself with the hypostatic union, so that there was no moment of time in which the flesh of Christ existed, when it was not united to the Word. At once flesh, says St. John Damascene, at once the flesh of the Word of God, at once flesh animated with a rational and intellectual soul.

From this and from what was explained before, we may understand how this conception had three grand prerogatives. It was a conception without original sin; it was not a conception of a mere man, but of a Man-God; it was a conception from a virgin, which did not thereby destroy, but enhanced beyond all idea the flower of her virginity. But if it is so, it may be asked, how is such conception to be styled, natural or miraculous? Considered on the part of the matter, it was all natural, for the reason that this came from the mother just as in the generation of any man. Considered on the part of the active power, it was all miraculous, for this was the supernatural power of the Holy Ghost. But everything has to be judged and named, rather from what regards it as to the active part, than from what regards it as to the passive part. The conception of Christ, therefore, should be styled miraculous, rather than natural: miraculous simply; natural with restriction, only as to the passive part.

Singular perfections with which Christ was adorned.

Let us ponder over the most singular perfections with which Christ was adorned from the first moment of his conception. They were principally four.

First. The plenitude of sanctifying grace; for this is derived from the union itself with the Word, just as light from the sun. Now the Word, as we have seen, was united to the humanity of Christ in the first moment of his conception, from which time, therefore, the divine light of grace enlightened and sanctified his soul and his body.

Second. The perfect use of his free will; for the exalted dignity of human nature assumed by the Word required, that its spiritual perfection from the very beginning should not be defective, but entire. Now the ultimate perfection is not in the power alone, or in the habit, but in the act, which is like the ripe fruit that completes the perfection of the tree on which it was grown, and on which it hangs. We must say, then, that from the first instant Christ had the operation of his intellect and will, in which the use of free will is found.

Third. In that same instant he could merit, and did really merit, the glory of immortality. In order to understand how this is true, we must notice that sanctification is of two kinds: the one of adults, who are sanctified by their own acts; the other of infants, who are sanctified, not by their own acts, but by the acts of others. Of these two the first sanctification is the more perfect, the second less perfect, because the first is not only habitual, but also actual; the second is habitual only. The first has its origin in some way from the subject itself which is sanctified, not as from a principal cause, which is God alone, but as from a secundary cause. The second comes all from without. All this being evident, no one can deny that Christ's sanctification in his conception was most perfect, for he was sanctified to that eminent degree which became him, who was to be the sanctifier of all others. Consequently, his sanctification was by his own act, seeing that from the first moment his free will turned towards God with all its might. But such a movement of the free will has the nature of merit, as is clear. Therefore, he truly merited in that first instant. Some one perhaps may object that, if Christ merited the glorification of his body with this first act, how then can it be said that he merited this same glorification with the other acts of his life, and especially of his passion? It can be said with all truth, as nothing prevents a thing from belonging to a person by several titles; for example, a kingdom by right of birth, and by right of conquest. And thus Christ could merit the glory of the body by that first act, and could merit it also by subsequent acts. Not that the first merit was imperfect; it was most perfect. But the other merits caused that glory to be not more due to Christ, but due by more titles.

Fourth Christ from the first instant of his conception was fully possessed of the beatific vision; for of him it is written, that 'God doth not give the Spirit by measure' (John III, 34). God does not give him the gifts of the Holy Ghost by measure, that is, with restriction, but above all measure, that is to say, with the greatest abundance possible in the present order of providence. Now the grace of wayfarers is of a lower degree than that of those who enjoy the beatific vision. Hence it is, that to Christ was communicated the grace which pertains to the blessed in heaven, not only in habit, but also in act; not only as great as that of all the blessed united together, but far greater and sublimer, such as became him who is the Supreme Lord of them all. And he had this in the same moment in which he was conceived, for the reason that all this was due to his humanity in virtue of the most admirable union with the Word which was effected at that juncture.

Chapter LXIV.

The Nativity of Christ.

As there are two natures in Christ, the divine and the human, one of which he had from his Father in eternity, the other from his mother in time, so two births are to be distinguished in him: one by which he is born eternally of the Father, the other by which he was born in time of the mother. Nor must we be astonished when we hear that two births are ascribed to the same person, so that we say that he was born twice. For what inconsistency is there in the same man walking, or sitting, or doing any other action twice at two different times? But if there is no incongruity in this, much less will there be, that the same person according to two different natures be born twice, the first birth being in eternity, the second in time, as time and eternity are far more different from each other than are the various parts of time.

Christ born in Bethlehem.

Christ willed to be born in Bethlehem, and that for four reasons especially. First, to show from the very place of his birth that he was 'of the seed of David according to the flesh' (Rom. I, 3), and that he came to fulfil the special promises made by God to the same David concerning the future Messiah. The second reason was, because, as

Pope St. Gregory observes, Bethlehem signifies the 'house of bread', and it is Christ who affirmed of himself: "I am the living bread, who came down from heaven." The same saint adds: "Rightly too is he born in Bethlehem, for Bethlehem is interpreted the house of bread, since it is he himself who says: "I am the living bread who came down from heaven." The third reason was, to confound the vain glory of men, who are accustomed to boast of being born in some great and noble city, whilst Christ, on the contrary, chose to be born in an obscure village. The fourth reason was, to make the power of his divinity far more prominent, which becomes the more manifest the more human means are wanting. On this account, he chose for himself poor parents, and a poor native place. "The foolish things of the world hath God chosen that he may confound the wise, and the weak things of the world hath God chosen, that he may confound the strong: and the mean things of the world hath God chosen, and things that are not, that he might destroy the things that are" (1 Cor. I, 27, 28).

We see, then, how Jesus Christ, both in his birth and in his death, willed to resemble David, his prophet and figure. David's native place was Bethlehem, and he chose Jerusalem for his royal and sacerdotal city, as in it he established the capital of his kingdom, and wished to erect the temple of God. Christ, in like manner, chose Bethlehem for his nativity, and for his passion he chose Jerusalem, in which and for which he founded his kingdom, and consummated his priesthood.

The time in which Christ was born.

Observe the time in which Christ was born; for even this was not by chance, nor determined by the necessary laws of nature, but chosen freely by divine wisdom, because most suitable to the end for which Christ came into the world, for which reason it was called by the Apostle the fulness of time: "But when the fulness of the time was come, God sent his Son made of a woman, made under the law" (Gal. IV, 4).

He willed, therefore, to be born when the Hebrew people were subject to the dominion of a foreign prince, so that the prophecy of Jacob might be fulfilled: "The sceptre shall not be taken away from Juda, nor a ruler from his thigh till he come who is to be sent" (Gen. XLIX, 10). He willed to be born at that time, when by order of Cesar the census of all his subjects was being made, in order to pass himself from the first moment as a servant of an earthly monarch, and thus by means of his servitude to effect our liberation. He willed to be born at a time when one prince held sway throughout the whole world, to signify that he had come to collect all his own together, in such a way that there would no longer be but one only flock and one only shepherd. He willed to be born when the greatest peace reigned over the whole earth, to signify that he is our peace: "For he is our peace, who hath made both one" (Eph. II, 14); to signify also that he appeared in this world to guide our steps in the way of peace: "To direct our feet into the way of peace" (Luke I, 79). He willed to be born in the bleakest season and without protection from the cold, so that his immaculate body might begin at once to suffer and to be immolated for us. Finally, he willed to be born in the depth of the night, to signify that he was the sun rising from on high, that came to enlighten those that lay in the darkness and shadow of death: "The Orient from on high hath visited us to enlighten them that sit in darkness, and in the shadow of death" (Luke I, 79).

The manner of Christ's birth.

As to the manner of Christ's birth, it was without pain to his most holy Mother; for the pain inflicted by God on the first Eve, the transgressor, "In sorrow shalt thou bring forth children", was not for the second Eve, immaculate from the first moment of her conception, and become a mother by the sole power of the divine Spirit. As Christ at his resurrection issued from the sepulchre, leaving it closed and intact, so at his birth he issued from the virginal bosom of his most pure mother without causing her injury or labor of any kind, just as a ray of light, in passing through a very clear crystal, does not dim it nor stain it nor injure it in the least, but renders its purity more conspicuous. Nor is this all. The Virgin, so far from experiencing any pain in this her divine delivery, was even filled with the sweetest, most chaste and altogether heavenly joy. Mary, therefore, was truly that happy land mentioned by

Isaias, as a solitary land not cultivated nor used by any man, and therefore a virgin land, which bloomed as a lily, rejoiced and skipped along blooming. She sent forth her bud, and in budding exulted, full of gladness, and singing praises to the Lord, and verifying the words of the prophet: "The wilderness shall rejoice, and shall flourish like the lily. It shall bud forth, and blossom, and shall rejoice with joy and praise" (Is. XXXV, 1, 2).

CHAPTER XLV.

Mary the Mother of God.

The most holy Virgin can and ought to be called Mother of God by all means, for the reason that Jesus Christ, who is her Son according to the flesh, is at the same time 'God over all things, blessed forever' (Rom. IX, 5). To understand how this is true, consider when it is that a woman is said to be the mother of some one. It is when she has conceived him in her womb and brought him forth to light. Now Mary really conceived and bore in her bosom, and begot according to humanity the Son of God, him who was also God, as is the Father and the Holy Ghost. What doubt then can there be, that to her with all propriety belongs the most glorious title of Mother of God?

Some one may perhaps object, and say, that although Mary begot the human nature, still she did not beget the divine person of the Word, which was begotten by the Father from all eternity. Note well, in order not to mistake, which in this matter would be very pernicious, note well I say, that in every generation it is necessary to distinguish two terms, the complete term or the subject of the generation, and the formal term. The complete term is the person, or hypostasis, which is generated; the formal term is the nature in which the person or hypostasis subsists. Now generation applies properly to the complete term, and not to the formal one. Nor even in ordinary language would any one say, for example, that the human nature of Peter is born, but Peter is born, who is the person subsisting in that nature. Now in the generation of Christ, the formal term is the humanity, but the complete term is the divine person of the Word, in as much as it subsists in the human nature. And therefore we must attribute to the same person of the Word his generation according to the divine nature, to be from the Father from eternity, so also his generation according to human nature, to be from his Mother in time. Nor are we to be astonished at hearing that one and the same person is begotten twice and by different persons. Whenever the person has but one nature, it is evident that it can have only one generation, by which it receives that one sole nature which belongs to it. But suppose the case that there were a man who had two distinct human natures, it is manifest that he could be generated twice, once according to one nature, another time according to the other, and from different genitors, one of them communicating to him one nature, and the other the other nature. And for this reason the same person would be at the same time the son of both, but according to distinct natures. Now what does not happen in a mere creature, really took place in Christ, in whom two distinct and different natures, the divine and the human, are united in an inexplicable, but most true manner in one sole person, who is the divine person of the Son of God. Hence it follows that this same person could have a double generation according to the two natures which belong to it, and be the Son of God according to the divinity, and the Son of Mary according to the humanity. From all this we can easily conceive the import of the word God when it is asserted that Mary is the Mother of God. It does not denote the divine nature, but the person; nor all the three divine persons, or any of them indiscriminately, but solely the person of the Word made flesh, because Mary is not the mother of the Divinity, nor is she mother of the whole Trinity, nor of the divine Father, nor of the Holy Ghost, but of the divine Son, who was conceived by her and born of her according to the flesh.

Mary's dignity as Mother of God.

Let us weigh the inexpressible dignity which the B. Virgin derives from this her prerogative of Mother of God. The mother begets a son from her substance to the likeness of her own nature, whence arises a natural and most intimate tie of affinity between the mother and the son. So in virtue of her divine maternity Mary also contracted a like affinity with the Son of God made man. And because, by the identity of nature, the Son of God is the same thing as the Father and as the Holy Ghost, in this intimate affinity of the Virgin with her divine Son there is included also a most singular and wonderful relation, and a parentage, as it were, between her and God the Father, who according to the divine nature begets that same

Son, who according to the human nature was begotten by her; between her also and the Holy Ghost, of whom her same Son is the principle according to the divinity, the fruit and effect according to the humanity. Wherefore St. Bernard, addressing the divine Mother, exclaims: "Not only Lord the Son is with thee, whom thou clothest with thy flesh, but Lord the Holy Ghost also, by whom thou conceivest, and Lord the Father too is with thee, who begot him whom thou conceivest. The Father, I say, is with thee, who makes the Son his and thine. The Son is with thee. . . . The Holy Ghost is with thee, who with the Father and the Son sanctifies thy womb." Who, then, can express how great a dignity accrues to Mary from this maternal affinity with the Son of God? Truly it may be affirmed that in its kind, that is, in the kind of maternity, it passes all limit, and is infinite, for the reason that the dignity of the mother as such has for its source and measure the dignity of the son, of whom she is the mother, and, therefore, the greater his dignity the greater is hers; and where the dignity of the son is divine, and infinite, the dignity of the mother also will be infinite.

This prerogative of Mary, the source of all her blessings.

Reflect how this most sublime prerogative of the Mother of God was for her the prime and most prolific root of all the gifts of sanctification and of glorification, that are found united in her. From this her immaculate conception. From this her

17

preservation from every personal fault, even the slightest. From this the freedom from any fomes, or propensity to sin. From this the fulness of sanctifying and actual grace, the gifts of the Holy Ghost, and of gratuitous graces. From this the joys of motherhood joined with the purity of the rarest virginity. From this the title and office of our co-redemptress, of our advocate, our hope, our mother, of treasurer and dispenser of heavenly favors, all of which are poured on us so abundantly by her hands. From this the supereminent bliss with which her soul is inundated, the brightest splendor with which her body is surrounded, and the august diadem crowning her brow as queen of heaven and of earth, and the highest seat of glory to which she has been exalted above all the saints and angels of paradise. All these her most special prerogatives have her maternity for their foundation. All germinate, as we have said, from this prime root, because from it comes the inconceivable immensity of her dignity, to which the divine goodness and wisdom has proportioned the immensity of its gifts of grace and glory.

Chapter XLVI.

Manifestation of Christ's Nativity.

You may ask why the Nativity of Christ was not to be made known to all men immediately. First, because that would have impeded the work of human redemption, which, according to the design of divine wisdom, had to be accomplished by Christ's crucifixion: "For if they had known it, they never would have crucified the Lord of glory" (1 Cor. II, 8). Besides, it would have lessened the merit of faith, which is the very thing by which men attain their justification: because "The justice of God is by faith of Jesus Christ" (Rom. III, 22). Again, if the divinity had been shown openly from the beginning to the eyes of men, it would have rendered the verity of the human nature in Christ less evident by its most vivid light.

But notice the difference between the first and the second coming of Christ. The second will be most manifest to the whole world: "As the lightning cometh out of the east, and appeareth even unto the west, so shall also the coming of the Son of man be" (Mat. XXIV, 27). The reason is, because then Christ will come to judge; and for judgment it is required that the authority of the judge be certain and manifested to all. But the first coming was to bring salvation to men, which is to be obtained by means of faith. But faith regards those things which are not seen: "Now faith is the substance of things hoped for, the conviction of things that appear not" (Heb. XI, 1). It was necessary, therefore, that this his first coming should be secret, not in the sense that no one should know it, for in that case it would have been useless; but that only some should know it, who might afterwards impart the knowledge of it to others. For this is the order observed by divine wisdom in the revelation of like supernatural truths. We see, too, that it happened thus in the mystery of the resurrection of the same Christ, as is testified in the Acts: "Him God raised up the third day, and gave him to be made manifest, not to all the people, but to witnesses preordained by God" (Acts X, 40, 41).

Who the witnesses of Christ's nativity were.

Those chosen by God to be witnesses of his nativity, were particularly the shepherds and the magi. The shepherds were Jews, poor, simple, and rude: the magi were Gentiles, rich, wise, and distinguished; to signify that Christ came to bring salvation to men of every condition, and that, therefore, with regard to him there is no difference between Jew and Gentile, 'where there is neither Gentile nor Jew, circumcision or uncircumcision, Barbarian nor Scythian, bond nor free, but Christ is all in all' (Colos. III, 11). The shepherds first, and the magi afterwards; for the reason that he wished that this manifestation of his nativity should be a figure of the more complete manifestation, which would afterwards be made of his coming, and of the redemption wrought by him. Accordingly, as this was to be made first to the Jews and afterwards to the Gentiles, so in like manner he disposed that his nativity should be announced first to the shepherds, who were the first fruits of the Jews, and afterwards to the magi, who were the first fruits of the Gentiles.

How this manifestation was made.

This manifestation was made to the shepherds by means of angels; to the magi by means of a star. The reason for that was, because the manifestation of any object whatever needs to be made by way of signs that are proportioned, both to the object manifested, and to the person to whom the manifestation is made. Hence it is, chiefly, that both the signs were heavenly and miraculous, as the nativity signified was a thing not merely earthly and natural, but celestial and miraculous; and both signs were accompanied with splendor, as they indicated the birth of him, who from eternity is the splendor of the glory of the Father. Hence also comes the diversity of the signs which God used with the shepherds and with the magi, as that sign was given to both which was most suitable to their conditions and customs. The shepherds were Jews, and on that account with them God made use of angels, since he was accustomed to reveal his secrets and to give his laws to his own people by means of angels: "You have

received the law by the disposition of angels"
(Acts VII, 53). The magi were pagans, and for
that reason God did not make use of angels, who
to these people were unknown. As they were
accustomed to study the course of the stars, God
called and guided them by means of a star.

Chapter XLVII.

Christ's Circumcision.

As Christ, who had no sin in himself, willed nevertheless to assume our death which is the effect of sin, in order to deliver us from death and make us die spiritually to sin, so also he willed to submit to the law of circumcision, which was the remedy for original sin, although he had not contracted it, so that he might free us from the yoke of the law, and effect a spiritual circumcision in our hearts, of which St. Paul says in his letter to the Romans, 'the circumcision is that of the heart in the spirit': and in the one to the Colossians: "In whom also you are circumcised with a circumcision not made by hand in the despoiling of the body of the flesh, but in the circumcision of Christ" (Colos. II, 11). But besides this, for other motives also, Christ willed to be circumcised. 1st. To show that his was a body not in appearance only, but real and composed of human flesh like ours. 2nd. To sanction the law of circumcision as instituted by God. 3rd. To make it openly seen that he was descended from Abraham, to whom the precept of circumcision had been given. 4th. To take away from the Jews the excuse for not receiving him on account of not being circumcised. 5th. To give by his example a greater value to the virtue of

(263)

obedience, on which account he willed to be circumcised in the time and according to the rite, which was prescribed by the law. 6th. To make himself like unto us, where there would be no sin, as he the Lord of the universe and the Saint of saints had for love of us put on the form of a servant, and willed to appear 'in the likeness of sinful flesh'.

Circumcised and named on the same day.

Consider how on the same day on which he was circumcised, he was also, according to the custom of the Jews, given a name, and was called Jesus: "And after eight days were accomplished that the child should be circumcised, his name was called Jesus, which was called by the angel before he was conceived in the womb" (Luke II, 21). Here, too, ponder attentively why this name Jesus should be given to Christ. The names that are given by men are usually taken from some circumstance connected with the person that is named. Sometimes they are taken from the time; as when the name of some saint is given to one born on the feast-day of the saint. Sometimes from kindred, as when the son is given the name of the father, or of some other relative. At other times from some event that is to be held in special remembrance. Thus the patriarch Joseph applied to his first-born son the name of Manasses, which means one who causes to forget: "And he called the name of the first-born Manasses, saying: God hath me to forget all my labors and my father's house" (Gen. XLI, 51). In like manner there are other particulars which accompany the birth of a person, and from which he is named. But the names which are assigned by God, always denote some gratuitous gift bestowed by the divine bounty upon the person to whom they are given. For example, Abram was called Abraham by God, which signifies 'high father of the multitude', to show that he was destined to be the progenitor of many people: "Neither shall thy name be called any more Abram; but thou shalt be called Abraham, because I have made thee the father of many nations" (Gen. XVII, 5). In a similar way Simon was called Peter, to signify that he was chosen by God to be the foundation stone of his Church: "And I say to thee, thou art Peter, and on this rock I will build my Church" (Mat. XVI, 18). For the reason, therefore, that this office and most gracious gift of the infinite munificence, viz., that through him all might be saved, was conferred on Christ, most justly was he called Jesus, that is, Saviour. If others also bore this name, they did not have it in the same sense as Christ. They were called so, as being imperfect saviours, that is, in some particular and temporal way. But the name of Jesus in its full signification means a perfect, universal and spiritual Saviour, and is proper only of Christ. With reason, then, is he given a new name: "Thou shalt be called by a new name, which the mouth of the Lord shall name" (Is. LXII, 2).

All the other names of the Messiah are included in the name Jesus.

All the other names attributed by the prophets to the Messiah are included in the name of Jesus, because they all express in some way the work of our salvation. He was called Emmanuel, which means God with us: "Behold a virgin shall conceive, and bear a son, and his name shall be called Emmanuel" (Is. VII, 7), showing by this the cause of our salvation, which is the hypostatic union of the Son of God with human nature, by virtue of which union it was verified with all strictness that God is with us. They named him: "Hasten to take away the spoils; make haste to take away the prey" (Is. VIII, 3); thus bringing to mind the slavery from which he saved us, by despoiling the infernal principalities and powers of their conquests, according to the expression of the Apostle: "Divesting principalities and powers, he made a show of them confidently" (Colos. II, 15). Isaias says: "And his name shall be called Wonderful, Counsellor, God, the Mighty, the Father of the world to come, the Prince of peace"; showing with these names the manner and the term of our salvation, namely, how by the most wonderful counsel and incomprehensible power of the divinity, we are raised up to enjoy the inheritance of the world to come, in which there shall be the perfect peace of the adopted children of God; and the prince of this kingdom of peace shall be his same natural and only-begotten Son. He was also named the Orient: "Behold a man, the Orient is his name" (Zach. VI, 12); indicating likewise the mystery of the incarnation, which was the cause and beginning of our salvation, for by it, whilst we lay buried in darkness, the Son of God, the sun of justice, arose to enlighten the right in heart: "To the righteous a light is risen up in darkness" (Ps. CXI, 4).

CHAPTER XLVIII.

Presentation of Christ in the Temple.

As the Son of God was made man, and was circumcised, not for his own need or advantage, but for us, to make us by the power of his grace sons of God and circumcised spiritually, so also for our sake he wished to be presented to God in the temple, so that we might learn to dedicate ourselves to the Lord; and he willed that this should be done after the circumcision, to teach us that no one is worthy of the divine sight, whose heart is not circumcised of his vices.

There were two precepts contained in the ancient law concerning a new-born child. The first was general for all, and was, that counting the days appointed for the purification of the mother, there should be two victims offered in sacrifice, the one as a holocaust, and the other in expiation of sin: "And when the days of her purification are expired, for a son or for a daughter, she shall bring to the door of the tabernacle of the testimony a lamb of a year old for a holocaust, and a young pigeon or a turtle for sin, and shall deliver them to the priest." The other precept regarded the first-born males both of men and of beasts, all which were to be consecrated to God in a particular way: "And the Lord spoke to Moses, saying:

(267)

Sanctify unto me every first-born that openeth the womb among the children of Israel, as well of men as of beasts, for they are all mine" (Exod. XIII, 1, 2). On this account the Son of God, who wished to make himself subject to the law, 'that he might redeem those who were under the law', submitted also to these two precepts, and therefore fulfilled them both punctually. As to the one of primogeniture, St. Luke relates that 'they carried him to Jerusalem to present him to the Lord'; as to the other, which was common to all, 'and to offer a sacrifice according as it is written in the law of the Lord, a pair of turtle-doves or two young pigeons' (Luke I, 24).

What was prescribed in Leviticus.

We read in Leviticus that it was ordained that a lamb and a turtle or a pigeon should be offered for sacrifice, but if any one were not able to offer a lamb, she should present two turtle-doves or two pigeons: "And if her hand find not sufficiency, and is not able to offer a lamb, she shall take two turtles, or two young pigeons, one for a holocaust and another for sin" (Levit. XII, 8). Now our Lord chose for himself the offering common to the poor, just as at his birth he had willed to be wrapped in poor rags, and to lie on hard straw in a manger. So although infinitely rich, for us he became poor, that by his poverty we might become rich: "For you know the grace of our Lord Jesus Christ, that being rich, he became poor for your sakes, that through his poverty you might be rich"

(2 Cor. VIII, 9). Accordingly two turtles or pigeons were offered for Christ. Nor was this without mystery, as both the turtle-doves and the pigeons are very well adapted to figure the perfections of Christ and of his members. The turtle is chatty, chaste, solitary; and thereby represents the preaching and confession of faith, the purity of manners, the contemplative life. The pigeon is simple, mild, sociable, and represents simplicity, gentleness and the active life. Both are plaintive, and thereby symbolize the wailings of the saints in the present life. But the turtle sends forth its plaintive sounds in solitude, and signifies the secret tears of private prayer. The pigeon does the same in union with its mates, and signifies the moanings of the Church in public prayer. And of both not one alone is offered, but two, to show that our sanctity and consecration to God ought to be, not of the soul alone, but of the soul together with the body.

The Blessed Virgin needed no purification for herself.

The B. Virgin had no need of purification for herself, for she was not defiled with any uncleanness either of sin or of legal irregularity, from which to be cleansed. Nay, her virginal candor had by the conception and birth of this divine child become a thousand times more pure and more estimable. The words in Leviticus show clearly that she was not comprised in that law, for there a woman is spoken of, who becomes a mother in the ordinary course of nature: "If a woman having

received seed, bear a man-child, she shall be unclean seven days" (Levit. XII, 2).   Here there is
no allusion to her, who by the supernatural power
of the Holy Ghost, is made prolific without any
prejudice to her integrity.   Nevertheless, Mary
spontaneously complied even with this observance;
and for the same reasons for which her divine Son
willed to submit to circumcision and the other
burdens of the law, in order to sanction thereby
the law itself, to remove all occasion of calumny
on the part of the Jews, and to give us a bright
example of obedience; but, above all, to give us an
example of the most profound humility.   Thus it
was befitting that the Mother should conform with
the humility of the Son, that she might be more
conformable with him also in the fulness of grace,
for God gives his grace to the humble, and gives
it the more, the more humble they are: "God re-
sisteth the proud, but giveth grace to the humble"
(James IV, 6).

CHAPTER XLIX.

The Baptism of Christ.

John's baptism was not of itself a sacrament, but was rather a sacramental, as it were, which prepared the way for the baptism of Christ. Wherefore it did not imprint a character, or confer grace, but only disposed to this in three ways. First, by the teachings of the Baptist, which led to the faith of Christ; second, by accustoming men to the rite of baptism; third, by moving them to penance, by which they would be made themselves worthy of receiving the effect of Christ's baptism. On this account John's baptism was called the baptism of water and of penance, whereas the baptism of Christ is the baptism of the Holy Ghost and of fire; for the grace of the Holy Ghost purifies souls from the dross of sin, like fire, and illumines and inflames them with charity. John himself said: "I indeed baptize you with water, but he, who is to come after me, will baptize you with the Holy Ghost and with fire."

Why Christ willed to receive John's baptism.

Let us dwell here on the reasons why Christ willed to receive the baptism of John. First of all, it was not to be cleansed himself, but to cleanse and sanctify the waters with the contact of his immaculate flesh, and to infuse into them the virtue of washing our souls from sin. In the next place, it was to show that he assumed our same nature, which in him, it is true, was most innocent, yet in others is sinful, and on that account needful of the waters of baptism. In the third place, it was to do first himself, what he would afterwards prescribe for all of us, and in this way, by his example itself, induce us also more efficaciously and sweetly to receive baptism. For it became Christ to fulfil all justice: "For so it becometh us to fulfil all justice" (Mat. III, 15). And this is to be understood not merely of the old law, but likewise of the new, seeing that Christ had to give completion to the old law, and inaugurate the new law. Hence it is, that he willed to be not only circumcised, but also baptized. He willed, however, to be baptized with the baptism of John, and not with his own, for the reason that John's baptism was in water only, whilst his baptism was in the Holy Ghost. Now he was overflowing with the grace of the Holy Ghost from the first moment of his conception.

The time and place of Christ's baptism.

The time was when he was at the age of thirty years, that is, at the age of perfect manhood. By this he wished us to know how baptism begets perfect men in the spiritual life, who are wanting in no grace and other supernatural gifts that are required in such a life. The place was in the Jordan through which the children of Israel entered into the promised land. And this, because the baptism of Christ has this property in respect to all baptisms, both of the Jews and of the Baptist, that it alone possesses the power of introducing into the kingdom of God, which was represented by the promised land. "Unless a man be born again of water and the Holy Ghost, he cannot enter into the kingdom of God" (John III, 5). Wherefore we also read in the second book of Kings, that Elias divided the waters of the Jordan, crossed the river, and was carried thence to heaven in a chariot of fire. What is the meaning of that? It means that those likewise, who pass through the waters of Christ's baptism, have access to heaven, in virtue of the fire of the Holy Ghost.

An objection may be made that the red sea also was a figure of baptism. True. But it was a figure of it as to its less principal effect, which is to drown sins with its waters, as the red sea with its waters drowned the Egyptians ; whereas the Jordan represented it as to its more noble effect, which is to open the gates of the heavenly country: Hence, without doubt, it was more beseeming that Christ should be baptized in the Jordan than in the red sea.

At the baptism of Christ the heavens were thrown open:

"And behold the heavens were opened to him" (Mat. III, 16). "Jesus being baptized and praying, heaven was opened" (Luke III, 21). For what reason ? To point out to us three things. The first is, that the invisible virtue, from which baptism has the effect of cleansing and sanctifying souls, is the heavenly virtue of grace. The second

18

is, that for the efficacy of baptism faith also is required, by which we raise our looks from sensible and earthly goods to fix them on heavenly goods. Hence it is, that those who approach baptism make a profession of faith; and baptism is called the sacrament of faith. The third thing is, that the entrance to the heavenly country, which was closed to the first man for his sin, and in him and by him to the whole human race, is opened to those who by this sacrament partake of the boon of baptism and of the passion of Christ.

St. Luke adds, that heaven was opened whilst Jesus was praying: 'Jesus being baptized and praying'; and this for our instruction also. First, to teach us that after baptism assiduous prayer is necessary for the faithful, that they may really enter into heaven. For although in baptism the sins are blotted out, still there remains the propensity to sin, which makes war inwardly; there remain the world and the devil, which assail us outwardly; nor shall we be able to withstand such and so many enemies without prayer, without incessant prayer. In the second place, to teach us that if our baptism opens heaven for us, this is owing to the prayer of Christ. St. Matthew, therefore, says that 'the heavens were opened to him'. Not that they will not be opened to us, but that they will be opened to us all, on his account.

Christ being baptized, the Holy Ghost descended upon him in the form of a dove.

Christ having been baptized, while still praying, the Holy Ghost descended upon him in the form of a dove: "The Holy Ghost descended in a bodily shape as a dove upon him" (Luke III, 22). Let us examine attentively all the particulars of this fact, and the mysteries which are included in it.

The Holy Ghost came upon Christ, to show in him what would afterwards be realized in all those who would be baptized with the baptism of Christ, who would all likewise receive the Holy Ghost, provided they were not wanting in the due dispositions. He came under a visible shape, 'a bodily shape', in order that his invisible coming upon all the others baptized might be more easily and more firmly believed by us. For God, by accommodating himself to our nature, wished to introduce us to the knowledge of insensible and supersensible things by means of the sensible. He came descending from on high, to signify that 'every best gift is from above, coming down from the Father of lights' (James I, 17). He came in the form of a dove for four reasons. First, because the dove is simple, not having fraud or deceit, and so expresses the disposition required for one who approaches baptism, that is, that he come with a sincere mind, and not deceitfully: "For the holy spirit of discipline will flee from the deceitful" (Wisd. I, 5). Second, the dove is gentle and peaceful, and shows thereby the effect of baptism, which is to reconcile us with God. Third, the dove is all loving and does not live solitary, but in company with others, and is therefore a symbol of the society of the faithful, or the Church, for which reason in the Canticles the Church is called a dove: 'One is my dove.' But the constitution of the

Church is the fruit of baptism, since by baptism men become her members, and are incorporated in Christ her head; and she has in it that salutary bath, and that word of life, which purifies and sanctifies and renders her without spot or wrinkle, all beautiful, all glorious, and worthy therefore of Jesus Christ her divine Spouse: "Christ loved the Church, and delivered himself up for it, that he might sanctify it, cleansing it by the laver of water in the word of life, that he might present to himself a glorious Church, not having spot or wrinkle, nor any such thing, but that it should be holy and without blemish" (Eph. V, 25 . . . 27). Fourth, because the dove serves wonderfully by its natural qualities to express the seven gifts of the Holy Ghost. It loves to dwell near streams, and often dives into their waters; and this property serves to express the gift of wisdom, in virtue of which the saints abide willingly near the streams of the holy scriptures, and by diving into the understanding of them, attain a very deep knowledge of divine things. The dove selects for itself the better grains and rejects the inferior; and this property serves to express the gift of knowledge, in virtue of which the saints know how to distinguish sound from unsound doctrines, and by these alone they are nourished. The dove, too, hatches and kindly feeds broods that are not its own; and this property serves to express the gift of counsel, in virtue of which the saints are wont with instruction and example to feed those even, who by their sins have become an alien progeny, that is, no longer children of God, but of the demon: "He that committeth sin, is of the devil" (1 John III, 8). "You are of your father the devil, and the desires of your father you will do" (John VIII, 14). The dove does not lacerate, nor injure with its bill; and this property serves to express the gift of understanding, in virtue of which the word of God proceeds from the mouth of the saints whole and unadulterated, not torn or maimed, nor corrupted in a thousand shapes as from the mouth of heretics. The dove is without gall, is not cross, not fierce, but quite agreeable; and this property serves to express the gift of piety, in virtue of which the saints also are without all bitterness, and all unreasonable anger against their neighbors. The dove loves to make its nest in the clefts of a rock, and this property serves to express the gift of fortitude, in virtue of which the saints willingly dwell in the wounds of Christ, which are a most solid rock: "But the rock was Christ" (1 Cor. X, 4). Here they place their nest, that is, here they have their refuge, their comfort, their hope: "My dove in the clefts of the rock, in the hollow places of the wall" (Cant. II, 14). The dove has a plaint for its song, and lastly this property serves to express the gift of fear, in virtue of which the saints never cease to mourn and bewail their errors.

As soon as Christ was baptized, a voice was heard from heaven.

As soon as Christ was baptized, a voice from heaven was heard, saying, 'This is my beloved Son, in whom I am well pleased'. Thus in the

baptism of Christ all the three persons of the most
holy Trinity manifested themselves in some manner: the Holy Ghost in the likeness of a dove; the
Father in the voice that resounded from on high;
the Son in the human nature assumed by him.
And why so?   Because the baptism of Christ was
the model of ours, which was to be conferred
explicitly in the name and in the power of the
three divine persons: "Go ye, therefore, and teach
all nations, baptizing them in the name of the
Father, and of the Son, and of the Holy Ghost"
(Mat. XXVIII, 19).   But see how fittingly the
Father willed to be pointed out with the sound of
the voice.   For it is proper of the Father to produce the Word, that is, to speak his eternal word.
And this word, which the Father speaks from all
eternity, is the substantial word, the infinite word,
and the adequate expression of the whole perfection
of the Father, who utters it, and is nought else
than his only-begotten Son.   We see from this,
that the voice of the Father proclaimed precisely
the filiation of his beloved Word by saying: 'This
is my beloved Son'.   But why especially at Christ's
baptism did the Father proclaim his sonship?   It
was to disclose to us the wonderful regeneration
that is wrought in us at our baptism, by which we
are born again adopted children of God, and
adopted children to the likeness of the natural Son
of God, whose second-born brethren we become:
"For whom he foreknew, he also predestinated to
be made conformable to the image of his Son, that
he might be the first-born among many brethren"
(Rom. VIII, 29).

CHAPTER L.

Christ's Intercourse on Earth.

Christ did not wish to lead a solitary life on earth, but wished to treat with men: "After this he was seen on earth and conversed with men" (Baruch III, 38). The reason of this was because the tenor of his life had to be conformable to the end of the incarnation, for which he had come into this world. Now why had he come into the world? First of all to manifest the truth. He himself says: "For this was I born, and for this cause came I into the world, that I should give testimony to the truth" (John XVIII, 37). It was proper, therefore, that he should not be concealed, but should go forth in public and propound his doctrines publicly. He was come to deliver men from sin: "Christ Jesus came into this world to save sinners" (1 Tim. I, 15). It was proper, therefore, for our example and for our comprehending much better the ardor of his charity, that he should go himself from city to city, from village to village, in search of poor sinners, as a good physician who comes in person near the sick whom he wishes to cure, or like a good shepherd who goes himself in search of the strayed sheep, without waiting for it to return to the fold of itslf. Lastly, he had come, that through him we might have

access to the divine Father: "For through him we
have both access in one spirit to the Father"
(Eph. II, 18). It was well, then, that he should
treat familiarly with men, that they might approach
him with all confidence, notwithstanding the sins
that may have defiled them. That he succeeded
in his purpose, is evident from what the gospel
relates: "And it came to pass, as he was at table
in the house, behold many publicans and sinners
came and sat down with Jesus and his disciples"
(Mat. IX, 10).

Still it is true that Christ was accustomed to
withdraw from time to time from the crowds, and
retire into solitude. He did this for three reasons,
as we read. Sometimes to recruit the body, as
when he invited the disciples to go aside with him
to rest a little from the fatigues which they had
borne: "Come ye apart into a desert place and rest
a little; for there were many coming and going,
and they had not so much as time to eat" (Mark
VI, 31). Sometimes to avoid the vain honors of
men: "When he perceived that they would come
and take him by force, and make him king, he
fled again into the mountain himself alone" (John
VI, 15). Most frequently for the sake of praying:
"And it came to pass in those days, that he went
out into a mountain to pray, and he passed the
whole night in the prayer of God" (Luke VI, 12).
All these things he did too for our instruction; but
especially that men devoted to the ministry of the
apostleship might learn from his example, to retire
from time to time from public, for some of the
reasons we have above mentioned.

In what respect Christ differed from the Baptist.

As Christ did not wish to live in the desert like the Baptist, so neither did he wish to appear like him, clothed with hair-cloth, in continual fasts, constant watchings and other such rigors of penance. Hence he himself declared that John had come 'neither eating nor drinking', whilst the Son of man had come 'eating and drinking'. Christ, therefore, chose a kind of life less austere, as that was more suitable to his design. He wished, as we have seen, to live and converse with us. Now is there anything that contributes so much to gain the love and confidence of those, with whom we live, as to adapt ourselves as much as possible to their manner of life? Look at the great Apostle St. Paul, how he made himself all to all, just to win the minds of those with whom he dealt, and thus to save them: "To the weak I became weak, that I might gain the weak. I became all things to all men, that I might save all" (1 Cor. IX, 22). For this reason, then, Christ also was pleased to live the ordinary mode of life of men. He would eat like them, dress like them, be present at their conversations, at their feasts, at their banquets, even at their weddings. In a word, he wished as far as possible to be like them, in order to make them like to himself.

Christ chose for himself a poor life.

Christ chose for himself a poor life to such an extent, that he could say, 'the foxes have their holes, and the birds of the air nests, but the Son of man hath not where to lay his head' (Mat.

VIII, 20). Thus was it expedient that he should do: First, to teach us that he who makes profession of preaching the word of God, in order that he may be able to attend more freely and more earnestly to this ministry, should be untrammeled with the cares and anxieties of the world, a thing not possible for him who possesses riches. On this account, when Christ sent his disciples to preach, he said to them: "Do not possess gold, nor silver, nor money in your purses" (Mat. X, 9). Secondly, because, as he underwent corporal death to give us spiritual life, so he wished to sustain corporal poverty to confer on us spiritual riches: "For you know the grace of our Lord Jesus Christ, that being rich, he became poor for your sakes, that through his poverty you might be rich" (2 Cor. VIII, 9). Thirdly, lest some men, at seeing him rich, might believe that his riches were the fruit which he derived, and the end which he had in his preaching. He wished, therefore, with his poverty to remove from them all occasion of being mistaken, or of calumniating him on this point. Fourthly, that the more he was unprovided with human means, by condition of his poverty, the more conspicuous might the power of the divinity appear in the accomplishment of the great work he did of redeeming and renewing the world.

Christ willed to demean himself according to the law.

In his life Christ willed to demean himself in all things according to the precepts of the law, as one who was come, not to destroy the law, but to fulfil it: "Think not, that I am come to destroy the law or the prophets. I am not come to destroy, but to fulfil" (Mat. V, 17). To signify this, he even wished to be circumcised, as circumcision was, as it were, a public protest of wishing to observe the law. Hence St. Paul had to say that he who was circumcised was a debtor of the whole law: "And I testify again to every man that circumciseth himself, that he is a debtor to do the whole law" (Gal. V, 3). But Christ was superior to all law. Why then did he thus submit to it? To show that he did not disapprove, but even approved of the ancient law; to take from the Jews every pretext of maligning him, and to bring men back from the slavery of the law to the freedom of the children of God: "God sent his Son made of a woman, made under the law, that he might redeem those who were under the law, that we might receive the adoption of sons" (Gal. IV, 4, 5). But above all, to let us see that he was come, as has been said, not to destroy the law by violating its precepts, but to give it its completion. This he did by observing it himself, who was the principle of the law and the term to which it was ordained, by verifying in himself what had been foretold and promised in its figures, and by transforming it from the imperfection of the old covenant into the perfection of the new; from the law of types and of shadows into the law of truth and of light; from the law of fear into the law of love; from the weak and inefficacious law, in which sin therefore abounded, into the most powerful and most efficacious law, in which the divine power of divine grace abounded and superabounded: "Now the law entered in, that sin might abound; but where sin abounded, grace hath abounded more" (Rom. V, 20).

CHAPTER LI.

Christ's Temptations.

Let us reflect a while on the temptations of
Christ, and why he willed to be tempted by the
devil. First, it was for our aid against temptations.
With his temptations he wished to overcome our
temptations, as with his death he overcame our
death. For as St. Gregory in one of his homilies
says: "It was not unworthy of our Redeemer, who
had come to be put to death, that he willed to be
tempted. For it was just, that he should overcome
our temptations with his temptations, as he had
come to conquer our death by his death."
Secondly, it was to make us more cautious, so that
no one, however holy he may be, may deem himself secure and exempt from temptation. For this
reason also he wished to be tempted after baptism,
that we might understand, as St. Hilary says, that
in us, who are sanctified, the attacks of the devil
are the fiercest, because a victory over the saints
is more to his liking, and that hence the more we
strive to dedicate ourselves to the divine service,
the more prepared we should be to sustain the
assaults of the tempter, according to that counsel
of Ecclesiasticus: "Son, when thou comest to the
service of God, stand in justice and in fear, and
prepare thy soul for temptation" (Eccl. II, 1).

(285)

Thirdly, that from his example we might learn in what way we can and must repel and overcome the temptations of the enemy. "Christ", says St. Augustine, "exposed himself to the devil to be tempted, that he might be a mediator to overcome his temptations, not only by assistance, but also by example." Fourthly, that we might conceive more confidence of obtaining from him mercy and seasonable aid in our weakness, whilst we behold him also our Pontiff, although most High and Divine, yet suffering and being tempted even as ourselves: "For we have not a high-priest, who cannot have compassion on our infirmities, but one tempted in all things like as we are, yet without sin. Let us go, therefore, with confidence to the throne of grace, that we may obtain mercy, and find grace in seasonable aid" (Heb. IV, 15, 16).

The place in which Christ was tempted was the desert.

He who is solitary is usually attacked with the most violence by the malignant spirit. For this reason, therefore, Christ willed to go into the desert, in order to enter, as it were, into the battle-field to contend with the enemy. St. Ambrose in discoursing on this point says: "Christ was led into the desert designedly, that he might provoke the devil. For unless he had combated, he would not have conquered for me." Besides, as the same St. Ambrose observes, Christ wished by this to point out to us the opposition that exists between the old Adam and himself the new Adam. The former was tempted in the earthly paradise, and overcome by the temptation; in punishment he was exiled from thence with all his descendants, and driven into a desert land, that was cursed and strewn with brambles and thorns. Christ, on the contrary, was tempted in a desert, and having gained a complete victory over the devil, freed the first Adam and his race from exile, and opened for them the gates of paradise, not of the earthly, but, what is incomparably more, of the celestial paradise. Finally, the divine Saviour wished that we should learn from his example, that not every occasion of temptation is to be avoided. To understand this rightly, we must distinguish well two occasions of temptations. One is on our own part, and is that in which the demon tempts us for the reason, that in it he finds us to be weaker, more ready to fall, more liable to be taken in his snares, and this, as is evident, is at the same time an occasion of temptation and an occasion of sin, and consequently is to be avoided by us with all care. The other is on the part of the demon, and is that in which he tempts us through rage and envy, which he feels more furious when seeing us engaged at some work of more signal virtue. Who does not see that such an occasion is not to be avoided? We should rather meet it courageously, trusting in the help of God, for it is the Holy Spirit that counsels and urges us to encounter it. Hence it is written of Jesus himself, that he was led, that he was urged by the Holy Spirit into the desert, that is to say, into the place where he was to be tempted: "Then Jesus was led by the Spirit into the desert to be tempted by the devil" (Mat. IV, 1). "And immediately the Spirit drove him out into the desert" (Mark I, 12).

The time in which Christ was tempted.

The time in which the temptation of Christ took place, was after he had fasted forty days and forty nights: "And when he had fasted forty days and forty nights, he was afterwards hungry. And the tempter coming, said to him: 'If thou be the Son of God, command that these stones be made bread'." (Mat. IV, 2, 3.) What did he intend tc teach us by this? First, that those who apply seriously to subdue their flesh with long and vigorous fasts, should not on that account flatter themselves, that they also have not to suffer molestations from the adversary, but are even frequently attacked by him with more fury. Secondly, that the devil, especially with the more perfect, is wont to watch very cunningly, and choose the time which is most favorable for him to attack them. Notice what he did with Christ. During all those forty days he did not approach him. When was it that he advanced to tempt him? It was when Christ began to feel the pangs of hunger: "He was afterwards hungry. And the tempter coming, said to him, etc." Thirdly. But more than all Christ by his example wished to make us understand, how important it is, that we also should arm ourselves against temptations with fasting, and in general by mortifying our bodies by bringing them under subjection, and how necessary this is especially for those who have the office of preaching to others, so that it might not happen to them, as the Apostle feared for himself, that after having preached to others they should become reprobate themselves: "I chastise my body and bring it into subjection, lest perhaps, when I have preached to others, I myself should become reprobate" (1 Cor. IX, 27).

The manner and order of Christ's temptations.

As the devil is very cunning, he does not proceed with all alike in proposing his suggestions, but differently according to the various conditions and different circumstances in which those are found, whom he wishes to tempt. Hence it is, that at the first onset he does not suggest grievous sins to spiritual persons, but begins with smaller ones, and then advances step by step, by drawing them into greater. We see he acted thus with our first parents. First he solicited them to taste the forbidden apple, saying: "Why hath God commanded you that you should not eat of every tree of paradise?" Next he tempted them with vain glory, saying: "Your eyes will be opened." Lastly he tempted them with pride, by adding: "You shall be like gods, knowing good and evil." This same order he observed also in the temptation of Christ. He began with that which, within certain limits, may be sought for even by spiritual men, namely, food proper for the sustenance of the body. He then proceeded on to that in which spiritual men also fail sometimes, which is to perform some work, good indeed in itself, but done

19

for ostentation. Lastly he ended with that which cannot take place in spiritual men, but only in carnal men, which is to love riches and the glory of this world so far as to the contempt of God. Notice, in fact, that in this third temptation he did not say, as in the two preceding ones: "If thou be the Son of God", because in this he proposed a thing, which is no longer consistent for one who is in the state of grace, and consequently a son of God by adoption. Still the divine Saviour willed to be tempted even in this guise, that every kind of temptation might be borne and overcome by us.

Here we should bear in mind two things regarding the manner in which Christ resisted the tempter. The first is that he repulsed him by opposing against him, not the force of his omnipotence, but the testimonies of the law. He did so, in order to bring more honor to man and more punishment to the devil, having conquered the enemy of the human race by fighting, not as God, but as man; or, as St. Leo in one of his sermons expresses the same thought: "That by this he might honor man the more, and punish the adversary the more, when the enemy of the human race was vanquished, not as though by God, but as though by man." The other thing is, that in the first and second temptation Jesus Christ answered the devil without becoming indignant or reprimanding him. But when the devil had the boldness to usurp the honor due to God, by saying: "All these will I give thee, if falling down thou wilt adore me," he became highly indignant and drove him away, saying: "Begone, Satan." By this Jesus wished to teach us, how we too should bear our injuries with longanimity; but as for injuries to God we are not to allow ourselves even to listen to them.

Chapter LII.

Christ's Preaching.

Christ willed to confine his preaching to the Jews only, and not to extend it also to the gentiles; and chiefly for four reasons. First, to show that his coming brought the fulfilment of the ancient promises made to the Jews, not to the gentiles: "For I say that Christ Jesus was minister of the circumcision, that is to say, apostle and preacher of the circumcised, for the truth of God, to confirm the promises made to the fathers" (Rom. XV, 8). Secondly, to show that his coming was from God. For that, which proceeds from God, proceeds with order. Now due order required that the doctrine of Christ should be propounded first to the Jews, who were the nearest to God by faith and the worship of the only and true God, and then be transmitted from them to the gentiles. Thus in the celestial hierarchy the divine illustrations are communicated first to the higher angels, and then by their means to the lower angels. Nor did Christ himself intend to intimate anything else, when he said that he was not sent but to the lost sheep of the house of Israel: "I was not sent but to the sheep that are lost of the house of Israel" (Mat. XV, 24). In explaining these words, St. Jerome observes that he did not say this, as if he had not

(292)

been sent at all to the gentiles, but that he was sent to Israel first. Thirdly, that the Jews might have no excuse to shield their perfidy in rejecting the Saviour and his doctrine. The coming of Christ had to be announced to the Jews first, says the same St. Jerome, so that they might have no just excuse saying, that they had rejected the Lord for the reason that he had sent apostles to the nations and to the Samaritans. Fourthly, because Christ, by the victory which he gained on the cross, merited power and dominion over the nations: "And he that shall overcome . . . . to him I will give power over the nations . . . . even as I received from my Father" (Apoc. II, 26, 28). Christ himself spoke these words in the Apocalypse. St. Paul too testified that 'God also hath exalted him . . . . that in the name of Jesus every knee should bend . . . . and that every tongue should confess that the Lord Jesus Christ is in the glory of God the Father' (Philipp. II, 9, 10, 11). But why did he so much exalt him? Because 'he humbled himself, becoming obedient unto death, even the death of the cross.' For this reason, then, he did not wish that his doctrine should be preached to the nations before his passion; but after his passion, on the contrary, he said to his disciples: "Go ye, therefore, and teach all nations" (Mat. XXVIII, 19).

The prophecies of Isaias fulfilled.

Consider that in Christ was verified perfectly whatever the prophet Isaias had foretold of him: "Behold I have given thee to be the light of the

gentiles, that thou mayest be my salvation even to
the farthest ends of the earth" (Is. XLIX, 6).
And afterwards the holy old man Simeon exclaimed: "My eyes have seen thy salvation, which
thou hast prepared before the face of all people,
a light to the revelation of the gentiles and the
glory of thy people of Israel" (Luke II, 30, 31).
For, indeed, Christ was most truly a light and
salvation to the nations also, although he did not
preach to them himself directly, but by means of
his disciples. Nor does this redound to his dis-
credit, as though it implied weakness in him.
Quite the contrary. Neither is it a sign or an
effect of less, but of greater power, to be able to
act through others rather than by one's self. Thus,
for example, the power of a general who fights by
means of his soldiers is greater than that of the
soldiers themselves, who go to face the enemy.
Much more then is this proved, when he that
operates by means of others, communicates to them
the power which they have. Thus the power of
a monarch, who governs by means of his ministers,
is greater than that of the ministers, who govern
in virtue of the authority which they have received
from him. Wherefore, when Jesus Christ, to effect
the conversion of the gentiles, made use of his disciples as instruments, and could infuse into their
words so much force to draw people to him without number, although very far off, and in spite of
their being opposed by a thousand obstacles; when
I say, that Jesus operated in this manner, it is
plain that his divine power was not in the least

obscured, but appeared much more bright and much more admirable. Moreover, in preaching to the Jews, Christ manifested his power in many ways. St. Matthew says of him: "That he was teaching them as one having authority" (Mat. VII, 29). And St. Luke adds that "They were astonished at his doctrine, for his word was with power" (Luke IV, 32). He manifested it in the miracles which he performed in confirmation of his doctrine. He manifested it in the efficacy of persuading even the most obstinate, of confounding even the most arrogant. He manifested it in the authority with which he spoke, 'not as their Scribes and Pharisees', but as one having mastery over the law: "But I say to you" (Mat. V, 22). Finally he manifested it in the most holy examples of every virtue, with which he accompanied and confirmed the doctrines which he proposed with his words.

Christ was fearless in his preaching.

Christ in his preaching did not fear to meet the indignation and malicious scandal of the Scribes, the Pharisees and the chiefs of the Jewish people, for although they would not accept it, he ceased not to teach in public the truth so much hated by them, and to reprove their vices with severity. Nor is this to be wondered at, for it is certain that the good of a whole multitude is to be preferred to the peace of some individuals, particularly if it be an unjust and false peace. Whenever, therefore, there are those who by the debased life which they lead, and by the perverse maxims which they inculcate, impede the true good of the multitude, we have not to fear their resentment when providing for the public good, especially if one have the office of promulgator, or teacher of truth. Now the Scribes, the Pharisees and the chief priests were by their malice a great hindrance to the highest good, that is, to the spiritual welfare of the people, both by contradicting the doctrine of Christ, by which alone salvation could be found, and by corrupting the customs of the people with their depravity. On this account, therefore, the divine Saviour did not wish, nor did it become him, to shrink from drawing down their anger and envy against him. Hence, although he had come into the world to cause the sanctification of all, yet to these, through their own fault, he was a stumbling stone, and a scandal, a snare and a ruin; and very many of them dashed against this stone, fell, and were crushed, and very many remained entangled and sorely pressed in this snare, according to what Isaias had already foretold: "And he shall be a sanctification to you; but for a stone of stumbling, and for a rock of offence to the two houses of Israel, for a snare and a ruin to the inhabitants of Jerusalem. And very many of them shall stumble and fall, and shall be broken in pieces, and shall be snared and taken" (Is. VIII, 14, 15).

Christ's preaching was done in public.

Christ's preaching was not done in private; but was open and public, as he himself affirmed: "I

have spoken openly to the world . . . and in private
I have spoken nothing'' (John XVIII, 18). And
certainly it cannot be called secret either on his
part, or on the part of his hearers. Teaching is
said to be secret on the part of the teacher when
he intends that his doctrines may not come to the
knowledge of many, but remain secret. He may
desire this for two motives : either because he
wishes to have no rival in his knowledge, and on
that account is unwilling that others also should
get possession of it, or because the nature of his
doctrines being false or immoral, he does not think
fit to expose them to the clear light. But neither
of these things could happen in Christ. Without
envy he communicates the treasures of wisdom,
which he possesses, not feignedly but really and
infinitely, and conceals from no one its worth and
its beauty: "Which (wisdom) I have learned without guile, and communicate without envy, and her
riches I hide not" (Wisd. VII, 13). These words
of the Scripture are said in the person of Christ.
Neither can anything erroneous or less moral be
found in what he teaches, since he is truth itself,
and is come to bear testimony to the truth; he is
purity and sanctity itself, and is come into the
world to purify and to sanctify it. On the part of
the hearers teaching is secret, when those are few
to whom it is proposed. But Jesus Christ proposed
his doctrines either to crowds that thronged around
him in the greatest numbers, or to all his disciples
in common. Or if he also spoke sometimes to a
few, he did not speak only for those few, but that

his teachings might through their means come to the knowledge of many. The teaching of Christ, then, was in no way secret. To some, however, it may seem perhaps to have been so in regard to the manner in which he was accustomed to propound the spiritual mysteries, which he announced to them, namely, by way of similitudes and parables. But a little attentive reflection will convince them, that not even in this respect can his preaching be deservedly called secret. If he made use of parables, he did so to adapt himself to the capacity of those who heard him. Just as a good teacher does not propose the lessons in the same manner to the scholars of a more mature age as to those of a more tender age, but differently, suiting them to the relative capacity of both the older and younger; so also Jesus Christ showed the truth openly to his disciples already advanced in spiritual knowledge; but to others who were not so, he showed it under the veil of parables. If this veil rendered it less clear, it is not to be imputed to Christ, as wishing to keep it concealed, but to the condition of the hearers, who were incapable and unworthy of contemplating it openly. In the same wise, as when the sun at times sheds its rays more languidly on the earth, it is not because it is sparing of its light, but because the earth is not capable of receiving it in all its lustre, owing to the mists or clouds, with which it is overhung.

Christ did not commit his doctrine to writing.

Christ did not wish to commit his doctrine to writing; for thus, in the first place, it was most conformable to his dignity, since the mode of teaching has to be in proportion to the excellence of the master, and accordingly the more perfect, as the master is more perfect. To Christ, therefore, the most perfect of masters, belonged the most perfect mode of teaching, more perfect than of any other: which is to imprint his doctrine not on paper, but in the hearts of the hearers, for which purpose writing itself is ordained, as a means to its end. Wherefore St. Paul in a letter to the faithful of Corinth writes thus: "You being made manifest, that you are the epistle of Christ, ministered by us and written not with ink, but with the spirit of the living God, not in tables of stone, but in fleshy tables of the heart" (2 Cor. III, 3). Thus also, in the second place, it became the dignity itself of Christ's doctrine, which is so sublime, profound, vast, and in a word so divine, that there is no writing that is sufficient to contain and express it. For this reason, what St. John said of the works done by Christ, that 'if they were written every one, the world itself, I think, would not be able to contain the books that should be written' (John XXI, 25), with all reason should be repeated of the doctrines given by him. But if he had put these doctrines of his in writing, men might have been easily induced to believe that all was included in that writing, and that there was nothing outside of it. Lastly, this was required also, so that the promulgation of Christ's doctrine might proceed with order from him to all men. For he promulgated it directly to his disciples, and

they with voice and with writings spread it afterwards through the whole world.   In this manner
was verified what is said in the Proverbs regarding
divine wisdom, that 'she hath sent her maids to
invite to the tower' (Prov. IX, 3).   Jesus Christ,
the Wisdom of God, sent the maids. who were the
word and the writings of the apostles, to call the
peoples into the very strong and lofty fortress of
his church.   But if he himself had written, his
doctrine would have passed immediately from him
to all the others, and there would have remained
no longer any place for the ministry of the maids.

CHAPTER LIII.

Christ's Miracles in General.

We shall here study the motives for which Christ willed to perform many miracles: "What do we, for this man doeth many miracles?" (John XI, 47.) God is wont to grant men the power of working miracles for two ends. First and principally, for confirmation of the truth which they teach. As the mysteries of faith exceed the natural capacity of the human understanding, they cannot on that account be proved by human reason, but the argument of divine omnipotence must come in to confirm them, so that it may be believed, that as the works which he does who announces them are from God, so also the truths which he announces are from God. When we see a letter bearing the stamp of the king's ring, we judge by this that what is written in the letter comes on the part of the king. Well, now the holy teacher who works miracles is a speaking letter sent by God, and the miracle is God's stamp which guarantees that what he says, he says on the part of God, and cannot therefore be but the truth. The other end for which God is accustomed to grant some one the gift of performing miracles, is to show that the Holy Ghost is present in him by his grace, so that the works themselves which he does, wonderful and proper of God alone, may be a clear indication that God dwells in him, not merely by his essence, presence and power, as he does in every other creature, but moreover in a most singular and altogether divine manner, as is the indwelling by supernatural grace.   Now it was necessary that in regard to Christ men should have a certainty of these two things, namely, that his doctrine was from God, and therefore undoubtedly true; and that God dwelt in him, not by the grace of adoption, but of union, and consequently by the plenitude of all the gifts of the Holy Ghost.   Here, then, we see what were the motives for which Christ willed to work miracles in great number, both open and public, so that his works might render certain testimony of both these things, and that there might be no excuse for obstinacy in not being willing to believe him: "The works themselves, which I do, give testimony of me that the Father hath sent me" (John V, 36).   And again: "If I do not the works of my Father, believe me not: but if I do, though you will not believe me, believe the works that you may know and believe that the Father is in me, and I in the Father" (John X, 38).

Christ's miracles the effect of divine power.

There can be no doubt that Christ's miracles were the effect of divine power, when we consider that they were certainly true, and not merely in appearance.   But true miracles cannot proceed but from the supreme power of God.   The reason of this is evidently drawn from the very essence of a miracle. For what is a miracle? It is an effect which exceeds the order and the forces of nature; still not of every particular nature, for in that case every time that we throw a stone up in the air, it would be a miracle, since that stone being heavy by the nature of its body, tends to fall downwards, and not to mount upwards. That effect, then, is to be understood, which transcends the order and forces of all created nature whatever. Now who does not see that whatsoever effect, which is produced not by the divine power but by a created power, will for this very reason never be above the order and the forces of all created nature? Hence a true miracle can proceed only from the uncreated power of God.

The term miracle implies the same, if we ponder its signification attentively. For what is the meaning of miracle? It means a fact which is worthy of admiration. But when is it, that admiration is aroused? It is when the effect is seen, but the cause remains hidden. Sometimes, however, the cause is hidden to some only, and known to others, and in that case the effect will be wonderful to those who are ignorant of the cause, but not universally; and for that reason it cannot be properly called a miracle. When does it justly deserve the name? When the cause is altogether and essentially hidden and incomprehensible to every created mind; for then, indeed, the effect will of itself be absolutely wonderful. It is plain that a cause of this kind can be no other than God. The power, therefore, which produces miracles is divine. And as it is in every other, so too it was in Christ. On this account he himself said openly to his disciples, that his Father, who was in him, did the wonderful works which they witnessed: "But the Father, who abideth in me, he doth the works" (John XIV, 10). Still this does not prevent us from holding that Christ also wrought miracles by his own power. For the Father is in him, it is true, yet he also is in the Father. The Father works, but he too works at the same time, so that the works of the Father are also his; for he and the Father are one and the same thing, and therefore the divine power with which the Father works, is the same divine power with which the Son works: "Believe you not, that I am in the Father, and the Father in me?" (John XIV, 11). "My Father worketh until now, and I work" (John V, 17). And again: "If I do not the works of my Father, believe me not." "I and the Father are one." (John X, 37 and 30.)

Here, finally, we must be careful not to mistake when we hear that Christ performed miracles with the divine power, judging therefore that in them his divinity alone worked the whole, and his humanity nothing at all. It was not so: the humanity also cooperated there, as far as the creature can cooperate with God. But the divinity acted as the principal cause, and the humanity as the instrumental cause. Hence it is, that the humanity shared the power of the divine nature, as the instrument shares the power of its principal cause, and was therefore enabled to produce effects superior to its own forces and proportioned to the forces of the divine nature; as when with the touch, or with spittle, or simply with words, he cured the sick, resuscitated the dead, expelled demons, or calmed the tempest. Thus, for instance, the chisel in the hand of the sculptor forms a statue, which is an effect superior to its own power, and proportioned to the power of the artist who handles it; and it does not make it similar to itself, but according to the ideal form which exists in the artist's mind. Thus the wild olive, engrafted on the domestic olive, produces fruits superior to its own power, and proportioned to the good olive in which it has been engrafted, and whose vital vigor it partakes. Thus too the water of baptism, which of its natural virtue would avail only to wash a body, yet as the instrument of the Holy Ghost it washes also the soul from the stains of sin, and confers grace.

Christ's miracles sufficient to prove his divinity.

The miracles of Christ were amply sufficient to prove his divinity; and for three reasons. First, by the very quality of the works which he did, for they exceeded all created power, and therefore it was evident that they could not proceed from any other than the divine power. Observe how astonished the blind man was at the incredulity of the Pharisees, when he received his eye-sight, repeating to them: "From the beginning of the world it hath not been heard, that any man hath opened the

20

eyes of one born blind. Unless this man were of
God, he could not do anything" (John IX, 32, 33).
And what did Nicodemus the Pharisee, yet a man
of upright and loyal heart, say to Christ when he
came by night to visit him? "Rabbi," said he,
"we know thou art come a teacher from God,"
and he added the reason: "for no man can do
these miracles which thou doest unless God were
with him" (John III, 2). Secondly, by the manner in which Christ worked miracles; not like
others, by praying, but by commanding, and as
one who acts by his own authority and power.
Hence it is written of him, 'that virtue went out
from him, and healed all' (Luke VI, 19), to signify, as St. Cyril explains, that 'he did not receive
the power of another, but as he was naturally God,
he showed his own power over the sick, and for
this reason performed innumerable miracles.'
Thirdly, by the doctrine which he joined to the
miracles, teaching openly by them that he was
God. Had this not been true, the divine omnipotence would never have concurred in confirming
it with miracles.

CHAPTER LIV.

The Miracles of Christ in Particular.

Reflect on the miracles which Christ wrought on spiritual substances by freeing the possessed from devilish spirits, with which they were oppressed, and thus fulfilling what God had foretold by the mouth of the prophet Zachary: "I will take away the unclean spirit out of the earth" (Zach. XIII, 2). Among his other miracles Christ willed also to work these, to show his dominion over the powers of darkness, and that he was come to deliver men from the slavery of the devil, who until then had been reigning in the world as a sovereign, but now by the divine power of the Redeemer was to be hurled from his throne and cast out: "Now shall the prince of this world be cast out" (John XII, 31).

Here we should bear in mind two circumstances, which usually accompanied such miracles of Christ. The first is, that whenever the evil spirits proclaimed him the Son of God, or uttered other words that tended to his praise, he did not allow them to speak, but enjoined them to keep silence: "And Jesus rebuked him, saying: 'Hold thy peace, and go out of him' . . . . And he rebuking them, suffered them not to speak, for they knew that he was Christ" (Luke IV, 35, 41).

Why so? To teach us that we should not make any account of what the devil may say, even when he seems to speak the truth; for there is always danger of his blending truth with falsehood. Besides, it was not becoming that the glories and mysteries of the divine Redeemer should be published by a tongue so foul: "For praise is not seemly in the mouth of a sinner" (Eccl. XV, 9).

The second circumstance is, that sometimes Christ permitted the demons expelled by him to inflict some injury on men, either by tormenting their body, as did that deaf and dumb spirit, which although it went out of him that was possessed, yet 'greatly tearing him, he went out of him' (Mark IX, 25), or by injuring their property, as when they entered the swine, and caused them all to perish in the sea. He permitted these things for the greater welfare of souls, which was the chief end he had in view in his preaching, and in the miracles which he performed. He was desirous that by this means men might be always more convinced of the malice of the demon, and of the furious rage which he has against them, and of the evil he would do to them, if the divine goodness did not prevent him; and especially, that he then multiplies his snares, and rages with greater fury, when after having been harbored in a soul by sin, he finds himself constrained to leave against his will.

Christ's miracles on the heavenly bodies.

Christ willed to work miracles on the heavenly bodies, for the reason that being more marvelous,

more evident, and more portentous, they were likewise more suited to make known his divinity, and
especially to show that he was the Lord, not only
of earth, but also of heaven. We read that Christ
performed miracles of this kind on two occasions,
in the beginning and at the end of his life. In the
beginning, when he caused the star to appear
which called and guided the Magi to Bethlehem.
At the end, when he caused the sun to be darkened,
and covered the whole face of the earth with darkness. Thus it was befitting; for then, above all,
it was necessary to make known the power of the
divine nature with more striking prodigies, when
the weakness of human nature was more apparent.
Now such a weakness was exhibited particularly
on these two occasions. In the beginning it was
shown in the extreme weakness, littleness, and
want of everything in a most poor infant, scarcely
born. At the end, in the opprobriums, nudity, and
torments of the passion, and last of all in agony
and death on the cross. For this reason, then, at
these two periods the manifestations of the divinity
were the most striking: in the passion even more
than in the nativity, because in the passion Christ's
humanity descended to utter abasement, even so
far as to be overwhelmed with torments and un-
done by death.

Christ's miracles on men.

Is it not true, that the means have to be proportioned to the end? But what was the end of
Christ's coming, and of his preaching? Not, indeed, to save the angels who had no need of it; not

the demons who were not worthy of it; not irrational creatures who were not capable of it; but men who were capable of it, and in the utmost necessity of it. For this reason, therefore, Christ wished to exercise his divine power on men in a special way, by miraculously curing their infirmities, and by thus making it known that he was the spiritual and universal Saviour of mankind. Who can recount the number and variety of such miracles? But there are three things in particular to be noted concerning them.

First, in restoring health to the sick, frequently he did not employ his divine power alone by curing them, as he might have done, with a simple command, but joined with it some act of his humanity, either by placing his hands upon them, or by touching the diseased part, or by applying saliva, or in some other like manner. What did he mean by this? To make us know, that as his humanity had a part in restoring health to the bodies, so also it should have part in restoring health to the souls, since he had come to save the world, not by the power of his omnipotence alone, but by the mystery of his incarnation.

Secondly, in curing the bodies, he cured the souls at the same time, for 'the works of God are perfect' (Deuter. XXXII, 4). But that is not perfect which does not attain its end; and the end of the external curing effected by Christ was the internal curing of souls. This he himself sometimes declared plainly, as in the case of the paralytic, to whom he said: "Thy sins are forgiven thee" (Mat. IX, 2), even before curing his body. But in the other cases also, although he did not express it, we may believe that he did the same for the reason pointed out.

Thirdly, he not only exercised his divine power on souls by justifying and enlightening them with grace, which was not a miracle properly, being only the end of the miracles wrought by him, but he also worked true and evident miracles on them, especially when by divinely moving their lower or sensitive faculties, he excited affections in them which the sole forces of nature would never have been able to produce. Thus, for example, by a simple look he at one time inflamed the multitude with so much love and desire of him, that they ran after him, forgetful of everything else, and even of taking necessary nourishment. At another time with the words "Follow me" he induced Matthew to abandon his treasures at once, and to follow him, and he changed the publican instantly into an apostle. In the temple he alone, with nothing more in his hand than a whip made of cords, put the profaners to flight, who were in great numbers, and cast such a dread into the minds of all, that no one dared to oppose the least resistance. In the garden with the words "I am he" he sent such stupor and consternation into his persecutors, that they all went backwards instantly, and fell prostrate on their backs. At other times also he produced in souls, in a similar way, other effects like these, which evidently surpassed the forces of natural causes, and manifested the power of his Divinity,

and may therefore with all rigor be counted among
miracles.

Christ's miracles on other creatures.

Christ was desirous that men should understand
well how all things created are subject to his divine power, and therefore he willed to perform
miracles even on irrational and insensible creatures
of every kind.   By reading the holy Scriptures, we
find that there is no kind of such creatures in
which he did not show his divine power with
prodigies.   He showed it in the animals, as when
he caused the fish several times to collect together
spontaneously, and fill the nets of his apostles.
He showed it in the trees, as when he cursed the
barren fig-tree, and it withered in an instant.   He
showed it in the loaves and fishes, which he multiplied, and in the water which he changed into
wine.   He showed it in the air and the sea, when
he commanded the winds and the sea, and there
came a great calm: ''Then rising up, he commanded the wind and the sea, and there came a
great calm'' (Mat. VIII, 26).

But especially on Calvary he displayed his
divine power more fully.   Then it was that he rent
in twain the veil of the temple from top to bottom,
to show that by his passion the mysteries of the
law were disclosed and the gates of heaven opened.
Then it was that he opened the tombs of many, to
signify that his death was the cause of resurrection
and life to those who were dead corporally and
spiritually.   Then it was that he rent the rocks,

to show that, in virtue of his blood shed upon the cross, the hardest hearts would become softened and converted to God with sincere contrition. Then it was that he shook the entire earth, to signify that the whole world would experience the power of his sacrifice, and would be roused from the mortal lethargy in which it lay buried.

CHAPTER LV.

Christ's Transfiguration.

In the beginning of the 17th chapter of St. Matthew we read as follows: "Jesus taketh unto him Peter and James, and John his brother, and bringeth them up into a high mountain apart, and he was transfigured before them, and his face did shine as the sun, and his garments became white as snow." What was the motive of this transfiguration? Christ had foretold his passion to the disciples, and had exhorted them also to walk in his foot-steps by following him in the way of suffering. Now how does a man walk aright in the way he is pursuing? By knowing in some manner beforehand the terminus he should reach. In the same way, the archer, in order to direct his aim straight, must first look at the mark which he has to hit. This is necessary and useful, particularly when the way is difficult and rough, the journey tiresome, and the terminus on the contrary delightful. This being so, what was the terminus which Christ reached by his passion? It was the full and perfect glory of his humanity, that is to say, not only that glory belonging to his soul, which he possessed from the beginning of his conception, but that also of his body: "Ought not Christ to have suffered these things, and so to enter into his

(314)

glory?" (Luke XXIV, 26). This likewise is the terminus to which he conducts all those who follow him in the same way of his passion: "For that through many tribulations we must enter into the kingdom of God" (Acts XIV, 21). In order, therefore, that his disciples might enter upon and go forward on this way with security and great courage, he willed that in his transfiguration they should see something of the terminus, at which they were to arrive. Here then is the reason why he let a ray of his glory shine upon them, by which they might argue what also would be the glory of their own bodies, when they too should be transformed, and raised up from their present abjection to be similar in brightness to the glorious body of Christ: "Who will reform the body of our lowness, made like to the body of his glory" (Philipp. III, 21).

The brightness of Christ's transfiguration was essentially the same as that of the glorified.

The brightness of Christ in the transfiguration was the very brightness of heavenly glory as to essence, but not as to manner. As to essence it was the same, because the brightness of a glorified body is but a reflection of the spiritual brightness of the soul; and in like manner the brightness of Christ's body in the transfiguration was a reflection of the spiritual brightness, first of his divinity, and then of his blessed soul also. It is true, that the soul of Christ had its glory from the first moment of its existence, as was said, but it did not transfuse it into the body at once, owing to a particular ordination of God, who willed that Christ should accomplish the mysteries of our redemption in a passible body.   Nevertheless the power was not wanting in him, to communicate also to his body the beatitude of his soul, when it was pleasing to him.   This he did in the transfiguration, not in respect to all the gifts of glory, but in respect to brightness.   Still this brightness was not in the transfigured body of Christ in the same manner as in glorified bodies.   In glorified bodies the brightness of the soul redounds as a property stable and inherent to the body itself ; and therefore to shine like a sun, is not a miracle in a glorified body, but a quality connatural to the state in which it is. Whereas in the transfigured body of Christ the brightness proceeded from the divinity and from his soul as a quality not permanent, but transient, and superior to the condition of a passible and mortal body, and therefore that light, with which Christ's body was resplendent, was miraculous.

Lastly, take notice that this brightness appeared not only in the body of Christ, but also in his garments, and in the cloud which overshadowed the disciples: "And his face did shine as the sun" (Mat. XVII, 2).   "And his garments became shining exceeding white as snow" (Mark IX, 2). "Behold a bright cloud overshadowed them" (Mat. XVII, 5).   All this did not take place without mystery.   The splendor which was in the transfigured body of Christ represented the future splendor of that same body glorified.   The brilliant splendor of his garments represented the future clarity of the saints, which will be surpassed by the clarity of Christ, as the whiteness of snow is surpassed by the brilliancy of the sun, since under the name of garments the just are pointed out, adorned with their virtues, with which Christ shall be vested, and the Church, his beloved spouse, adorned as with a nuptial dress. ''The garments of Christ,'' says Pope St. Gregory, ''have been made splendid, for all the saints refulgent with the light of justice, shall cleave to him in the height of supernal brightness.'' And Isaias: "As I live, saith the Lord, thou shalt be clothed with all these as with an ornament, and as a bride thou shalt put them about thee" (Is. XLIX, 18). Thus spoke the Lord to Sion, which was a figure of the Church. Finally the luminous cloud, which overshadowed the disciples, signifies the glory of the Holy Ghost, as we shall presently see.

Witnesses of the transfiguration.

Those who were chosen to be the witnesses of Christ's transfiguration, were Moses, Elias, and the three disciples Peter, John, and James. For what reason were these chosen? Jesus Christ was transfigured, to give men a taste of his glory, and thus stimulate them to desire it also for themselves. Now not only men of the new covenant, but those also of the old, are conducted by Christ to the glory of eternal bliss, for there is for all but one fountain of salvation, and that is Christ himself. He willed therefore to choose some from both covenants, to be spectators of his glory. He did not will to have the angels as witnesses, because in the transfiguration he manifested the glory of his body, a thing which appertained to men only. He chose Moses and Elias from among those of the ancient testament for the following reasons adduced by the holy doctors: First, to show that he was not Elias, nor any of the prophets, but the Lord of all the prophets: he willed, therefore, that the chiefs of the prophets should appear to glorify him. Second, because Moses gave the law, and Elias showed a great zeal for the glory of God, and therefore by their presence they refuted the stupid calumnies of the Jews, who accused Christ of being a transgressor of the law, and the usurper of the glory of God. Third, to show that he has power over life and death, and is the judge of the living and the dead; and therefore he took with him Moses already dead, and Elias still living. Fourth, to comfort the minds of his disciples, who were dismayed at the announcement of his approaching passion, and therefore he made Moses and Elias, both of whom had exposed their life for the honor of God, Moses by presenting himself to Pharoe, and Elias to King Achab, to appear and speak of his passion. Fifth, because he was desirous that his disciples should imitate the meekness of Moses, and the zeal of Elias. Sixth, to signify that he had been foretold both by the law of which Moses was the herald, and by the prophets, among whom Elias held the first place.

Among the apostles he gave the preference to Peter, John and James, because, as St. Chrysostom observes, all three were distinguished above the others for some special prerogative. Peter for the ardor of love with which he was inflamed towards his divine Master, and for his dignity as head and foundation stone of the Church. John for the singular love which Jesus showed him on account of his virginity, and for the prerogative of evangelical doctrine. James, because he was to be the first among all the apostles to give testimony with his blood to his faith and love for Jesus Christ.

Why the Eternal Father in the transfiguration willed to attest the divine Sonship of Christ, as he had already done in baptism.

Men's adoption as sons of God lies in some conformity to the natural Son of God. Now this conformity is obtained in two ways: imperfectly by grace in the present life, perfectly by glory in the life to come. "Dearly beloved we are now the sons of God; and it hath not appeared what we shall be. We know that when he shall appear, we shall be like to him, because we shall see him as he is" (1 John III, 2). Since, then, we obtain grace by baptism, and have been allowed to see in the transfiguration the brightness of future glory, it was proper that both in baptism and in the transfiguration the testimony of the Father should intervene, to manifest the natural Sonship of Christ, for the reason that the Father alone is fully cognizant of such a divine generation, and with him the Son and the Holy Ghost.

Observe, moreover, that as in the baptism, in

which the mystery of the first regeneration was declared, all the three divine persons manifested themselves in some manner, the Father in the voice which was heard from heaven, the Son in the flesh assumed by him, and the Holy Ghost in the dove, so in like manner in the transfiguration, which was the sign and pledge of the second regeneration, the whole Trinity appeared: the Father in the voice, the Son in human nature, and the Holy Ghost in the resplendent cloud which covered and overshadowed the disciples. But why did not the Holy Ghost show himself under the same form in the baptism and in the transfiguration? To point out the different gifts, which he bestows in the first, and in the second regeneration. In the first he gives innocence, which is symbolized by the simplicity of the dove; in the second he will give to his elect the brightness of glory, and relief from all afflictions; which things are figured by the cloud, which was shining and at the same time protected the disciples with its shadow.

But the excellence of this glory is such, and so greatly above any sense and faculties of mortals, that their frailty cannot sustain it. Hence it is written: "For man shall not see me, and live" (Exod. XXXIII, 20). For this reason it is, that the disciples on entering the cloud, and hearing the voice of the divine Father, fell prostrate on the ground, and had great fear: "And they were afraid when they entered into the cloud" (Luke IX, 34). "And the disciples hearing, fell upon their face and were very much afraid" (Mat. XVII, 6).

But men shall be cured of such frailty by Christ himself, when he shall introduce them into his glory. And this is what he intended to signify, when, approaching his disciples, he touched them and said to them, "Arise and be not afraid" (Mat. XVII, 7).

Chapter LVI.

Christ's Passion.

We shall meditate on the motives for which Jesus willed to submit to the dolors of the passion. To liberate us from sin, it was not necessary that he should sustain so cruel a passion and death. A simple act of divine clemency, such as, I pardon you, had sufficed. But that was not enough for the most ardent charity of Jesus. He not only wished to redeem us from the slavery of sin, but was desirous also that his redemption should be plentiful, should superabound with other most precious goods for us: and for this he chose to suffer and to die. And what are those goods which he wished to procure for us at so great a cost? It is only by attentive reflection that we can understand a little of his excessive love towards us.

The first good was to make us know this his love for us, and by this means to excite us to return his love. For Jesus takes it greatly to heart that we should love him very much; not for any advantage to himself, but solely for our benefit. He knows well that the whole perfection of our welfare is placed in loving him. Therefore, to incite us gently and strongly to such a love, he wished by the most atrocious pains of his passion, borne by him, our God, for us his creatures and his enemies, to give us a sensible proof and some measure of his immeasurable love: "But God commendeth his charity towards us, because when we were yet sinners . . . Christ died for us" (Rom. V, 8, 9).

The second good was the brightest examples of obedience, humility, constancy, justice, and of other virtues, which Jesus Christ gave us in his passion: "Christ suffered for us, leaving you an example that you should follow his steps" (1 Peter II, 21). We had great need of learning well and of desiring efficaciously the practice of these virtues. And the example of Christ was doubtless the manner most adapted to enlighten our minds and move our wills. On this account he wished these virtues to figure so admirably in his passion, and to shine with a light so brilliant, that even the most blind might see them, and even the most sluggish might be aroused by them.

In the third place, as a father and a mother, who most tenderly love a son, who has been cast into a foul prison, are not contented with seeing him at last merely free from his imprisonment, but also wish to clothe him with precious garments, to procure for him conveniences and honors, and provide for him a rich patrimony, and would desire, if they could, to make him sovereign of the world, so also the most loving Jesus was not content to see us merely free from sin, but wished besides this to merit for us by his passion the divine garment of justification, the inheritance of glory and the kingdom of heaven.

In the fourth place, it was not enough for the

sweetest heart of Jesus to relieve us from present misery, without fortifying us in advance against future relapses. He wished, therefore, to spend for our ransom all his blood and his life, so that, reflecting that we have been purchased at 'a great price', we might understand better the gravity of the evil in which we were sunk, and become more solicitous in future to avoid it: "For you are bought with a great price: glorify and bear God in your body" (1 Cor. VI, 20).

Lastly, the most amiable Jesus wished to restore and ennoble the dignity of human nature, which had been debased and trodden on in the first man. It was right, therefore, that the devil, who had overcome man, should in turn be overcome by man; and as the first Adam by his disobedience merited death, so the second Adam dying through obedience should triumph over death.

Christ sustained every kind of pain in his passion.

The sufferings to which human nature can be subjected in this land of exile and sorrow, may be considered as to their species or genus. As to the species, not all could concur in the passion of Christ, for there are many among them contrary to each other, and others that were not becoming his divine person. But as to their genus, we may say with all truth that Christ willed for our example and encouragement, and to show us the ardor of his charity, that every genus of sufferings should combine together to inundate and overwhelm his most sacred humanity in a most bitter sea.

And first those, who met together to torment him, were persons of every class, Gentiles and Jews, men and women, rich and poor, nobles and plebeans, learned and unlearned, soldiers, ministers, priests, princes and kings of the earth, according to the words of the psalmist: "Why have the gentiles raged and the people devised vain things ? The kings of the earth stood up, and the princes met together against the Lord and against his Christ" (Ps. II, 1, 2). And among the rest, even those who had been most benefited by him; also some of his most intimate friends; some of his apostles, too, one of whom betrayed, and another denied him. In addition to this, all hell broke loose and was infuriated in his executioners against him. Even his heavenly Father did not spare him: "He spared not his own Son, but delivered him up for us all" (Rom. VIII, 32), and abandoned him a prey to his persecutors: "My God, my God, why hast thou forsaken me ?" (Mat. XXVII, 46). And he willed to see him crushed under the weight of our iniquities and his just vengeance: "And the Lord hath laid on him the iniquity of us all. . . . And the Lord was pleased to bruise him in infirmity" (Is. LIII, 6. 10).

In the second place Jesus Christ suffered in all those things in which a man is capable of suffering. In his body, which was made one whole wound from the top of his head to the sole of his feet: "From the sole of the foot unto the top of the head there is no soundness therein" (Is. I, 6). In his soul, oppressed with fear, with sadness and deadly disgust: "My soul is sorrowful even unto death" (Mat. XXVI, 38). In his goods, being so reduced, as not to have clothing to cover him, nor a span of earth on which to place his foot. In his friends, by whom he was abandoned: "The disciples all leaving him, fled away" (Mat. XXVI, 56). In his reputation, by the calumnies and horrid blasphemies uttered against him. In his honor, by the derisions and insults of every kind, of which he was made the target, so as to be saturated with them: "He shall be filled with reproaches" (Jerem. Lamen. III, 30).

Notice, in fine, how notably in the immaculate body of Jesus every part had its own peculiar torment. The head penetrated with thorns; the hands and feet pierced through with nails; the face bruised with buffeting, and befouled with spittle; all his members lacerated by the blows of the scourges; his heart thrust open with a spear; his blood scattered and trampled on; his throat parched and seared; his taste embittered with gall; his hearing harassed with the shouts of those who were cursing and deriding him; his vision saddened by the sight of his mother and the beloved disciple, who stood sorrowing at the foot of the cross.

We see, then, how true it is that Jesus suffered pains of every genus, for he suffered from all, in all things, and in all parts of his body.

The extension and intensity of Christ's sufferings.

The suffering of Jesus Christ in his passion, both externally in the body and internally in the soul, was not only most vast in extension, but was also

extreme in intensity, so much so, that it far surpassed all the sufferings of the present life. Four
things conspired to render his suffering the greatest.
First, the causes, which were as to his body the
most grievous torments of every kind, and especially
the death on the cross, most agonizing on account
of the transpiercing of the hands and feet, parts
that are so full of nerves and so exquisitely sensitive; also on account of the weight of the body,
which always enlarges the wounds, and increases
the convulsions; and owing to the length of time,
for death does not come till after several hours of
the most painful agony. Besides this, to these
sufferings of Jesus were added the sharpest prick-
ing of thorns, the deep and agonizing wounds with
which he was furrowed from head to foot. Then,
too, as to his soul, the first and most atrocious
cause of pain was the sins of the human race,
which he regarded as his own, as when he exclaimed, 'the words of my sins' (Ps. XXI, 2).
If then some holy penitents, while meditating on
their sins, felt their hearts break with sorrow, and
some even died of sheer contrition, who shall be
able to tell what was Christ's sorrow? There is
no doubt, that it surpassed without comparison the
sorrow of all penitents, both because it proceeded
from wisdom and charity incomparably more perfect, and because it was a sorrow for all the sins
together of mankind, according to what the prophet
Isaias said of him: "Surely he hath carried our
sorrows" (Is. LIII, 4). Another cause of most
intense grief to the soul of Jesus was the cowardice

and ingratitude of the disciples dismayed and scandalized by his passion, the obstinate perfidy of the Jews, and the foreknowledge of the tremendous chastisements which awaited them. Moreover, to increase his internal martyrdom, there was united also the natural horror of death; for Jesus naturally and most justly loved his corporal life, which being most holy and most precious, especially on account of union with the divinity, was most worthy of love and most undeserving of death. Therefore the loss of such a life, even for a brief instant only, ought to be justly accounted a greater evil, and deplored more bitterly, than the loss of the life of any other man whatever, and for any length of time.

In the second place, the suffering of Christ was the greatest, owing to the quality of his human nature, which, having been formed immediately by the operation of the Holy Ghost, was most perfect both in body and in soul. Wherefore the complexion of his body was most delicate, and consequently most susceptible to every pain. The interior powers of his soul were likewise most lively, and therefore adapted to lay hold with the greatest effect on all the causes of sadness, and to experience all the distress they produce.

In the third place, the suffering of Christ was the greatest on account of the way in which he suffered, since he willed to suffer in such a manner that his might be pure suffering. In others who suffer, the superior part brings some relief to the inferior part, which lightens the inward pain and

also the external.   But it was not so in Jesus; for
while his superior part enjoyed a perfect calm, he
abandoned the inferior part and his body to the full
power of the fierce storm, which caused him to
sweat blood and to agonize in the garden, and
brought death to him on Calvary.

In the fourth place, the suffering of Christ was
the greatest by reason of the end which he proposed
in submitting voluntarily to the passion, which
was to free men from sin.   For although it is true,
that even the least of his sufferings had an unspeakable value from the union of the divinity,
yet he did not wish to effect our salvation by the
sole might of his power, but also in accordance
with the rigor of justice, and for that reason he
burdened himself with as much suffering as would
be proportioned to the enormous weight of all the
sins of men together.

If we consider attentively the four circumstances mentioned, which united to render Christ's
suffering the greatest, we shall see with how much
reason he himself challenges us to find a sorrow
that can be compared to his: "Attend and see if
there be any sorrow like unto my sorrow" (Jer.
Lam. I, 12).

CHAPTER LVII.

The Death of Christ.

Jesus was not satisfied by suffering for us the most atrocious torments, unheard of humiliations and every kind of outrage, but wished to drink the chalice to the dregs. So he, who is life and the fountain of life as God, willed as man to submit to the dissolution of death, by which his most holy soul was truly separated from his body, although both remained indivisibly united to the divine person. But what were the reasons, for which Jesus wished to submit to death? They were the five following especially. First, because the human race had been condemned to death on account of sin: "For in what day soever thou shalt eat of it, thou shalt die the death" (Gen. II, 17). Therefore he, who was come to satisfy for us, willed to take upon himself, who was innocence itself, the same punishment as was due to us sinners: "Christ died once for our sins, the just for the unjust" (1 Pet. III, 18). Second, to show us thus more and more the verity of the human nature assumed by him. He knew well how necessary it would be for our salvation, to believe this truth with the greatest firmness, and for that reason he wished in addition to the other proofs of it already given, to add also this the greatest one, that of death.

(330)

Third, "that through death . . . . he might deliver them who, through the fear of death, were all their life-time subject to slavery" (Heb. II, 14, 15). As a valiant captain marches in front, to meet the enemy in order to encourage his soldiers, so he willed to encounter death to deliver us from the fear of death. Fourth, in order that the sight of his corporal death, undergone for the chastisement of sins not his, might serve to teach us and incite us also to die spiritually to sin, to the world and its vanities, to die to the flesh and its allurements, to the devil and his suggestions, to die to the inordinate love of ourselves, that we may love him alone, and live for him alone: "For in that he died to sin, he died once, but in that he liveth, he liveth unto God. So also do you reckon yourselves to be dead indeed to sin, but alive to God" (Rom. VI, 10, 11). Fifth, to make known to us afterwards his divine power by his resurrection, and the triumph which he had won over death, and to give us a secure hope of rising also ourselves, of rising, if we put no hindrance, as he rose to true life, to a blessed life, an eternal life: "Now if Christ be preached, that he arose again from the dead, how do some among you say, that there is no resurrection of the dead ?" (1 Cor. XV, 12).

Christ suffered and died through obedience.

Jesus Christ suffered and died through obedience to his divine Father: "Becoming obedient unto death" (Philip. II, 8). Thus it accorded, first, with the work of men's justification, which had to be the fruit of Christ's obedience, as their condemnation was the fruit of Adam's disobedience: "For as by the disobedience of one man, many were made sinners, so also by the obedience of one, many shall be made just" (Rom. V, 19). Secondly it accorded with God's reconciliation with men, for Christ's sacrifice was the more acceptable to God, and the more available to reconcile him with us, as it proceeded from obedience, which to God is dearer than all sacrifices: "Obedience is better than victims" (1 Kings XV, 22). Thirdly it accorded with Christ's victory over death, and over the author of death, for a soldier conquers by obeying his commander, and thus Christ as man gained the victory by obeying God, proving in this way even in himself the truth of the proverb, which says: 'An obedient man shall speak of victory.' Nor did this prevent Christ from suffering and dying for love, as he obeyed for love and loved for obedience.

Jesus by dying fulfilled the whole ancient law.

By dying, Jesus not only obeyed the Father, but also perfectly fulfilled all the precepts of the old law, whether moral, ceremonial, or judicial. He fulfilled the moral, as the moral precepts are all founded on the love of God and of our neighbor, and Jesus Christ went to death through love of his divine Father: "But that the world may know that I love the Father, and as the Father hath given me commandment, so I do. Arise, let us go hence" (John XIV, 31). He went to death also for love of each one of us: "He loved me and delivered himself for me" (Gal. II, 20). He fulfilled the ceremonial precepts, as these were ordained principally for the sacrifices, which were nothing more than a shadaw and figure of the true sacrifice, which Jesus Christ offered by dying for us. He fulfilled the judicial precepts, as these were intended most of all, to render satisfaction to those who had suffered wrong, and Jesus Christ died expressly to pay the debt contracted by us by sinning, and to make amends for the outrage offered by us to the honor of God. From this we see, how in the death of Christ the whole law was consummated, that is to say, had its complete fulfilment, as Jesus himself intended to signify when a little before rendering up his last sigh, he uttered these words: "It is consummated" (John XIX, 30).

The circumstances of Christ's death.

Jesus Christ chose for his passion and death those circumstances which would be most suitable for our instruction, and for satisfying and manifesting his inflamed love towards us.

First. He willed to die on the most cruel and infamous frame of the cross. First of all, for our encouragement, so that we, beholding his example, might not have an utter horror of undergoing any kind of death. As a most loving mother who, to encourage her sick child to take a nauseous medicine, wishes to taste it first herself, so Jesus wished to taste the bitterness of the most painful death, to **induce us** to accept freely from the hands of God whatever kind of death it may please him to send us, which, however painful it may be, can never be compared to his. In the next place, because such a kind of death was the most suited to satisfy for the sin of the first man, for he had prevaricated by detaching the forbidden apple from the tree, and Jesus, by suffering himself to be fastened to the tree of the cross, restored as it were with the most ample usury that which Adam had taken, according to the words of the psalm: "Then did I pay that which I took not away" (Ps. LXVIII). In the third place, that the reality might correspond to the figures, as the salutary wood of the cross had in many ways been prefigured by various symbols which preceded it. Such were the arc of wood, which saved the human race from the deluge; the rod of Moses which divided the waters of the sea, submerged Pharao and delivered God's people from bondage, and drew water from the rock; the wood with which Moses converted the bitter waters of Mara into sweet; the arc of wood which contained the tables of the law; and the altar of holocausts composed also of wood.

Secondly. He willed to die in the prime of life. In this we must admire especially the exquisite delicacy of his love. A kind friend, who wishes to offer an apple as a present to his friend, plucks it when it is quite ripe and luscious; so Jesus, desirous of sacrificing his life for us, willed to do so when it was in its greatest bloom.

Thirdly. He willed to die in Jerusalem, that there the true Lamb of God might be immolated, where the legal victims were wont to be offered, which figured and predicted that Lamb. But not in the temple, so that the Jews might not attribute his sacrifice to themselves alone. But outside of the city, so that all might be verified which was represented and prophecied by the typical sacrifices of the calf and the goat, the bodies of which, according to the prescription of the law, had to be burned outside the habitations: "The bodies of those beasts, whose blood for sin is brought into the sanctuary by the high-priest, are burned without the camp. Wherefore Jesus, also that he might sanctify the people with his own blood, suffered without the gate" (Heb. XIII, 11, 12). On the height of Calvary, and in the midst of a throng of people of every condition, and of every nation, so that the ignominy of his death might be greater and more public, and thus his humility might be better satisfied; and also to show that he died for the sins, not of one people alone, but of all the men in the world, as they were all the object of his most ardent charity.

Fourthly. He willed to be crucified between two thieves, to show that he was come to seek sinners, and he gave his life for them. To show that he is the judge, and therefore upon the cross as from a tribunal he absolved and condemned, promised paradise to the good thief, and sentenced the impenitent thief to hell. To signify what he shall do on the last day, when he will come to judge the living and the dead, when he will place the good at his right and the wicked at his left, and will invite the former to ascend with him to heaven, and cast the latter together with the demons into everlasting fire.

Fifthly. He willed that together with the Jews the gentiles also should cooperate in his passion, in order that these two might have part in the precious fruit of the prayer, which he addressed to his eternal Father on the cross, asking pardon for his persecutors. And, moreover, that in the same manner as his passion, its effect might be prefigured also. For as the passion began with the Jews, and ended by the hand of the gentiles, so the effect of salvation was to be communicated first to the Jews, and afterwards to pass on to the nations. Thus, whilst men were thinking of nothing but of doing him evil, Jesus Christ with the tenderest solicitude, was arranging and ordaining these and all the other circumstances of his passion and death for their greater good.

CHAPTER LVIII.

The Effects of Christ's Passion.

The first effect of the passion of Christ was to free us from sin: "He hath loved us, and washed us from our sins in his own blood" (Apoc. I, 5). He so loved us, that he wished to make a salutary bath of his most precious blood, to cleanse us from the stains of our loathsome sins.

The passion of Christ is the true and proper cause of the remission of sins, in three ways. First by enkindling in our hearts the beautiful flame of charity, which instantly consumes all filthiness of sin. Truly the meditation on Christ, who suffers and dies for us sinners, helps wonderfully to make us understand the ineffable charity of God towards us: "But God commendeth his charity towards us . . . . because when as yet we were sinners . . . . Christ died for us" (Rom. V, 8, 9), and consequently arouses in us sentiments of gratitude and love towards him, who loved us so excessively and rendered good to us, when we were most unworthy of it. In virtue of this love we obtain the pardon of our sins, as Jesus himself attested of the penitent Magdalen: "Many sins are forgiven her, because she hath loved much" (Luke VII, 47).

Second. By way of redemption. We were the servants of sin, because 'whosoever committeth sin

22 (337)

is the servant of sin' (John VIII, 34). But Jesus by his passion has redeemed us from such a servitude, by giving as the price not silver and gold, but his immaculate blood: "You were not redeemed with corruptible gold or silver .... but with the precious blood of Christ, as of a lamb unspotted and undefiled" (1 Pet. I, 18, 19). It is true that the ransom price was his, and the sin was ours; but Jesus is our head, and we are his members. And as in the same man a meritorious work done by one member of the body, as for instance by the hand, acquits him of a sin committed by another member, for example by the tongue, so the passion sustained through the charity and obedience by Christ our head, ransomed us his members from the slavery of sin. And his ransom was commensurate with his love and his dignity, that is, it was most abundant and most sufficient to free us not only from the sin of Adam common to all, but also from past, present and future personal sins, provided the fruit of redemption be applied to each individual by faith and the sacraments.

Third. By way of efficient cause, in virtue of the divinity, of which the most sacred flesh of Christ, which suffered in the passion, was the instrument. For as a clear crystal, when struck by the rays of the sun, becomes itself brilliant with light, so the immaculate flesh of Jesus, by union with the divine nature, was made capable of producing in its actions and sufferings divine effects, one of which is to drive away from our souls the darkness of sin. This is what the Apostle intended to indicate with these words: "That, which *appeareth* weakness of God, is stronger than men" (1 Cor. I, 25), that is, what is most weak in Christ, and a sign and effect of weakness, namely, his flesh and his passion, has, in as much as it is of God, a more than human, yea infinite power.

The second effect of Christ's passion.

The second effect of Christ's passion was to free us from the power of the devil: "Now shall the prince of this world be cast out. And I, if I be lifted up from the earth, will draw all things to myself" (John XII, 31, 32). By virtue of Christ's passion the prince of this world was cast down from his throne; and when Jesus was raised up on the cross, he drew all men to him, for he drew them from the slavery of the devil to the liberty and dignity of the children of God. His most merciful love willed also that our deliverance should be full, and therefore he stripped the devil of all the three titles which he had for exercising his tyranny over mankind. The first title was on the part of man, who by his sin had deserved to fall into the power of the enemy, who had overcome him: "By whom a man is overcome, of the same also is he the slave" (2 Pet. II, 19). But Jesus with his passion canceled sin, and so annulled this first title. The second title was on the part of God, who being justly angered by the offence received from man, had in punishment left him subject to the servitude of Satan. But the passion of Christ appeased the divine anger, and thus did away with this second title. The third title was on the part of the devil himself, who by his most wicked will and the rabid hatred which he bears towards the human race, labored to keep it oppressed under his cruel yoke. But this title also ceased through Christ's passion; not that Satan's rage against us ceased or diminished in the least, but because having abused the power given him by God, by plotting death against the divine Redeemer, who being most innocent did not deserve death, he was with reason deprived of the power which he had even over those who deserved to remain subject to him. In this way did Christ's passion chain the devil, and free us from his chains, and furnish us also with the means of guarding ourselves against his snares, of blunting his arms, and of healing the wounds that he may sometimes inflict upon us. So, unless it be through our fault, he will not be able to do us any real harm, but all his temptations and all his vexations will turn to our good, to his greater hurt, and to the greater glory of Jesus our liberator.

The third effect of Christ's passion.

The third effect of Christ's passion was to free us from the punishment of sin. In two ways Jesus released us from the debt of punishment, which we owed the divine justice; directly, by satisfying most fully for the sins of the whole human race; indirectly, by removing the sin itself, which was the foundation of it. Nor was the satisfaction most sufficient only, which he made to his divine Father, but was beyond measure superabundant, for three reasons especially.   By the immense and most perfect charity with which he suffered, and which without comparison surpassed the malice of all sinners; by the value of the price which he paid, which was his life, a life not only the most innocent and most holy, but of infinite dignity, because the life of a God; and by the amount and weight of sufferings to which he willed to be subjected, which were of every kind and the very greatest.

The fourth effect of Christ's passion.

The fourth effect of Christ's passion was to reconcile us with God: "We were reconciled to God by the death of his Son" (Rom. V, 10). The passion of the Saviour was the cause of our reconciliation with God in two ways. First of all, by purifying our souls from sin, which made us enemies of God, and deserving of his hatred, for 'the Highest hateth sinners' (Eccli. XII, 3). In the second place, because reconciliation with God is the proper effect of sacrifice. Now the passion and death of Christ was a most true sacrifice, in which he was at the same time both priest and victim, he accepting it as God, and offering it as man, and he being the head for us his members: "He hath delivered himself for us, an oblation and a sacrifice to God for an odor of sweetness" (Eph. V, 2). It was a most perfect sacrifice, of which all the imperfect sacrifices of the ancient law were a figure, and from which they had their value. It was a most suitable sacrifice, as his flesh was most adapted to be offered for men, because it was human; and to be immolated, because it was passible and mortal; to cleanse us from sin, because it was most pure and born of the virginal bosom of Mary without contagion of carnal concupiscence; and to appease the divine anger, because it was most acceptable to God, as belonging to Christ himself, who offered it, and on account of the inexplicable charity with which he offered it. Hence his passion and death reconciled us completely with God. Indeed, the reconciliation effected by his sacrifice was not only most complete, but was beyond expression superabundant. For Christ's oblation was more pleasing to God, than the offences of all men are hateful to him, and could therefore allay his indignation much more, than our iniquities could provoke it. His most tender charity willed and did so much, to the end that at the sight of our wickedness and abjection we might never lose courage, nor despair of obtaining pardon. However grievous and deserving of divine vengeance our offences may be, we can always obtain pardon, through the merits of Christ's passion, provided we comply with the conditions required to have part in it.

The fifth effect of Christ's passion.

The fifth effect of Christ's passion was to open for us the gates of heaven: "Having a confidence in the entering into the sanctuary by the blood of Christ" (Heb. X, 19). The gates of the heavenly kingdom were closed for men; nor would we ever have been able with our own power to open them, nay, rather our demerits would always have kept them inexorably closed against us. But our most loving Redeemer in virtue of his passion threw them open, so that all those who share the precious fruit of his blood, shall enter with confidence into the holy temple of his glory. What, indeed, was the obstacle which prevented entrance into heaven? It was sin; before all, the sin of our first parent, common to the whole human nature, then the personal sins of each individual. Covered with this twofold leprosy, it was not possible for us to have access where nothing defiled can enter: "A way shall be there, and it shall be called the holy way, and the unclean shall not pass over it" (Isaias XXXV, 8). But the passion of Christ removed this impediment, by obtaining for us deliverance from the guilt and from the penalty, both of original and actual sin; and thus opened the gates of heaven, and opened them in such a way that they are never more to be closed.

As to the saints, who preceded the coming of Christ, they too by faith in his future passion, together with works of justice, obtained the kingdom of heaven: "Who through faith subdued kingdoms, wrought justice" (Heb. XI, 33). This same faith also cleansed them from their personal sins. But neither their faith nor their justice availed to remove the guilt which weighed on the whole human family. No one, then, could ascend to glory until the Messiah came to pay the price of redemption, and put us himself in possession of the heavenly country.

The sixth effect of Christ's passion.

The sixth effect of the passion of Christ was to merit the exaltation of Christ himself: "He humbled himself, becoming obedient unto death, even the death on the cross. Wherefore God also hath exalted him" (Philipp. II, 8, 9). The more he abused himself in his passion beneath his dignity, the more by a just recompense was he exalted. In four things particularly we may observe Christ's abasement, and the exaltation which he had in return. First, he abased himself by willing to endure pains and death, which were not due to him, who was most innocent; and for this he merited to be exalted with the glory of the resurrection. Secondly, he abased himself by willing that his body should lie in the sepulchre, and his soul descend into hell; and on that account he merited to be exalted with the triumph of the ascension into heaven: "Now that he ascended, what is it but because he descended first into the lower parts of the earth? He who descended is the same also who ascended above all the heavens" (Eph. IV, 9, 10). Thirdly, he abased himself by willing to bear infamy and revilings of every sort; and therefore he merited to be exalted even to sit at the right hand of his heavenly Father, and that at his name every knee should bend in heaven, on earth, and in hell, and that all should recognize and adore his divinity.

Fourthly, he abased himself by willing to submit to the tribunal of human power, and by that he merited to receive the authority of supreme and universal judge: "Thy cause hath been judged as that of the wicked: cause and judgment thou shalt recover" (Job XXXVI, 17).

Chapter LIX.

Christ's Burial.

Jesus Christ, through love for us, willed also to bear the humiliation and obscurity of the tomb. First, that thus the truth of his death might be better proved; for a body is not enclosed in the tomb, except when death is clearly manifest. Secondly, that by seeing him rise from his sepulchre, we too might take confidence of rising from ours by the power of his voice, which shall recall us to life: "The dead shall hear the voice of the Son of God, and they that hear shall live" (John V, 25). "All that are in the graves shall hear the voice of the Son of God" (John V, 28). For the example of those who, by virtue of his death, die spiritually to sin, and live with him and in him, hidden to the turbulence of the world: "For you are dead, and your life is hidden with Christ in God" (Colos. III, 3).

Christ ordained all the circumstances of his burial.

Jesus, moved likewise by his love for us, ordained all the various circumstances of his burial for our advantage and instruction. The honors, which were rendered to him, show his dignity and power, for contrary to the perverse intentions of his murderers, he was buried with honor, they prefigured also the devotion of the faithful, who in

(346)

after-time would render homage to Christ. The white linen shroud denotes to us the purity of mind and heart, with which we should dispose ourselves to receive him within us. The myrrh and aloes signify to us the bitterness of penance, with which we may be able to keep him in our hearts without the corruption of sin. The fragrance of the spices expresses to us the good odor of virtue, which the life of those should exhale who by baptism are buried with Christ: ''For we are buried together with him unto death'' (Rom. VI, 4). The garden, in which he was buried, reminds us of the terrestrial paradise, in which Adam prevaricated. The new monument is a symbol for us of the virginal womb of the most holy Mary, and also of our renovation, the fruit of the death and interment of Christ. The sepulchre was not his own; to make us understand always better, how dear to him was poverty, which he wished as a companion even after death. It was excavated in a rock, enclosed with a huge stone, nor did it contain other corpses, in order that the certainty of his resurrection might be more evident. His body remained uncorrupt, to show that his death did not happen by natural dissolution, but by his spontaneous will, and also to manifest the divine power to which it was united.

Jesus remained two nights and one day in the sepulchre.

Jesus willed to remain two nights and one day in the sepulchre, to manifest also in this way the salutary effect of his death. And truly was the

human race darkened with the obscurity of a
double death, the death of the soul by sin, and the
death of the body in punishment of sin, both of
which deaths are represented by the two nights
during which our Lord remained in the tomb.
But the death of Christ, figured by the day, as it
did not proceed from sin, but from the most lively
charity, scattered with its triumphant light the
darkness of the two nights with which we were
enveloped; and thus by the death of the Redeemer
was our death overcome and swallowed up, that is,
destroyed: "Death is swallowed up in victory"
(1 Cor. XV, 54).

Chapter LX.

Christ's Descent into Hell.

The same love which moved Jesus to die for us, induced him also to descend with his soul into hell after death. First for the reason that, as his death had delivered us from death, so his descent into hell might preserve us from falling into it; and in this way the prophecy of Osee might be fulfilled, that he would be death to death, and bite to hell: "O death, I will be thy death; O hell, I will be thy bite" (Osee XIII, 14). In the second place, for the reason that, having discomfited the devil by his passion, it was proper for him to take away his prey, and restore those to liberty who were held by him in imprisonment: "Thou also by the blood of thy testament", that is, by virtue of the blood shed by thee in the passion, "hast sent forth thy prisoners out of the pit" (Zach. IX, 11); "divesting principalities and powers", that is, the infernal ones, "he hath exposed them confidently in open show" (Colos. II, 15), in other words, he has led away the souls of the just with the confidence and authority of a conqueror and a master. In the third place, to make his power known also in hell, as he had already shown it on earth while living and dying; so that at the name

(349)

of Jesus every knee should bend, not only in heaven and on earth, but also in hell.

Christ descended into hell instantly after his death.

Scarcely was his sacrifice consummated, when Jesus Christ descended into hell, for his most loving heart could not brook that the communication of the salutary fruit of redemption should be delayed even for an instant. He wished, therefore, to release the souls of those just ones from the penalty of original sin without delay; and by enlightening them with the light of glory, he made them perfectly happy, so that, although they remained in limbo in company with his most holy soul as long as his sacred body remained in the tomb, as seems at least most probable, still their liberation from hell was effected immediately, as that place was no longer a prison or a hell for them, but a true and most delightful paradise; and in fact Jesus himself called it so, when he promised the good thief, that on that very day he would be with him in paradise: "This day thou shalt be with me in paradise" (Luke XXIII, 43).

The effect of Christ's descent was felt in every part of hell.

Although the soul of Christ, as to its essence, was present only in the limbo of the holy fathers, yet the effect of his visit was felt in all the various regions of hell, but in a different manner, according to the different condition of those who were confined there. The damned had an increase of confusion and torment, at seeing their incredulity and malice confounded. The souls in purgatory received consolation and comfort by the certain hope of near beatitude, and many also, either because sufficiently purified, or because more deserving, especially by faith and devotion shown to the passion and death of the Saviour, were admitted at once to share in the glory and triumph of Christ. As regards the souls of children who died with the original sin, they too in some manner were to feel the coming of Jesus. But they were not liberated from Limbo, nor made partakers of the vision of God, for the reason that Christ's descent into hell operated in virtue of his passion, and therefore produced the effect of deliverance on those only, who by faith and charity were found united to the merit of his passion. Now the souls of those children were without such faith and charity. Consequently they were incapable of sharing in the fruit of redemption. Besides, they were deprived of grace, without which it is impossible for any one to be admitted into everlasting life.

Chapter LXI.

Christ's Resurrection.

Let us ponder the reasons why it was necessary that Christ should rise from death: "It behooved Christ to suffer, and to rise again from the dead the third day" (Luke XXIV, 46). The principal reasons were the following. First, for the glorification of the divine justice, whose property is to put down the proud and to exalt those who humble themselves for God, and to exalt them the higher, the more they lower themselves: "He hath put down the mighty from their seat, and hath exalted the humble" (Luke I, 52). Since then Christ through love and obedience had humbled himself even unto the death of the cross, it was necessary that he should be exalted by God even to the glory of the resurrection. Hence he is made to say in the psalms: "Thou hast known my sitting down, and my rising up" (Ps. CXXXVIII, 1). In other words, thou hast approved my abasement in the passion, and my exaltation in the resurrection. Secondly, to strengthen our faith, so necessary for us, in his divinity, as by the power of the divinity he arose and lives immortal: "For though he was crucified through weakness, yet he liveth by the power of God" (2 Cor. XIII, 4). Thirdly, to confirm in us the hope of our future resurrection, while we see Jesus our head already risen, so that every one of us can and should with reason repeat those words of Job: "I know that my Redeemer liveth, and in the last day I shall rise out of the earth. . . . This my hope is laid up in my bosom" (Job XIX, 25, 27). Fourthly, to teach us that we also can, and should, after his example and through his merits, from now on rise to a new and perfect life by dying to sin, and living to God alone: "That as Christ is risen from the dead by the glory of the Father, so we also may walk in newness of life . . . . so do you also reckon yourselves to be dead indeed to sin, but alive to God" (Rom. VI, 4, 11). Fifthly, to give completion to the work of our salvation; for as his death brought death to our evils, so his resurrection to a glorious life brought life to our goods and initiated our glory: "He was delivered up for our sins, and rose again for our justification" (Rom. IV, 25). That means, he was delivered up to destroy our sins, and he rose to vivify us with grace, and to beatify us afterwards with glory.

Jesus rose on the third day.

Jesus rose on the third day, as he himself had several times foretold. Not before, in order that our faith in his humanity and death might be the more undoubted; not after, in order that our faith in his divinity might be more firm, since both these truths are of the greatest importance; nor is it enough to believe the one without the other. He wished also to signify to us, that after the first period of the world, which was before the law, and after the second, which was under the law, he commenced the third period by his resurrection, which is the present one of grace. Moreover, he wished to show us that with the triumphant light of his resurrection the third state of his saints dawned, as the first was under the figures of the law, the second is at present in the truth of faith, and the third will be in the eternity of glory, to which, by rising again, he gave the beginning. For this reason he rose at early dawn, to denote to us that his rising was for us the dawn of a most splendid and perpetual day of heavenly glory.

Christ the first of the dead that rose to true life.

Christ is called by St. Paul 'the first fruits of them that sleep', the first of the dead that rose, although several others returned to life before him, as Lazarus and others brought back to life by Jesus himself. It is true that these also rose again to life, but with an imperfect resurrection, for they rose to a passible life, to a life that was still subject to the dominion of death. But Jesus was the first that rose with a true and perfect resurrection, that is, to an impassible, immortal and blessed life: "Christ rising again from the dead, dieth now no more; death shall no more have dominion over him" (Rom. VI, 9). And thus it was befitting, for he was the author of the resurrection and glory of all others that shall be resuscitated and glorified.

Christ effected his resurrection of himself.

It can be said with all truth that Christ effected his resurrection of himself, as he himself testified:

"No man taketh it [my life] away from me, but I lay it down of myself, ... and I have power to take it up again" (John X, 18). For by the power of the divinity united to both, the body again assumed the soul, which it had left, and the soul again assumed the body from which it had been separated, and thus by his divine power Jesus resuscitated himself. This, however, does not make void the truth that Christ was resuscitated by God, or by the Father. He was resuscitated by God; for if the body and the soul of Christ be regarded merely as to the forces belonging to created nature, they were not able of themselves to reunite together, but it was necessary that the power of God should intervene. He was resuscitated by the Father, because the same divine power and operation with which Christ effected his resurrection, is common to all the three divine persons, and hence, by the very fact that Christ by his divine power resuscitated himself, the Father also with the same divine power, which is equally his, resuscitated Christ.

Chapter LXII.

The Body of Christ risen.

Let us consider and adore in Christ risen that same flesh which was torn, tormented and abused in so many ways for love of us during the passion; all that same blood which was shed for us, even to the last drop; that same whole and entire sacred body, which languished in agony and succumbed to death; for all that same has risen in the resurrection, in the same nature but with another glory. That is said to rise, says St. John Damascene, which was fallen. And St. Gregory, in his 26th Homily on the gospels, writes thus: "Our Redeemer showed himself both incorruptible and palpable, so that he might prove that his body after the resurrection was indeed of the same nature and of an other glory."

The body of Christ rose perfectly glorious.

The body of Christ rose perfectly glorious, for which reason it was called by the Apostle a 'body of glory' in contradistinction to ours, which he calls a 'body of lowness': "Who will reform the body of our lowness, made like to the body of his glory" (Philipp. III, 21). Such a glory was due to the body of Christ for three reasons especially. First, because he had deserved it, chiefly by the

(356)

humiliation of his passion and death. Next, because Christ's resurrection was the model and cause of our resurrection. Now if the body of the just, which at present is 'sown in dishonor, shall afterwards rise in glory' (1 Cor. XV, 43), much more should the body of Jesus Christ rise again in glory, since the perfection of the effect and of the copy should with greater reason be found in the cause and original. Lastly, because the soul of Christ from the first moment of its existence enjoyed the vision and fruition of the divinity. That his beatitude did not also redound into his body, was by a particular disposition of divine wisdom, which made an exception to the common law in Christ, for the reason that it had ordained, that he should accomplish the mystery of our redemption by his passion. But that mystery having been accomplished, the glory of Christ's soul overflowed instantly into his reassumed body, just as the waters of a stream, when the dikes are removed, at once begin to inundate the surrounding country.

The particular properties of the risen body of Christ.

We shall now examine more distinctly the properties of the glory with which the body of Christ is adorned when risen. There are four gifts of glorified bodies enumerated by St. Paul in his first epistle to the Corinthians. The first is impassibility, by which that body which was sown corruptible and corrupt in the grave, shall rise again incorrupt and incorruptible, not only because it will no longer be liable to the corruption of

death, but also because it will not and cannot be
subject any more to any hurtful or disagreeable
changes, which might come to it either from within
or from without: "It is sown in corruption, it will
rise in incorruption" (1 Cor. XV, 42). "They
shall not hunger nor thirst any more, neither shall
the sun fall on them, nor any heat" (Apoc. VII,
16). The second property is clarity, by which
that body which was sown obscure and squallid,
shall rise again shining with the most noble light.
"It is sown in dishonor, it shall rise in glory"
(1 Cor. XV, 43). "Then shall the just shine as
the sun in the kingdom of their Father" (Mat.
XIII, 43). The third is agility, by which that
body which was sown feeble, sluggish and inert,
so much so that it was a burden to the soul: "For
the corruptible body is a load upon the soul"
(Wisd. IX, 15), will rise full of vigor, most able
and ready to obey the soul in every movement and
operation: "It is sown in weakness, it will rise in
power" (1 Cor. XV, 43). "The just shall shine
and shall run to and fro like sparks among the
reeds" (Wisd. III, 7). "But they that hope in
the Lord, shall renew their strength, they shall
take wings as eagles, they shall run and not be
weary, they shall walk and not faint" (Isai. XL,
31). The fourth is subtility, by which that body
which was sown an animal body, and therefore
subject to the functions and imperfections of animal
life, shall rise, a body, it is true, but a body in a
certain way spiritualized, because made partaker,
according to its capacity, of the being and the

operating of pure spirits: "It is sown an animal, it shall rise a spiritual body" (1 Cor. XV, 44). These are the four properties of every glorified body, and are derived from the soul itself glorified. And, indeed, it belongs to the soul to give being to the body; to vivify it and preserve it from corruption; to give it the forms and the complexion, that is to say, its proper comeliness; to give it, in fine, its motion: and these four things the soul communicates to the body the more perfectly, according as the perfection of the soul itself is greater, and according as the dominion which it has over the body, is more perfect. Now in a glorified soul the perfection is most complete, and the dominion which it has over the body is most full. Consequently, the glorified soul gives to the body corporal being, but gives it in the most perfect manner, that is, in a manner most resembling a spiritual existence, and therefore it confers on it the property of subtility. It vivifies the body, and preserves it from corruption, but it does this also in a most perfect manner, that is, in such a way as to render it forever exempt from death and from any suffering whatever. Hence it confers on it the property of impassibility. It gives to the body its proper beauty, but gives it in a most perfect manner, that is, refulgent with the most brilliant splendors. Hence it confers on it the property of clarity. It gives to the body its movement, but gives it in the most perfect manner, so that the body is in every respect docile and ready to execute every desire of the soul, and hence it imparts to it the property of agility.

It is true that every one of the blessed souls confers on the body these four gifts, yet not all confer them in the same degree, but each one in the degree proportionate to its glory. The reason is clear; for the glory of the body is the effect of the glory of the soul, and the effect must be proportionate to its cause.   Hence it is that in a glorious body the glory of the soul can be seen, just as in a vase of pure crystal may be seen the color and splendor of what is within.   But if it is so, what then should we say of the glory of Christ's body? What must be the subtility, impassibility, the agility and clarity that belong to it?   We may argue it from the glory of his soul, and from the glory of his divinity; because the flesh of Christ is united substantially and immediately not only to the soul, but also to the divine person, and therefore its glory is a ray not only of the ineffable clarity of that most blessed soul, but also of the infinite majesty of the Word, which is the candor of eternal light and the splendor of God's glory.

Another cause of the glory of Christ's body risen.

In the blessed there is, besides the essential reward called the *aurea*, an accidental reward which is called the *aureola*. The essential reward belongs to all, the accidental not to all, but only to those who have gained a more signal victory over their enemies, which are the world, the devil, and the flesh. Now there are three different aureolas: that of the virgins who have gained a perfect victory over the flesh; that of the martyrs who have triumphed with a perfect victory over the world; and the third of the doctors who have triumphed with a complete victory over the devil, discomfiting him not only in themselves, but also in others. The aureolas are properly the reward of the soul, which feels a special joy in the works for which the aureola is owing. But it extends likewise to the body, in which there results a particular beauty and brightness corresponding to that accidental glory of the soul. In the body of the virgins there will be the beauty and brightness of virginity; in the body of the martyrs, the beauty and brightness of martyrdom; in the body of the doctors, the beauty and brightness of doctrine. Now apply all this to Christ. Notice well, however, that although in Christ is found whatever perfection there is in the aureolas of the saints, yet nothing of the imperfection which they have. The aureola, as the word itself implies, means a crown, but a smaller crown, and therefore it relates, it is true, to those who are victors and kings, but victors and kings in an inferior degree, namely, by participation and in imitation of him in whom the victory and royal dignity are in all their fulness and as in their original source, and such is Christ. For this reason the aureolas, as such, do not apply to Christ, but the aurea of Christ contains in itself in a most excellent manner whatever there is precious in all the aureolas, and is the efficient origin and model of all the aureolas. Thus the light of the moon, as such, does not pertain to the sun, being as a pale reflex of the solar rays; but an incomparably greater one belongs to it, which is the source of all the moon's light. This being so, as from the aureola of the virgins, there are reflected to the body the beauty and brightness of virginity; as from the aureola of the martyrs, the beauty and brightness of martyrdom, and from the aureola of the doctors the beauty and brightness of doctrine, so from the aurea of Christ all these beauties and splendors are communicated to his body at the same time, and in a manner the most sublime and most divine beyond all understanding.

Jesus retained his wounds after his resurrection.

Here consider and admire the sweet love of Jesus, by which he wished to retain the scars of the wounds made by the nails and the spear, even after his resurrection. He wished to retain them: First, that they might be signs and perennial monuments of his triumph; for his greater exaltation; for the greater joy of the blessed; for our greater comfort, and for the greater terror of hell. Secondly, to make us understand that, as his wounds have no deformity, but rather the light and beauty of his glory shines in them more vividly, so likewise in his mystical body those members that shall have been more grievously wounded for his love, shall afterwards be more refulgent with his glory in paradise. Thirdly, to present them continually to his heavenly Father, and by thus recalling the merits of his passion and death, to appease his anger against us, and obtain his pardon, and draw down his graces upon us. Fourthly, to strengthen

the hearts of his disciples concerning the faith of
his resurrection; also to reveal more and more his
unspeakable mercy and incomprehensible charity,
and thus incite us to return his love. For his open
wounds are as so many mouths that speak to us
incessantly of his sufferings, of his bounty, of the
excesses of his love, and demand of us unceasingly
a correspondence of love. Fifthly, to show them
to his enemies at the last judgment for their greater
confusion. "Behold", he will say to them, "that
man whom you have crucified; see the wounds
which you yourselves have made; recognize the
side which you have pierced; behold that heart
which was opened by you and for you, but you
would not enter in." (St. Augustine.)

CHAPTER LXIII.

Manifestation of Christ's Resurrection.

The resurrection of Christ having been ordained for the common salvation of all, it was necessary that the knowledge of it should reach all, in such a way, that no one could reasonably doubt it. Still it was proper, that it should not be made known immediately 'to all the people, but to witnesses preordained of God' (Acts X, 41). For such is the rule observed by God respecting those truths which are of an order superior to the natural reach of the human understanding, such as that of the glorious resurrection of Christ, to reveal them first to some selected by him, that they may afterwards communicate them to others. For the same reason he willed that the first tidings of it should be given to men by the angels, as this is also the order established by him in the revelation of similar superhuman truths, that they be announced to men through means of the angels. Yet this did not hinder the apostles from being able to testify as ocular witnesses the resurrection of their master, as they had seen him truly risen. From this we understand also, why Christ after his resurrection did not appear always, nor to all in the same form; for it is peculiar to divine and supernatural things, that they are disclosed to men differently according to their different dispositions. Those who have a mind well disposed comprehend them according as they really are; but those who have it ill disposed, perceive them confusedly, and with a mixture of doubt and error, for 'the sensual man perceiveth not the things that are of the Spirit of God' (1 Cor. II, 14). For this reason, therefore, Jesus Christ appeared to some who were well disposed to believe, in his ordinary form, but to others who began to grow lukewarm and to waver in faith, he showed himself in a form not his own, as he did to the two disciples who were going to Emmaus. Nor did he do this to deceive them, but, as St. Gregory observes, 'he showed himself to them in his body as he was with them in their mind.'

Reasons why Jesus did not appear continually with his apostles after his resurrection.

We shall now examine the reasons why Jesus did not stay continually with his apostles after his resurrection, as he was wont before his death. For the reason that it was necessary for his apostles to understand well two things concerning his resurrection, the reality of his resurrection, and his glory when risen. The frequent visits which he made them were intended to manifest the reality of his resurrection, and to show the glorious life to which he was risen; he did not wish to treat with them continually, as in the past, in order that they might understand, as St. Bede remarks, that 'he was risen in the same flesh, but was not in the same mortality'. Still he promised them the consolation of his continual visible presence in the

future life, when they too would be partakers of
his glory: "I will see you again, and your heart
shall rejoice, and your joy no man shall take from
you" (John XVI, 22).

Jesus proved the truth of his resurrection in two ways.

Jesus proved the truth of his resurrection with
testimonies and with arguments or sensible signs,
either of which proofs was quite sufficient to remove
every doubt.   The testimonies were three, and
each one of them was such as not to admit of any
suspicion of error or deception.   The first is his
own, confirmed by miracles.   The second that of
the angels, who announced his resurrection to the
pious women.   The third that of the holy Scriptures adduced by himself: "All things must needs
be fulfilled which are written in the law of Moses,
and in the prophets and in the psalms concerning
me. . . .   Thus it is written, and thus it behooved
Christ to suffer, and to rise again from the dead
the third day" (Luke XXIV, 44, 46).   Again he
added most powerful arguments or evidences to
prove that his was a true and glorious resurrection.
As to his body, he showed that his was a true and
not a fantastical body, by its being solid and palpable: "Feel and see, for a spirit hath not flesh
and bones as you see me to have" (Luke XXIV,
39).   He showed that it was a human body by the
features which it presented visible to the eyes of
those to whom he appeared; that it was the same
as at first, by the scars of the wounds: "See my
hands and my feet, that it is I myself (Luke

XXIV, 39). As to his soul, he showed that it was really united to the body and vivified it, from the works of a three-fold nutritive, sensitive and intellective life, by eating and drinking with the disciples, by conversing with them, and by letting them see in many and most clear ways that it really exercised the acts of the various sensitive and intellective faculties. He showed his divinity by the miracles which he wrought, especially by the prodigious draught of fishes in the sea of Tiberias, and also by the ascent he made to heaven in presence of his disciples, as 'no man hath ascended into heaven, but he that descended from heaven, the Son of man who is in heaven' (John III, 13). In fine he showed his state of glory by entering through closed doors, by appearing and disappearing at his pleasure; since the gift of subtility, and the having it in his power to be seen or not seen, are prerogatives of glory.

Chapter LXIV.

Christ's Resurrection the cause of our Resurrection.

Jesus rose not only for himself, but also for our advantage, as his resurrection is also the cause of resurrection for us, just as the prevarication of Adam was the cause of death, not only to himself, but also to the whole human race: "For by a man *(came)* death and by a man the resurrection of the dead; and as in Adam all die, so also in Christ all shall be made alive" (1 Cor. XV, 21, 22). Christ's resurrection is therefore first of all the efficient cause of the resurrection of our bodies. And indeed, the Word of God, the Son of God, is the principle of life-giving: "With thee is the fountain of life" (Ps. XXV, 10), as is said of him in the psalms; and as he attested of himself, saying: "As the Father raiseth up the dead, and giveth life, so the Son also giveth life to whom he wills" (John V, 21). As the sun is the source of light, as the fire is the source of heat, so he is the source of life. And as the sun enlightens those bodies first which receive its light directly, and afterwards by their means the others on which its rays are reflected from the first; as the fire heats first the bodies which are nearest, and then by their means communicates its heat to those farther off, so the divine Word first imparts immortal life to that body which

(368)

is most closely and immediately united to himself, and wishes, then, that by it and from it, acting as an instrument of the divinity, life be communicated to and reflected on all the others. Note well, too, that this efficient virtue of Christ's resurrection regards not only the elect, but likewise the reprobate, since both have to be judged by him, and receive from him their reward or punishment in soul and body.

Christ's resurrection the model of the resurrection of our bodies.

The most perfect and most glorious resurrection of Jesus is moreover the exemplary cause of the resurrection of our bodies: "Who will reform the body of our lowness, made like to the body of his glory" (Philipp. III, 21). For Jesus Christ is our prototype, not only in the present life, but also in the future. Therefore, as we should in this passible and mortal life endeavor to resemble him, suffering and dying, so he wishes also that in like manner we resemble him risen in immortal life, provided our malice interposes no obstacle. Hence the glorious resurrection of Christ is properly the exemplary cause only in regard to the elect, but not in regard to the reprobate, for although all shall rise, yet only those in whom by grace the image of Jesus the Son of God shines, will be made worthy of imitating him in the glory of the resurrection: "For whom he foreknew, he also predestinated to be made conformable to the image of his Son . . . . them also he glorified" (Rom. VIII, 29, 30).

24

Christ's resurrection in regard to our souls.

Christ's resurrection is also the efficient and exemplary cause of the resurrection of our souls, and this is what the apostle meant to point out, when he said that Christ 'rose again for our justification', since the supernatural life of our souls consists precisely in justification. It is, therefore, the efficient cause, for it acts in virtue of the divinity, which gives life to the body and to the soul; to the body by the soul, and to the soul by grace. It is also the exemplary cause; for we should also in our souls become like to Jesus risen; so that as he rose again to a new life, so we too should 'walk in the newness of life'. And as he rose to lose life no more, so we should lose the life of the soul no more by sin. Jesus, too, on his part certainly desires that his resurrection be the cause of life to all. But all do not rightly respond to his love, and therefore all do not rise to the life of the soul, nor do all those who rise again, persevere in it with due constancy.

Chapter LXV.

Christ's Ascension into Heaven.

Jesus, after having in many ways for forty days proved the truth of his resurrection, and comforted his disciples, ascended to heaven to take the place which belonged to him near his Father and our Father: "I ascend to my Father and to your Father" (John XX, 17). He ascended to heaven, because the earth, a place of death and corruption, was no longer adapted to him, who lived an immortal and incorruptible life. He ascended, not according to the divine nature, which was, and is, and always will be essentially in every place, but according to the human nature, as it was only according to his human nature, that he had already descended 'into the lower parts of the earth'. He ascended by his own power: "Walking by the greatness of his strength" (Is. LXIII, 1); that is to say, in the first place, by the power of his divinity, and next by the power also of his blessed soul, which made it docile to every movement that it willed, not indeed naturally, but by the privilege of glory, which was communicated from it to the body. But it can be said also, that he was taken up to heaven by the Father: "He was taken up to heaven" (Mark. XVI, 19); for the divine power of the Father and Son are one and the same.

(371)

'He ascended above all the heavens', and above every principality and power, and above every other spiritual creature however sublime and perfect it may be: "Above all principality and power and virtue and dominion, and every name that is named, not only in this world, but also in that which is to come" (Eph. I, 21). For the dignity of his soul and also of his most sacred body, by union with his divine person, is immeasurably superior to that of any creature the most noble. And so Jesus departed from us as to his visible and corporal presence, remaining however with us 'all days even to the consummation of the world' (Mat. XXVIII, 20), not only with his divinity and with his grace, but by a most wonderful invention of his tender love, with his humanity also, although hidden under the veil of the eucharistic species, as was befitting the state in which we live at present, that is, in the obscurity of faith, not yet in the brightness of glory.

Christ's ascension was a cause of salvation to us.

Christ's ascension to heaven was a cause of salvation to us, as Jesus himself declared: "It is expedient for you that I go", that is, that I separate myself from you by ascending to heaven. Consider, then, how it was in the first place the cause of our salvation, if regarded on our side, that is, as to the effects which it produced in us. Since by it our faith is increased and rendered more meritorious and more perfect, for blessed are those who have not seen and have believed. By it our hope is enlivened, that we too shall be able to reach the place where our human nature is found exalted by him and in him. The affections and aspirations of our hearts are raised towards heavenly goods, so that we should now more than ever seek and relish no longer the things of earth, but only those which are above in heaven, where our Redeemer sits at the right hand of God, and should fix our heart where our true and only treasure is found. "Seek the things that are above, where Christ is sitting at the right hand of God; mind the things that are above, not the things that are on the earth" (Colos. III, 1). "Where thy treasure is, there is thy heart also" (Mat. VI, 21). Lastly, our reverence toward Christ is increased, whilst we no longer look upon him as an earthly man, but as a heavenly God.

Christ's ascension a source of salvation for us in an other way.

In the second place, the ascension of Christ was a source of salvation for us, if regarded on his part, that is, by what he has done for us by ascending to heaven. First of all, by his ascension he opened for us the way and prepared the place: "He shall go up, that shall open the way before them" (Mich. II, 13). "I go to prepare a place for you" (John XIV, 2). As he is our head, it is necessary that the members go where the head has preceded them. And as a sign and pledge of this, 'Ascending on high he led captivity captive' (Eph. IV, 8), conducting to heaven in his train the souls of the just, whom by his victory he had liberated from their captivity and made his most fortunate prey. Moreover, as in the ancient law the high-priest entered the sanctuary to make supplication to God for the people, so Christ entered heaven 'to intercede for us' (Hebr. VII, 25).   For the reason that the very presence of his sacred humanity in heaven is a continual intercession for us, most available to move the mercy of God, who willed that in him the human nature should be so much exalted in favor of those for whom the Son of God put on this same nature.   Finally, Jesus 'ascended above all the heavens, that he might fill all things' (Eph. IV, 10), so that seated on his heavenly throne as God and Lord, he might bountifully distribute his divine gifts upon all according to the most splendid magnificence and most fervent charity of his heart, in such a way that every one might be loaded with them.

CHAPTER LXVI.

Christ sits at the right Hand of the Father.

Here we shall weigh the meaning of that expression, Christ sits at the right hand of God the Father. To comprehend it rightly, it is necessary to understand well what the words 'sits' and 'right hand of God' signify here. It is plain that in God, a pure spirit, there can be no right or left hand materially. By the right hand of God then three things may be understood. First, with John Damascene we may understand the glory of the divinity, where he says: "We call the right hand of God the glory and honor of the divinity." In the second place, we may with St. Augustine understand it as the blessedness of the Father, when he says: "The right hand of the Father is the name of his blessedness." Hence it is said in the psalms: "At thy right hand are delights even to the end" (Ps. XV, 11). In the third place, it may be understood, with the same St. Augustine, to be the supreme power of judge: "Understand that right hand to be the power which that Man-God received, to come and judge, who had before come to be judged." To sit, then, implies two things, the quiet and steady abiding in some place: "Stay you in the city" (Luke XXIV, 49), or also the regal power, as we are wont to say of kings or of the supreme pontiffs, that they sat so many years, that is, they reigned so many years. This being now well understood, you may ask what is meant when we say that Christ sits at the right hand of the Father. Nothing else than that he possesses together with the Father the glory of the Divinity, the beatitude and the judicial power, and possesses these things immutably and regally.

Christ sits at the right hand of the Father both in his divine and human nature.

To sit at the right hand of the Father, applies to Christ both as to his divine and as to his human nature, but in a different manner. According to his divine nature, Jesus Christ, the Son of God, sits at the right hand of the Father, because he has the same nature as the Father: "I and the Father are one" (John X, 30). Hence the glory of the Divinity, the beatitude, the judicial and regal power of the Divinity belong to the Son in the same way as to the Father, that is, eternally and essentially; for although between the Father and the Son there is a personal distinction and order of origin, yet there is no difference in grade and in dignity, but perfect equality. According to the human nature, Christ is inferior to the Father: "The Father is greater than I" (John XIV, 28). Therefore, according to this nature, to sit at the right hand of the Father does not imply parity with the Father, but signifies a participation of the Father's goods greater than that of other creatures, in such a way that the human nature of Christ is endowed with a grace more abundant, with a beatitude more sublime, with a regal and judicial power over all the other creatures. St. Paul also intended to point out the same when he said of Christ, that 'he sitteth on the right hand of the majesty on high' (Heb. I, 3), that is, that he possesses the goods of God's majesty in the very greatest degree.

To sit at the right hand of the Father belongs to Christ alone.

To sit at the right hand of God the Father, is the property of Christ alone, because he alone is entitled to enjoy the Father's goods, whether by equality as to the divine nature, or by a participation more excellent than all the other creatures as to the human nature. This is what St. Paul affirms when he asks: "'To which of the angels said he at any time: 'Sit on my right hand'?'" (Heb. I, 13); meaning that he said it to none. Now if he said it to none of the angels, who are more perfect, much less did he say it to any of the other inferior creatures. Hence it is true that all the saints are at the right hand of God, as all are in his beatitude, but they do not sit at his right hand, for as has been explained, to sit at the right hand of God does not mean simply to have beatitude, but to have it with regal dominion and dignity, a thing which is becoming only to Christ. Nor is this contradicted by St. Paul when he says: "God . . . hath quickened us together in Christ . . . hath raised up together, and made us sit together in the heavenly places in Christ Jesus" (Eph. II, 4, 5, 6). He made us sit together, he says, for

Christ being our head, that which was conferred on him, was in him conferred also on us. And, therefore, as we have risen with Christ, not that we ourselves are already risen, but because he our head is risen, so we sit with Christ in the heavenly places, not in our own persons, but 'in Christ Jesus'.

CHAPTER LXVII.

Christ's Judiciary Power.

Although the power of judging be common to the whole Trinity, still by a certain appropriation it is ascribed to the Son. Because the rule of judgment is wisdom and truth, according to which judgment should be formed. Now the Son of God is wisdom begotten, and truth proceeding from the Father, which represent perfectly and contain all the perfections of the Father. Wherefore, as the Father produces all things by the Son, in as much as the Son is the art of the Father, so he judges all things by the Son, in as much as the Son is the wisdom and truth of the Father: "For neither doth the Father judge any man, but hath committed all judgment to the Son" (John V, 22).

The judiciary power belongs also to Christ's human nature.

The power of judging appertains to Christ, even as to his human nature, for according to this also he is the head of the whole Church. For this reason he himself said that 'the Father hath given him authority to execute judgment, because he is the Son of man' (John V, 27). By this he would give us to understand, that he had such authority, not simply because he was the Son of man, for otherwise all men would have it, but also as man,

(379)

for as such he is also the Lord of all, and consequently all are subject to his jurisdiction: "He hath put all things under his feet" (1 Cor. XV, 26), Nor is this the only title by which this authority is due to Christ as man, but he has besides gained it by his merits, by fighting and overcoming for the justice of God, especially in his passion, and by allowing himself to be judged unjustly by men. Wherefore St. Augustine with good reason says: "He will sit as judge, who stood beneath a judge; he will condemn the truly guilty, who was made guilty falsely."

Besides, the three following reasons will make it more clear how befitting all this was. First, the proportion and affinity which the human nature of Christ has with men, who have to be judged; since this is the sweet law of divine providence, to make use of the intermediate causes which are nearest to the effects. Thus it wills the fruit to be born from its plant, and the plant from its seed; that man be generated from a man, and therefore in a similar way, that man be judged by Christ as man. Secondly, because the final judgement is connected with the general resurrection of the dead, which was merited for us by Christ through the passion which he sustained in his humanity, and of which resurrection this same humanity is to be the cause as an instrument of the divinity. Thirdly, because, according to the observation of St. Augustine, it was proper that at the universal judgment all the good and bad should see their judge; the good in his two natures, divine and human, the bad in his human nature at least. It was proper, he says, that those to be judged should see the judge. . . . But good and bad were to be judged. . . . Therefore it remained that in the judgment the form of the servant should be shown both to the good and the bad, and that the form of God should be reserved for the good alone.

Christ's judiciary power extends to all human things.

The judiciary power of Jesus Christ extends to all human things without any exception. If we speak of Christ as to the divine nature, there can be no doubt of it, since, as was said before, the Father judges all things by the Word, as he executes all things by the Word. But of Christ as man, it must be said likewise that all human things are subject to his judgment. And this appears evident, if we bear in mind first of all the very close union of Christ's soul with the Word. For if it be true, that 'the spiritual man judges all things' (1 Cor. II, 15), because the spiritual man, by adhering to the Word of God which is truth itself, and by being enlightened by its light, becomes as it were a living justice and law to decide distinctly on all matters, how much more, then, does the soul of Christ, which is full of the Word's truth, 'judge all things', that is to say, have all things subordinate to its judgment. Again this same is deduced from the merit of Christ's death: "For to this end Christ died and rose again, that he might be Lord both of the dead and of the living" (Rom. XIV, 9). Therefore, as the apostle immediately adds, 'we shall all stand before the

judgment-seat of Christ'. And why shall we stand,
if not that he, according to that same nature in
which 'he died and rose again', may judge us all
and in all our concerns? Lastly, consider briefly
what is the relation which all human things have
in regard to our eternal salvation. This is the
end and those are the means; this is the principal
and those the accessories. Now to the judgment
of the man Christ it is reserved to admit to the
blessed life, which is our salvation, those who are
worthy of it, and to reject those who are unworthy
of it (Mat. XXV). Much more, then, are all
other human things subject to his judgment, since
he who has power over the end and over the principal, has it with greater reason over the means
and over the accessories.

All the angels, good and bad, are subject to Christ's judiciary authority.

All the angels also, both good and bad, are
subject to Christ's judiciary power, and not only
in as much as he is the Word of God, but also as
to his human nature, and chiefly for three reasons.
First, by reason of the closest proximity which the
assumed nature has with God, for 'nowhere doth
he take hold of the angels, but of the seed of
Abraham he taketh hold' (Heb. II, 16). On this
account the soul of Christ is filled with the power
of the Word, much more than any of the angelic
spirits, even the very highest, so that it belongs to
it to enlighten the angels, and also to judge them.
Secondly, on account of the abasement to which
the human nature in Christ submitted during the

passion, for which it merited to be exalted above all the angels, good and bad, in such a way that 'in the name of Jesus every knee should bend, of those that are in heaven, on earth, and in hell' (Philipp. II, 10).   Thirdly, by reason of the works which the angels perform for men, of whom Christ is in a particular manner the head; for all the angels are ministering spirits, sent to minister in favor of those who shall attain the inheritance of salvation: "Are they not all ministering spirits, sent to minister for those who shall receive the inheritance of salvation?" (Heb. I, 14).

But in what things precisely do the angels depend on the judgment of Christ? On three. First, as to the dispensation of the various offices and ministries which are performed by them, because such dispensation belongs to Christ also in his human nature, in which the angels in fact served him: "And behold, angels came and ministered to him" (Mat. IV, 11); and the devils entreated him to send them into the herd of swine: "And the devils besought him, saying, if thou cast us out hence, send us into the herd of swine" (Mat. VIII, 31). Secondly, as to the accidental rewards of the good angels, which are especially the joys that they feel for the salvation of men: "There shall be joy before the angels of God upon one sinner doing penance" (Luke XV, 10). And as to the accidental punishments, which Christ even as man inflicts on the devils, either by increasing their torments, or by putting them to flight and confining them in hell. Hence at his sight the devils cried out:

"What have we to do with thee, Jesus of Nazareth? Art thou come to destroy us?" (Mark. I, 24). "Art thou come hither to torment us before the time?" (Mat. VIII, 29). Thirdly, in regard to the essential reward of the good angels, which is eternal beatitude, and in regard to the essential punishment of the rebel angels, which is eternal damnation. But this was done by Christ as the Word of God, at the beginning of the world.

And here, finally, we may observe that, if Christ as man has the power of Lord and judge not only over men, but also over the angels, who are the most important among creatures, he has it therefore also universally over all creatures, because, as St. Augustine says, 'inferior things by a certain order are ruled by God through the superior things'. Consequently, it is proper to say that all creatures are ruled and governed by God through the humanity of Jesus Christ, which is above all men and all the angels, and all that is created: "Thou hast set him over the works of thy hands; thou hast put all things in subjection under his feet, for in that he subjected all things to him, he left nothing not subject to him" (Heb. II, 7, 8). And this supreme power of the Lamb of God all creatures acknowledge and confess in their own way: "And every creature which is in heaven, and on the earth, and under the earth, and such as are in the sea, and the things that are therein, I heard all saying, to him that sitteth on the throne, and to the Lamb, benediction and honor and glory and power for ever and ever" (Apoc. V, 13).

Chapter LXVIII.

The Final Judgment.

According to the teaching of Catholic faith, we have to admit two final judgments, one at the end of each man's life, and the other at the end of the world; one private, the other public; one proper to individuals, and which on that account is called particular, the other common to all, and therefore called universal. Both necessarily take place after death, not before: "It is appointed for men once to die, and after this the judgment" (Heb. IX, 27) For what reason? Because a definite judgment cannot be given of any thing subject to change, until it reaches its termination. Of a statue there can be no judgment made until its workmanship be finished; of a house until the building is completed; of a book until the writing is ended; and so of other things in like manner, which sometimes appear fair and good at first, but afterwards are admitted to be unseemly and hurtful; or at first they appear unseemly and hurtful, and are afterwards admitted to be fair and good. So, in a similar way, of man who is every hour changeable and every hour liable to pass from good to evil, and from evil to good, a perfect judgment cannot be given until he has ended his days. But having once ended them, he can be judged

25 (385)

immediately; and therefore also he shall be judged immediately in the particular judgment, in which he shall receive the retribution which is due to him according to his merits, either of eternal reward, or of eternal punishment.

But notice that, although with death the temporal life itself of man has its end, yet he continues on this earth to survive himself, so to say, in many of his effects. He survives in the memory of men, who, being often deceived, esteem him as good, whilst he is bad, and bad whilst he is good. He survives in his children, who are, as it were, a reproduction of their parents, according to the words of Ecclesiasticus: "His father is dead, and he is, as if he were not dead, for he has left one behind that is like himself" (Eccl. XXX, 4). And yet the children of many good parents are bad, and the children of many bad parents are good. He survives in the effects of his works: thus the heresy of Luther and of other heresiarchs continues still to occasion the unbelief and perdition of many, and the preaching of the apostles continues still to bring about the faith and salvation of many. He survives in his ashes, which sometimes enjoy an honorable sepulchre, when they ought to lie in the commons; and they lie in the commons, when they ought to have an honorable sepulchre. He survives in those things in which he fixed his love, for example, in some temporal goods, some of which last a very short time and others for a longer time. Therefore, that first judgment mentioned before cannot be so perfect and so full as it should be,

because at that time the man has ended living only
in himself. It is necessary, besides, that he end
living also in those things which he had outside of
himself, all of which are subject to the valuation
of the divine judgment; and then be judged again.
Hence it is, that there will be a second judgment,
in which a full judgment will be passed on all that
appertains to every man by whatsoever title; and
this judgment cannot take place until the end of
the world, that is, until the whole human generation on the earth shall have ceased to live, and to
survive: and the judgment shall be universal and
public, in order that all may manifestly see and
admire the wisdom, the goodness and justice of
God towards all and in all things.

On the last day all shall rise, both good and bad.

On the last day, at the voice of the Son of God,
at the sound of God's trumpet, all shall rise again,
good and bad; the good to live forever, the bad to
be condemned in soul and body to everlasting
death: "The hour cometh wherein all that are in
their graves shall hear the voice of the Son of God,
and they that have done good, shall come forth
unto the resurrection of life, but they that have
done evil, unto the resurrection of judgment"
(John V, 28, 29). "The Lord himself shall come
down from heaven with commandment, and with
the voice of the archangel, and with the trumpet
of God, and the dead who are in Christ shall rise
first" (1 Thes. IV, 15). What is meant here by
the voice of Christ? Remember that Christ's re-

surrection is the cause of our resurrection. Now
it is necessary that in some way the cause be joined
to the effect, and in a manner proportioned to the
quality of the effect. Hence it is, that Christ risen
will, in order to effect the general resurrection of
our bodies, make use of some corporeal sign perceptible to all, and this is what is called the voice
of the Son of God. According to some, it will be
really the living voice of Christ, who will command the dead to rise, as he formerly commanded
the sea and the winds to be still, and the tempest
ceased. According to others, this sign will be
nothing more than the appearance itself of the Son
of God, who like a flash of lightning shall instantly appear visible to the whole world: "For as the
lightning cometh out of the east, and appeareth
even unto the west, so shall also the coming of the
Son of man be" (Mat. XXIV, 27). This his appearance too is called a voice, because it will have
the force of a command, which all nature will obey
instantaneously. Hence it is also written that
'the Lord shall come with commandment'.

Notice, however, that this voice, in whatever
way it is to be understood, is called the sound of a
trumpet, to denote clearness and force, so that there
will be no one who shall not hear it. But chiefly
by analogy to the use which they made of the
trumpet in the old testament. They employed it
particularly in three cases. To assemble men to
meetings, to stir them up to war, and to call them
to the feasts. Now, on the last day, the risen will
be called to the great meeting of judgment; to the

great war in which God, and the entire universe with him, shall fight against the unwise: "And the whole world shall fight with him against the unwise" (Wisd. V, 21); and to the great feast of Christ's complete and everlasting triumph.

The conscience of every man will bear testimony of his past acts.

On that tremendous day, when God shall judge the secrets of men, the conscience of each one will render testimony of the acts he has done, both good and evil, and his very thoughts will come forward to accuse or to defend him: "Their conscience bearing witness to them, and their thoughts within themselves accusing them, or else defending them, in the day when God shall judge the secrets of men" (Rom. II, 15, 16). This means that on that day every man will have a complete knowledge of all the actions done by him, for in that judgment each and all of them have to be dealt with, and he that is witness, accuser and defender, needs to have a knowledge of those things which are to be the matter for judgment.

St. John wished to express the same with these words: "And I saw the dead, great and small, standing before the throne, and the books were opened; and an other book was opened which is the book of life; and the dead were judged by those things which were written in the books, according to their works" (Apoc. XX, 12). The many books are the consciences of men; and they are said to be open, to signify that nothing shall remain closed, nothing hidden, but that all shall be manifest.

By the book of life, also open, is meant the book of the divine law, which teaches us the way that leads to life; or that divine power by which all the doings of each one will be recalled to his memory; or also the sentence of the judge which will shine written in his mind.

But it may be objected that, if it is true that every one will recall to mind whatever he has done in life, then the saints too will recall to mind all their sins, and the damned likewise will remember their virtuous deeds. True enough; but the remembrance of evil done will not in the least diminish the joy of the saints, nor will the remembrance of good done lighten in the least the torment of the damned. On the contrary, both will be increased; the joy of the saints will be increased, because they will understand much better the many and great evils from which, by the divine mercy, they were freed; the torment of the damned will be increased, because they will understand much better the many and great goods, which through their own fault they have lost irreparably. Not only will each one see clearly his own merits or demerits, but will know at the same time the merits and demerits of all the others. This at least is the most probable and most common opinion of the holy doctors. And the reason is, because in the last and universal judgment it is necessary that the justice of God be plainly manifested to all, which at present most frequently remains concealed or unobserved. For this reason it is required that all should know, that the sentence which Christ pronounces on each one of them, is most just, and such as corresponds to their works, good or bad. Therefore, it is necessary that these same works be disclosed to all. Nor are we to think that a like manifestation of their sins will be a cause of pain and confusion to the just. Quite the contrary: it will even turn to their great glory and contentment, because together with the fault will be published the penance which they did for it; whilst on the other hand the manifestation of good performed by the reprobate will be for them a greater distress and reproach, because it will render their malignity, and the abuse which they made of God's gifts, plain and inexcusable.

Those who shall be present at the last judgment.

Those who shall be found present at the final judgment, will be all men good and bad, and likewise all the angels good and bad. All men, for the reason that the judiciary power was conferred on Christ in reward of the humility which he exercised in his passion. Now in the passion he humbled himself for all, he shed his blood for all. On this account it is just that all men be assembled together to contemplate his exaltation in the human nature, in which God has appointed him judge of the living and the dead: "It is he who hath been appointed by God to be the judge of the living and of the dead" (Acts X, 42). Not only the adults, but the infants also, who died before the use of reason, shall be present at the judgment, not to be judged, but to be spectators of the glory of Christ the judge.   In this way it shall come to pass, that at his appearance amid the clouds, there will be no eye that shall not see him : "Behold he cometh with the clouds, and every eye shall see him" (Apoc. I, 7).

But among men there will be some privileged ones, who will not only be present, but will sit in judgment together with Christ as his associates. These will be the apostles and their imitators in the perfect following of Christ, which consists in abandoning all things to follow him: "Amen I say to you, that you, who have followed me, in the regeneration, when the Son of man shall sit on the seat of his majesty, you also shall sit on twelve seats, judging the twelve tribes of Israel" (Mat. XIX, 28).   Let us examine diligently, what is implied by judging together with Christ.   It does not mean simply, that they will approve the sentence of Christ, for this improper mode of judging will be common to all the elect.   Neither does it mean that they will have a seat more eminent, nearer and more like to that of the judge; for even this is not properly to judge.   To judge is to pronounce definitive sentence, and this can be done in two ways, either by passing sentence by one's own authority, or by merely concurring in the sentence already passed by another's authority.   The first manner of judging belongs only to Christ.   The second manner will be that, which by a singular privilege will be given to the apostles and their followers.

Besides all men, there will be present also all

the angels of heaven, and all the demons of hell. All the angels of heaven, to form a retinue for the Son of man, who shall come in all his majesty: "And when the Son of man shall come in his majesty, and all the angels with him" (Mat. XXV, 31). But these shall be present in quality of ministers, not in quality of associate judges, because between the associate judges and the judge there should be conformity, and it is men that are conformed to Christ the Son of man, and not the angels. The demons, too, shall stand there, in spite of their unwillingness, for their shame and punishment, in quality of instruments to execute divine vengeance on the reprobate. Neither the angels, however, nor the demons shall be judges on that day directly, but indirectly; and it will be in this manner. In a judgment it is necessary to distinguish two sides, the discussion of merits or demerits, and the retribution of reward or punishment. In the angels, whether good or bad, the discussion cannot have place, since this occurs when there is mixture of good with evil. Now in the good angels there is only good, and in the bad angels there is only evil as regards judgment. As to retribution, one is that which corresponds to one's own merits or demerits, and the other that which corresponds to the merits or demerits of others. The retribution corresponding to the personal merits or demerits of the good and the bad angels was given them from the beginning, when the former were raised up to heavenly glory, and the latter were cast into the infernal abysses. The retribution corresponding to the merits or demerits of others, brought about through the same good or bad angels by inducing men to do good or to do evil, is that which shall be reserved for the last judgment, in as much as the good angels will then have more joy at the salvation of those whom they have assisted to good, and the bad angels will have more torment for the damnation of those whom they have incited to evil. It is owing to this indirect retribution, that it is said that the good and the wicked angels shall also be judged, but indirectly.

The manner in which Christ will appear as judge.

We may now consider in what manner Christ will come on the last day to exercise his authority as supreme judge. He will come with great power and majesty: "And then they shall see the Son of man coming in a cloud with great power and majesty" (Luke XXI, 27). And so his coming will be preceded by many and most singular prodigies, which will give men a sign of his near coming, and of his supreme dignity and power: "And there shall be signs in the sun and in the moon and in the stars" (Luke XXI, 25). "The sun shall be darkened, and the moon shall not give her light, and the stars shall fall from heaven, and the powers of the heavens shall be moved" (Mat. XXIV, 29). After that, when the time appointed by divine wisdom shall come, he himself will appear, and spread his rays like lightning from pole to pole, for his sacred humanity will be encompassed and beaming with all its glory. It will not be then any more as in his first coming. He then came to pay the Father our debts, and on that account appeared covered with our miseries himself. But the second time he will come to execute on us the justice of his Father in a most solemn manner, by rendering to each one publicly and fully the retribution deserved; the retribution of eternal happiness to the elect, both as to soul and body; the retribution of eternal punishment to the reprobate, both as to soul and body. So he will come loaded with the riches, the glory, the power, and the supreme and tremendous majesty of his divine Father.

The sight of the glorious humanity of Christ will bring great rejoicing to the good, but at the same time it will cause inexpressible terror and sadness in the wicked, for the glory and power of him that is loved, cheers and gladdens, whilst the glory and power of him that is hated saddens and terrifies. Moreover, the just shall contemplate also the glory of his divinity. Not so the wicked; yet from the effects which they will feel in themselves and see in others, they will be unable to doubt that Christ is God. At the same time there will appear with Christ in the heavens the sign of the Son of man, that is, the cross, as the fathers explain: "And then shall appear the sign of the Son of man in heaven" (Mat. XXIV, 30). And this, too, for the greater consolation of the just, who owe their eternal salvation to the cross of Christ, and for the greater anguish and confusion of the wicked, who trampled on that blood which Christ shed on the cross also for them.   To the same end, likewise, in the glorious body of Christ the scars of his wounds will appear shining with the most brilliant light, so that they may be as perpetual signs and monuments of his divine power, through which by suffering and dying he could gain over his enemies and ours a triumph so complete, and which will endure forever.   "Thanks be to God who hath given us the victory through our Lord Jesus Christ" (1 Cor. XV, 57).

CONCLUSION.

So, now, dear reader, we have reached the end of the present volume, and I think it will be profitable and at the same time agreeable to you to cast a look back, to review a little the road over which we have passed by following the footsteps of our faithful and most skilful guide. But first it will be well to consider what was the terminus at which we wished to arrive. The terminus was to know Jesus Christ the Incarnate Word better, that is, to have a clearer and more complete knowledge of him as far as is possible for us. With the eye fixed on this terminus, we began the journey behind our guide, being certain that we would be conducted by the most secure and direct way.

Therefore, after having exercised ourselves briefly in pondering in general on the great benefits of the study of Jesus Christ, we applied ourselves at once to the study first of Christ as the Word of God. And first of all we considered those titles which belong to the second person of the Trinity, because they express his personal character, and are especially the three following, of the Word, of the Son, and of the Image of the Father. Then we went on to consider those of the common attributes, which are wont most frequently to be ascribed to the Word by appropriation,

(397)

such as wisdom, power, the book of life, and the like. Lastly, we examined the relation which the Word has towards the other divine persons, as being sent or as sending, and also towards creatures, as to the term of his invisible or visible mission; the invisible which is accomplished by the gift of sanctifying grace; the visible which was accomplished by the mystery of the Incarnation. After this we proceeded to study Jesus Christ as the incarnate Word. First we endeavored to understand, as far as our mind strengthened by the light of faith can understand, the nature and the end of the most wonderful work of divine wisdom and goodness, which is the incarnation of the Son of God. We considered also its fitness under various respects. Next we turned our whole attention to examine in detail two things, into which the whole matter of our study was then divided; the first, what the divine Word assumed in uniting itself to human nature, and the consequences of this union; the second, what the incarnate Word wrought and suffered in this life by the humanity assumed by it, and what it obtained in the next life.

Regarding the first thing, we examined what was the nature which the Word assumed, and what were the perfections or imperfections which he put on together with it. As to the perfections, we saw that they are reduced to three heads. First, the grace, which besides the grace of union is twofold in Christ, namely the personal sanctifying grace with all the other gifts which accompany it, and the grace which regards him as head of the Church, his mystical body and virgin spouse. Secondly, the knowledge proper of Christ's soul, which is three-fold, that is, beatific, infused, and acquired knowledge. Thirdly, the active power with which the soul of Christ is adorned. With regard to the imperfections, which are inherent to the nature of fallen man, we saw that some were admitted by him, as that of being passible and mortal, and others not, as that of sin. From all this we concluded that Christ as man, during his life here upon earth, was not simply possessor of the beatific vision, nor simply a wayfarer, but was both at the same time.

Afterwards we went on to investigate the consequences which arise from such union between the divine person and the humanity, some of which regard Christ in himself, some regard him considered in relation to the Father, and others regard him in relation to us. The consequences which regard Christ in himself are his having a two-fold will, and a two-fold operation, for although there is only one person, yet it subsists in two natures, not confused nor defective, but distinct, and each perfect in its own degree. The consequences which regard Christ in relation to the Father, are his subjection and prayer to his divine Father, in as much as he was man; and his quality of Mediator, Priest, Victim and Predestinated of the Father. The consequence in regard to us is the adoration of latria, which we are bound to render him even according to his human nature. We pondered over all these consequences successively, and thus ended the first part of the matter which we undertook to treat.

Then we passed to the second part, which took in four points, that which appertains to the beginning, the progress, the end of the Saviour's life in this world, and his exaltation after death. To the first point belong Christ's conception, and birth, the manifestation of his birth to those who were chosen by God as the first-fruit of believers, the circumcision, the presentation in the temple, and lastly his baptism, in as much as it was the beginning, not of his human life absolutely, but of his public life. Thus we considered all these mysteries of the Redeemer's life separately. But before paying the tribute of our love to the flower, we allowed ourselves to pause a little, to contemplate and extol the most fortunate plant which produced it. I mean that woman, who was blessed among all women, because chosen among all to receive within her bosom the Word made flesh. Concerning her we brought to mind four things, which were closely connected with our subject, her most exalted sanctity, her perpetual and purest virginity, her conjugal union with St. Joseph without any detriment of her integrity, the annunciation of the angel, when as soon as she had given her consent, the ineffable mystery of the incarnation of the Son of God was effected in her bosom. And having meditated on the birth of Christ, we could not but at least cast a glance of complacency and of admiration on her by recognizing and venerating her as Mother of God.

We next proceeded to view attentively the divine Redeemer in the progress of his passible life. We observed particularly how he willed to dwell here on earth, how he deported himself in sustaining and repelling the temptation of the devil, how he preached his doctrine, and the miracles which he performed to confirm it. As to the miracles, we first considered them in general, and afterwards according to their different kinds, and finally we made a pause to contemplate the miracle of the transfiguration, in which Christ wished that his disciples should have a little foretaste of that glory which was reserved, even as to the body, both for him our head, and by him and to his likeness for us also, his members.

After this we went on to ponder on what Christ did and suffered on the end of his mortal life. We recalled to mind his passion, his death, the precious effects which flowed from it, and the mysteries which occurred after death in the Saviour's body and soul; in the body his burial, in the soul his descent into limbo.

Finally, we endeavored to represent to ourselves as well as we could, Christ's glorious exaltation, and to this end we considered it minutely in the five following things. In his resurrection, which for us also was the source of corporal and spiritual resurrection; in his ascension to the highest heavens; in the sublimest throne where he sits at the Father's right hand; in the power of supreme Lord and judge of all and of all things; and in the most solemn exercise of such power, which is to be

carried out at the end of the world, when Jesus
Christ shall appear encompassed with all his glory,
to judge the living and the dead, and shall have
a complete triumph over all his enemies.   Here
then we concluded, blessing and thanking God for
the victory of Christ, which is our victory also,
since he fought and conquered for love of us, and
for our sake.

Does it not seem now, kind reader, that we
have reached the terminus at which we aimed,
that is to know, not perfectly, for no finite intelligence can reach so far, but more clearly, more distinctly and more fully Jesus Christ, the Incarnate
Word ?   But if it be so, then we must thank our
kind guide for it, who not only pointed out the
way, but made it easy, by leveling, by clearing
and lighting it up with his superhuman wisdom.

Still we must not be contented with all this.
Besides knowing Jesus Christ, we must strive also
to love him: and this, too, has to be the ultimate
end of our study.   Therefore in this also, and in
this above all, it is necessary for us to follow the
example and invoke the patronage of the angelic
doctor St. Thomas, who if he had a very remarkable knowledge of Jesus Christ, had also a very
remarkable love for him.   This is perhaps what
Jesus himself intended that we should understand,
when he addressed him with those well known
words: "You have written well of me, Thomas."
He said that he had written well of him, not only
because he had written of him with clearness, with
fulness, and with the greatest profoundness, but

also and especially, because whilst his mind was studying, and his pen was writing about Jesus Christ, his heart was burning with the most lively and sincere love of him. In proof of this, notice what answer the saint made to our Lord, when asked by him what recompense he desired in return: "What recompense then will you receive?" He replied, that he desired no other recompense than him: "No other, Lord, but thyself", intimating by these words that the desire and the love of his heart was for Jesus Christ, all for Jesus Christ, and only for Jesus Christ.

References to the Works of St. Thomas

Chapter   I.—C. Gent. lib. I, c. 2.—Coloss. II, lect. 1.

    "   II.—I. q. 27, 54. — C. Gent. lib. IV, c. 11. — De Verit. q. 4, opusc. 12. — De diff. verbi div. et hum. Hebr. I, lect. 4.

    "   III.—I. q. 27.—III. q. 23.—C. Gent. lib. IV, c. 11, 13. — Comp. Theol. c. 57—44. — Rom. VIII, lect. 6.— Ephes. I, lect. 1.—Coloss. I, lect. 4.

    "   IV.—I. q. 35; q. 45, a. 7; q. 95.—I. dist. 3, qu. 2, a. 1. — C. Gent. lib. IV, c. 11. — I. Cor. XI, lect. 2.—Coloss. I, lect. 4.—Hebr. I, lect. 2.

    "   V.—I. q. 39, a. 7, 8. — I. II. q. 95.—C. Gent. lib. IV, c. 13, 13. — De Verit. q. 7, a. 3. — Rom. VIII, lect. 6. — I. Cor. I, lect. 3. — Hebr. I, lect. 2.

    "   VI.—I. q. 18, 24. — C. Gent. lib. IV, c. 11. — De Verit. q. 4, 7.—Hebr. XII, lect. 1.

    "   VII.—I. q. 5, a. 4; q. 39, a. 8. — I. II. q. 27, a. 1. —II. II. q. 145, a. 2; q. 180, a. 2.—I. dist. 31, q. 2, a. 1.

    " VIII.—I. q. 43.—I. dist. 15, 16.

    "   IX.—III. q. 1, a. 2, 4; q. 2.—C. Geut. lib. IV, c. 54.

    "   X.—III. q. 1, a. 1; q. 3, a. 5, 8.—C. Gent. lib. IV, c. 42.

    "   XI.—I. q. 64, a. 2.—III. q. 1, a. 2; q. 4, a. 1.

    "   XII.—III. q. 1, 5, 6.—C. Gent. lib. IV, c. 55.

    " XIII.—III. q. 4, a. 6; q. 5.

    " XIV.—III. q. 2, a. 10; q. 6, art. 6; q. 7, a. 11, 13.

    "   XV.—I. II. q. 110.—III. q. 7, a. 1, 9, 10, 11, 12.

    " XVI.—III. q. 7, a. 2, 3, 4.

(405)